The Demographic
Evolution
of Human
Populations

The Demographic Evolution of Human Populations

edited by **R. H. Ward**

Child Development and Mental Retardation Centre and Department of Anthropology, University of Washington, Seattle, Washington, U.S.A.

and **K. M. Weiss**

Centre for Demographic and Population Genetics, University of Texas, Houston, Texas, U.S.A.

1976

Academic Press

London   New York   San Francisco

A Subsidiary of Harcourt Brace Jovanovich, Publishers

ACADEMIC PRESS INC. (LONDON) LIMITED
24–28 Oval Road,
London NW1 7DX, England
(Registered Office)
(Registered number 598514)

U.S. edition published by
ACADEMIC PRESS INC.
111 Fifth Avenue,
New York,
New York 10003, U.S.A.

Copyright © 1976 Academic Press Inc. (London) Limited
LCCCN 76-3342
ISBN 0-12-735250-3

Printed in Northern Ireland at the Universities Press (Belfast) Ltd.

Foreword

From 15 to 30 August 1974 a Workshop and Advanced Study Institute on "Demographic Aspects of the Biology of Human Populations"* was held in Erice (Sicily) at the International School of Human Biology of the Center for Scientific Culture "Ettore Majorana".

The course was directed by G. W. Lasker of the Wayne State University who was able to get together a group of promising predoctoral and postdoctoral students and distinguished human biologists.

There was a surprisingly cohesive outcome of the workshop, despite the different interests represented. Almost all the participants agreed that for the purposes of studying biological consequences of demographic parameters it is necessary to combine three types of methods: (1) standard demographic methods (construction of birth rates fertility rates, death rates and life tables), (2) the formulations of the population geneticists and (3) the field work method of anthropology.

The present volume is the first cohesive result of this attempt; we all are obliged to Drs R. H. Ward and K. M. Weiss for their efforts in editing the present volume and we look for further cooperation in this important field of science.

B. CHIARELLI
Editor of the Journal of Human Evolution
and
Director of the International School of Human Biology of the Center for Scientific Culture "Ettore Majorana"

* The above Workshop and Institute has been financially supported by the Scientific Affairs Division of the North Atlantic Treaty Organization and by the U.S. National Science Foundation.

Preface

The importance of demographic parameters in affecting the differential survival of populations has long been realised in evolutionary theory. From the time of Darwin to the present, the concept of selection and genetic fitness has implicitly relied upon the assumption that successful populations will differ from unsuccessful ones in some key demographic parameters. There may be some debate as to whether components of differential mortality or differential fertility are the more effective in influencing rates of evolutionary change; there is no debate that some differences in demographic parameters must exist for the evolutionary process to occur.

Despite this concurrence, our evaluation of the importance of various demographic parameters in regulating the tempo of evolution, comes more from theoretical models than from observations derived from natural populations. In the past decade, there has dawned an awareness that a detailed study of the genetic consequences of demographic profiles in natural populations would repay the necessary effort. Of all species studied, we have accumulated the most demographic information about our own. This information is all too often fragmentary, inappropriate to evolutionary questions, and variable in reliability. Nevertheless, we do have at least some appreciation of the major temporal changes in demographic profiles in our species. The information that is available now warrants some general conclusions about the interrelationship between demographic parameters and process of evolutionary change. More importantly, it offers guidance to fruitful areas for further research. It is to these twin aims that this volume is directed. We do not claim that the contributions to this volume are an exhaustive set of all possible areas of demographic interest. We would claim that we have represented most major components of the evolutionary consequences of demographic change throughout much of our species' history.

The initial concept of this volume sprang out of a workshop on "Demographic Aspects of the Biology of Human Populations" held at Erice, Sicily, August 15–30, 1974. Many of the contributors were at that workshop and our fruitful discussion led to the inception of this volume. We should like to pay tribute to all participants of the workshop, especially Professor Lasker, Professor Chiarelli and Dr Kester who brought us together. If this volume can provide confirmation of the importance of just some of the themes that threaded their way through discussions at Erice, we shall be content.

Finally, we should like to express our deep gratitude to the contributors to this volume and to the many colleagues who gave enthusiastic support to our concept. Especially, we should like to thank Jack Kelso and David Greene of Boulder, Colorado, who provided a quiet haven to work in and sympathetic hospitality to revive our flagging spirits after a gruelling weekend of editorial responsibility. Our gratitude to Janis Dill and Jeryl Silverman is as deep as our admiration for the cheerful manner in which they typed the manuscripts. The financial support of the U.S. Institute of Health Research Grant, GM-19513-02 is also gratefully acknowledged.

R. H. WARD

K. M. WEISS

List of Contributors

L. L. Cavalli–Sforza   *Genetics Department, Stanford University, U.S.A.*

H. C. Harpending   *Department of Anthropology, University of New Mexico, Albuquerque, New Mexico 87131, U.S.A.*

M. Henneberg   *Department of Physical Anthropology, Adam Michiewicz University, 10, ul Fredry, 61–701, Poznan, Poland*

N. Howell   *Scarborough College, University of Toronto, West Hill, Ontario, Canada*

A. Jacquard   *Institut National d'Etudes Demographiques, 27 Rue de Commandeur, 75675 Paris, France*

L. B. Jorde   *Department of Anthropology, University of New Mexico, Albuquerque, New Mexico 87131, U.S.A.*

R. Meindl   *Department of Anthropology, University of Massachusetts, Amherst, Massachusetts 01002, U.S.A.*

M. Mohan   *Department of Human Genetics, University of Newcastle upon Tyne, Newcastle upon Tyne, NE2 4AA, U.K.*

A. Moroni   *Laboratorio di Ecologia, University of Parma, Parma, Italy*

D. F. Roberts   *Department of Human Genetics, University of Newcastle upon Tyne, Newcastle upon Tyne, NE2 4AA, U.K.*

E. Siri   *Laboratorio di Ecologia, University of Parma, Parma, Italy*

M. Skolnick   *Biophysics Department and Biology Department, University of Utah, Utah, U.S.A.*

P. E. Smouse   *Department of Human Genetics, University of Michigan, Ann Arbor, Michigan, U.S.A.*

A. Swedlund   *Department of Anthropology, University of Massachusetts, Amherst, Massachusetts 01002, U.S.A.*

H. Temkin   *Department of Anthropology, University of Massachusetts, Amherst, Massachusetts 01002, U.S.A.*

R. H. Ward   *Child Development and Mental Retardation Center and Department of Anthropology, University of Washington, Seattle, Washington 98195, U.S.A.*

K. M. Weiss   *Center for Demographic and Population Genetics, University of Texas, Houston, Texas 77025, U.S.A.*

H. M. Wobst   *Department of Anthropology, University of Massachusetts, Amherst, Massachusetts 01002, U.S.A.*

Contents

To the memory of
LUDWIK KRZYWICKI
A pioneer in the demographic analysis of anthropological populations

R. H. Ward

The Demographic Evolution of Human Populations

*CDMRC and Department of
Anthropology, University of
Washington, Seattle, Washington
98195, U.S.A.*

K. M. Weiss

*Center for Demographic and
Population Genetics, University of
Texas, Houston, Texas 77025, U.S.A.*

1. Introduction

From the standpoint of the population geneticist it is a virtual truism that evolutionary processes can only be fully understood if the mechanisms for genetic change are viewed in the context of the demographic structure of the evolving populations. In the Darwinian sense, evolution occurs as the consequence of the differential survival of populations constrained by environmental limitations and their interaction with other populations. The origin of new adaptive gene complexes due to natural selection arises through the processes of differential fertility and mortality. These factors need to be described in demographic terms before their impact can properly be appreciated in the evolutionary sense. Similarly, the outcome of selection is reflected in demographic parameters; e.g. population size, population density, intrinsic rates of increase, etc.

In formulating the calculus of genetic change through time, the models of population genetics implicitly incorporate this basic relationship between the demographic characteristics of a population and its evolutionary potential. However, for reasons of mathematical convenience, the great majority of such models deal with biologically simple populations comprised of haploid or diploid organisms, lacking age structure and other demographic complexities. Thus, this relationship is not made explicit as often as it should be, if the models of population genetics are to relate to real populations (cf. Pollack & Kempthorne, 1970, 1971). Perhaps the first clear statements of the evolutionary consequences of demographic structure are embodied in the papers by Norton (1926) and Haldane (1927), while Fisher's development of the "Fundamental Theorem" of natural selection (Fisher, 1929) rested on an explicit treatment of this relationship (see also Li, 1967; Edwards, 1967; Turner, 1970; Price, 1972; Price & Smith, 1972). Since this influential statement, the relationship between demographic structure and mechanisms for evolutionary change has not been a major concern for many workers in the field. Only a small proportion of papers have been concerned with extending these concepts for use in natural populations (e.g. Crow, 1958; Charlesworth, 1970 et seq.).

Hence, in attempting to understand the biological evolution of human populations it needs to be emphasised that the important aspects of the evolutionary process are fundamentally products of the demographic characteristics of the set of evolving human populations through time. To understand fully the evolution of our species we must understand how the demographic structure of hominid populations has changed through time, since the demographic structure provides the milieu within which agents of genetic change (selection, drift, migration and mutation) can operate. This statement is no less valid for other species. However, in our own species we have the opportunity for a rare insight into the workings of evolution by virtue of the fact that we have a closer understanding of the action of demographic parameters than in most other natural populations. Unfortunately, this opportunity is lessened by the fact that the demographic processes that operated during the bulk of our species' evolutionary history are not well understood: far less so than demographic processes operating today, because they fall outside the purview of classical demography.

By analogy with the extant tribal populations scattered in many parts of the globe, and by extrapolation from the meagre archaeological remains known to us, it is evident that the early evolving human populations differed in some important characteristics from modern national populations. Specifically, they were small and subject to a set of biological forces distinct from those operating today. The interaction with the biological ecosystem was modulated by the social organization of the population in a manner that can only be faintly discerned in a few tribal populations today. The data which bear most directly upon these ancient demographic processes are sparse and not directly interpretable in terms of the processes themselves, the models of classical demography which were developed to explain processes operating in large nation-states have little bearing on the analysis of the demographic attributes of the human species during the past few million years. The papers in this volume treat a variety of aspects of the demographic evolution of human populations and attempt to deal with some of the basic problems of inference that we are faced with if we are to understand the mechanisms of evolutionary change in our own species.

It seems most probable that human culture evolved from some form of simple band society through a variety of "tribal" levels of organisation to complex civilisations. It is important to determine whether the demographic characteristics of these types of culture differed in ways relevant to the biological evolution of man. We therefore require information about the following processes: the age distribution of deaths; the age distribution of fertility; the size and density of a population; the spatial distribution of subpopulations; interaction between individuals within and between populations with respect to mating; the regulation of population growth; and the modification of natural selection by cultural evolution. In each case, the way in which we approach the problem is severely constrained by the kinds of data available. The quantity and quality of data vary appreciably according to the process being studied and as a function of the temporal distance of the population being studied from the present. The logic of our investigations is also affected by the fact that we are forced to deal exclusively with inferences about the past rather than observing the processes directly. Our inferences are perforce based on models derived by analogy with extant primitive populations and assumptions drawn from population ecology. Even the best data which are available, i.e. archaeological data, are only reflections of the outcome of the processes and not of the processes themselves.

Opportunities for evolution arise through the demographic processes mentioned above. However, the existence of differential demographic processes may not inevitably lead to evolutionary changes if they are not a function of genetic differences. Demographic differentiation may have an evolutionary consequence in two general ways. On one hand, demographic differences within populations will influence the opportunity for selection among competing alleles in those populations. Hence, the rate of gene substitution within a population will be a direct function of the internal demographic differentiation of that population. On the other hand, demographic variability between populations can mediate the differential evolution of whole gene pools—even when this variability may not be related to specific genes distributed among the populations. For example, cultural differences may lead to the accelerated growth of one population relative to another, and yet this may have nothing whatever to do with genes. This is illustrated quite clearly by the radical change in certain gene frequencies in the islands of Fiji during the past 150 years—as a consequence of differential growth rates of Indians and Fijians (Roberts & Mohan, this volume). It would be inappropriate to argue that this rapid increase in the frequency of the allele for the B-blood group is due to genetic selection for that allele; rather, the Indians have lived in Fiji during this time with relative socio-economic advantages, allowing them to maintain much larger families. Therefore, it is important that we not only attempt to assess demographic variability through time, but that we also try to determine the genetic import of this variability. Failing this, we are left only with estimates of potential evolution.

2. Estimating Demographic Processes in Prehistoric Populations

In order to gain an evolutionary perspective of the demographic attributes of prehistoric human populations it is necessary to develop techniques whereby age-specific fertility rates and age-specific death rates can be estimated. It is only by gaining knowledge of the age schedules of fertility and mortality and thereby deriving information about differential reproduction that we can estimate the opportunity for selection. While it is extremely unlikely that we can ever identify specific components of selection with any precision, a detailed knowledge of the distribution of differential reproduction and its relationship to the demographic structure of a population *may* allow the opportunity for selection to be partitioned into biologically relevant components. It may also allow elimination of otherwise competing forms of selection from the set of potential selective forces postulated to account for the evolutionary characteristics of the population. Thus some method for determining the age-specific demographic schedules of prehistoric populations becomes a necessity if we are to chart their evolutionary course with any precision.

In populations with nonoverlapping discrete generations and but a single breeding season, differential reproduction is a much simpler function of viability and mortality than in a long-lived animal such as man. The longer life span of the human species not only allows a more complex set of competing causes of mortality to operate but the processes of mortality and fertility overlap during the life time of an individual. Thus, with a fixed fertility schedule, early mortality deprives an individual of more reproduction than does late mortality, and with a fixed mortality schedule earlier fertility is advantageous. This relationship between mortality and fertility schedules and the effect it has on the rate of allele substitution has been discussed at length by Charlesworth (1970, 1972, 1973, 1974). These findings are of central interest to attempts to evaluate the evolutionary consequences of demographic structure, since the age schedules of mortality and fertility are reflected in the age structure, or census, of the population. The age structure of a population is often our primary available data and allows reconstruction of the age-specific schedules of birth and death. From this we may estimate the *opportunity* for selection, even when the causes of mortality and their genetic relevance have not been determined.

The problems involved in such an endeavour are manifold and should not be lightly glossed over—only by their recognition and subsequent solution can we hope to make definitive statements regarding the selective forces operating in prehistoric populations. The problems that must be contended with are of two distinct types: (a) the adequacy of data from prehistoric populations, and (b) the validity of making demographic inferences from the type of data available to us.

(a) The data that are relevant to the demographic evolution of human populations can be classified into three distinct categories.

(i) Data such as skeletal series that yield direct evidence of the demographic structure of the prehistoric population. While such data are to be preferred there are some problems of reliability when using skeletal series to estimate demographic parameters (due to differential exhumation, differential preservation, biases inherent in the original processes of burial, etc.). In addition, while skeletal series yield an indication of overall mortality schedules of a prehistoric population, they give little indication of the cause of death and essentially *no* information regarding the fertility schedules of the population. Hence the reconstruction of fertility schedules is essentially unrelated to the data being examined and can only be assessed in terms of its concordance with the mortality schedules of the population and our assumptions as to how these two schedules should fit together (e.g. Weiss, 1973*a*).

(ii) Data that are demographic in nature, but indirect with respect to prehistoric populations. These are the data relative to the demographic structure of present tribal populations whose way of life is presumed to be similar to that of certain prehistoric populations. Here the problem is essentially a reversal of the skeletal situation for it is direct observations on the age at death that is lacking. Perinatal and infant death rates are most likely to be inaccurately assessed for tribal populations yet they are crucial to our understanding of the inter-relationship of fertility and mortality schedules (e.g. Neel & Weiss, 1975). Given the usually limited time for observations, one is forced to construct period life tables, deducing the age of death from the survivorship distributions and fertility schedules from the distribution of mothers and their living offspring. The translation of such period life tables into synthetic cohort life tables then depends upon a variety of assumptions (see below). In addition, just as the data from skeletal series were beset by problems due to inadequate sampling, sampling biases, etc., so too are observations from tribal populations. Here, however, gaps in the data base can be filled in with anamnestic information. There is also the possibility of resampling to clear up ambiguities. Thus data from existing tribal populations may make the greatest contribution to our understanding of the demographic evolution of the human species, particularly if it tends to corroborate the data actually derived from the past. This is reflected by the utilisation of principles derived from the study of existing tribal populations by many papers in this volume. However, it must be stated that the interpretation of past processes in terms of present phenomena should be made with considerable caution.

(iii) The third type of data requires mention, not because it yields any insight into demographic processes but only because it is so pervasive in the archaeological literature (e.g. Spooner, 1972). This is the collection of archaeological observations assumed to yield indirect evidence of total population size and hence allow speculation about rates of growth through time. Ranging from estimates of number of people per room through areal estimates of village (or city) size, it is obvious that such evidence adds little to our understanding of demographic processes. However, it does yield some information about the possible rates of growth of prehistoric populations for vast tracts of time during which we have no information, and may provide independent evidence against which data of the first type can be tested (e.g. Zubrow, 1971; Swedlund & Sessions, in press). For this reason they should not be rejected out of hand. In addition, Yellen & Harpending (1972), Williams (1974) and Wobst (this volume) have shown that such indirect evidence can reveal certain attributes of population structure (in terms of the distribution of demes within a given area) that is instructive from both an evolutionary and demographic perspective.

(b) Having considered some of the deficiencies in the data base we now consider the set of assumptions that must be made in translating our data observations into estimates of demographic structure.

Since data of either type 1 or type 2 will be most commonly used, the demographic structure of the population will derive from reconstructing vital rate schedules. This reconstruction hinges on the relationship between birth and death rates by age, or the age structure of the population, and the intrinsic rate of growth of the population. The standard Euler equation (Euler, 1760) will commonly be used to formalise this relationship for a given set of data, viz:

$$1 = \sum_x l_x b_x e^{-rx} \qquad\qquad (1)$$

and a companion equation

$$c_x = b l_x e^{-rx}$$

where l_x is the probability of surviving from birth to age x, b_x is the birth rate at age x, c_x the proportion of the population at age x, b the crude birth rate, and r is the annual growth rate of the population; the summation is over all ages. Lacking direct observations of either the ages at death in living populations or of fertility schedules for skeletal populations we are forced to utilise models which assume the stability and constancy of the basic demographic process. In practice most analyses depend on deriving the best estimate for r and assuming that the relative pattern of age-specific fertility is essentially invariant in time and space (Weiss, 1973b). With these two parameters fixed, a mortality schedule and average annual birth rate can then be used to reconstruct vital rates with some precision (e.g. Weiss, 1973a). However, the validity of the assumptions inherent in this procedure are crucial to our ability to make such reconstructions and they need to be carefully examined. Failure to realise the pervasive nature of these assumptions in reconstructing demographic schedules and the uncritical application of demographic techniques developed for large modern nation-states to prehistoric or tribal populations will only result in misleading conclusions. (For some discussion about this point see Petersen (1975) and the accompanying comments).

The two most widespread assumptions in standard demographic models (excepting the contentious opinion that r has rarely risen above 0.1% in man's history) are (a) age-specific birth and death rates are essentially independent of other parameters in the population (i.e. no density regulated feedback) and (b) birth and death rates are intrinsic parameters of a population not subject to statistical fluctuations (thereby yielding the stability of age structure necessary for the derivation of the Euler equation). However, if the first assumption were true then the vital rates would be subject to chance fluctuations about these expected values to the extent that small populations with more extreme fluctuations would be highly susceptible to chance extinction. With fluctuations in both birth and death rates as populations become small, there is always the chance that every member of the population will die without issue. If we add to this the increasing restriction in eligible mates as a consequence of decreasing size in a population with various marriages being prohibited, then the likelihood of the continued existence of human population groups smaller than 200 becomes small indeed. However, such populations do survive and do exhibit variability in birth and death rates. As a consequence, some authors have claimed that the variable age structure derived from prehistoric (or primitive) populations are too severely distorted to be reliable (e.g. Angel, 1969). The extent of the variability in vital estimates under a density independent model, can be shown to be sufficiently great (e.g. Moore *et al.*, 1975) that model life tables such as those found in Coale & Demeny (1965), Acsádi & Nemeskéri (1970) or Weiss (1973*a*) seem inappropriate. However, if the vital rates are dependent on population density (i.e. violating the first assumption) the birth and death rates, as well as the age distribution tend to be stable for long periods of time (Weiss & Smouse, this volume). Furthermore, using a non-stochastic density dependent model, Weiss has shown that even relatively major demographic disturbances do not severely disrupt the demographic structure of even quite small populations, provided the disturbances last only a few years (Weiss, 1975). Hence if vital rates are density dependent, as seems most probable by analogy with other biological populations (e.g. Wynne–Edwards, 1962; McLaren, 1971), then even for populations as small as 100, the age distribution becomes remarkably stable and the fluctuations of birth and death rates about their expected values are well within the tolerance required by evolutionary studies. Thus model life tables can be used with some confidence to estimate the underlying vital rates from prehistoric populations since the density dependent fluctuations about these rates will usually be small.

The density dependent model not only gives stable demographic rates that are realistic for small populations but also has some implications for evolutionary theory. If density dependent rates have tended to regulate population size over long time periods then the importance of genetic "bottlenecks" in contributing to gene frequency drift (e.g. Wright, 1948) may have been greatly overemphasised. This is certainly a point worth further study, as is the implication that density dependent vital rates may give rise to constantly changing selective coefficients through time. Thus the existence of density dependent selective coefficients as a result of changing vital rates may yield radically different predictions of the amount of genetic variability in small populations than that estimated by standard Markov models assuming constancy of selection coefficients along with invariant vital rates.

Earlier we referred to the fact that the study of the demographic evolution of human populations assumes that models drawn from population ecology are applicable and that analogies drawn from extant tribal populations are valid. These assumptions which essentially state that present processes can be applied to the past are part of the principle of "uniformitarianism" to which Howell's paper is addressed. We assume that during the evolution of the human species, as simple band societies gave way to larger population aggregates with more complex social organisations, population structure underwent a series of transitions comparable to the shift that would be required to move from one level of cultural complexity to another amongst present day tribal populations; much as stages of biological evolution are conceived of in terms of modern day taxa. Thus as Howell clearly shows, the pattern of vital rates found in today's populations with a given level of cultural organisation can be expected to be characteristic of extinct populations exhibiting similar aspects of cultural complexity. More importantly, the kind of biological processes that are identified as contributing to the regulation of vital rates in extant tribal populations can be presumed to have prevailed in the past amongst populations with similar levels of social organisation existing in similar ecological contexts. Specifically, Howell argues that mortality patterns found in modern hunter-gatherers such as the San are representative of those found in prehistoric populations with a similar level of cultural organisation. Such a position is strengthened by the observation that several studies surveying anthropological data have found similar patterns of mortality among both living populations as well as in skeletal series (Acsádi & Nemeskéri, 1970; Weiss, 1973a). Further, we can argue that the fertility schedules and the factors which modify or regulate basic parameters of fertility (especially probabilities of ovulation, conception and successful termination of pregnancy) observed in such populations have had a long evolutionary history in human populations by accepting Howell's premise that there has been a long standing persistence of physiological mechanisms effecting the age-specific distribution of fertility in a defined way. Hence the principle of uniformitarianism not only allows us to estimate age schedules of fertility (e.g. Weiss, 1973b; Henneberg, this volume) but also allows us to incorporate relatively sophisticated models of fertility control (e.g. Potter, 1970; Goodman, 1971; Ginsberg, 1973; Poole, 1973) into our analyses of the biological factors involved in demographic changes over-time.

3. Evolutionary Aspects of Changes in Differential Mortality and Fertility

Having examined the kinds of assumptions on which paleodemographic work is generally based, we can go on to consider the uses to which this work has been put. One of the major areas of inference is the contribution of differential mortality and fertility to human evolutionary history.

Age-specific vital rates affect the opportunity for selection in a variety of ways. As first discussed by Haldane (1927) and Norton (1926), and recently elaborated by other workers (Charlesworth, 1970, et seq.; Charlesworth & Giesel, 1972a, 1972b; Anderson & King, 1970; Pollak & Kempthorne, 1970, 1971) the schedules of age-specific birth and death rates offer the opportunity for differential rates of growth of alleles. If the total reproduction of genotype (ij) is given by the standard formula for overlapping generations

$$R_{ij} = \sum_{x} l_{ij.x} f_{ij.x} \qquad (2)$$

where R_{ij} is the total number of female offspring produced per female of type (ij), $l_{ij.x}$ is the chance of surviving to age x (a direct reflection of mortality) and $f_{ij.x}$ is the number of female offspring produced by a carrier of genotype (ij) in the xth year of life, then the genotype with the highest R_{ij} will have the highest mean fitness and expand at the expense of others. Following Fisher's definition of fitness as the Malthusian parameter in a population, we can express this as follows:

$$1 = \sum_x l_{ij,x} f_{ij,x} e^{-r_{ij}x} \tag{3}$$

where r_{ij} is that growth rate (Malthusian parameter) which satisfies this standard equation for stable populations. The resulting changes in gene frequencies can be computed from the relative values of the genotype-specific Malthusian parameters, after some approximations have been made (e.g. Jacquard, 1974).

There can be changes in gene frequencies which are simply due to overall demographic changes in the population (Charlesworth & Giesel, 1972a); if we define mean fitness of genotypes in a mixed population of genotypes by:

$$W_{ij} = \sum_x l_{ij,x} f_{ij,x} e^{-rx} \tag{4}$$

with r the overall population growth rate, then the fitness of a given genotype will change simply by virtue of changes in total population growth rate (which may be unrelated to an allele's probability of survival). In a growing population, genotypes which reproduce relatively earlier in life than others will increase in frequency relative to others; conversely in a declining population alleles with a later pattern of reproduction will increase in frequency. Charlesworth & Giesel (1972b) have also dealt with the case in which the vital rates are density dependent, and again changes in allelic proportions may arise as a consequence of changes in population density, rather than changes in intrinsic physiological properties. Thus the fertility and mortality schedules of genotypes in populations with overlapping generations are directly related to changes in allele frequencies.

In addition to the evolutionary opportunity afforded by differential age-specific vital rate schedules for alleles, the opportunity for selection to act is modified by mortality schedules in a different way. Populations with different mortality schedules (up to and including the period of reproduction) offer different opportunities for the action of genetic selection. If premenopausal mortality is distributed over a long time interval then the opportunity for genetic death to compete with causes of nongenetic (e.g. accidental) death will be greater (i.e. corresponding to the concept of "soft selection" (Wallace, 1970)) than in populations in which prereproductive mortality is concentrated into a short interval. The more extended the period of attrition experienced by cohort before it completes its reproduction, the greater the variety of environmental constraints it experiences and the greater the opportunity for different selective causes to act. In populations with concentrated mortality schedules the opportunity for the action of a diverse set of selective forces is reduced. Under such mortality regimes, where "hard selection" operates it is inherently unlikely that the proportion of deaths solely due to genetic causes will be as high as in situations where mortality is extended and soft selection prevails. Thus the detection of age-specific mortality schedules in prehistoric populations allows some inference to be drawn concerning the existence of regimes of "hard" or "soft" selection, and hence the magnitude of the genetic load experienced by the population as well as the possible rate of allelic change due to the operation of selective forces.

An alternative approach to evaluating the evolutionary consequences of demographic processes derives from Fisher's Fundamental Theorem of Natural Selection (Fisher, 1929). Since the theorem states that selective intensity (or relative increase in fitness) is related to variability in fitness (biologically expressed in terms of variability of offspring produced), then the parameters of differential mortality and fertility exhibited by a population can be used to derive the opportunity for an increase in relative fitness in successive generations (Crow, 1958, 1966). The resulting Index of the Opportunity for Selection, I_t, can be conceived as the ratio of the variance in number of offspring to all individuals ever born divided by the square of the mean number of offspring produced per individual ever born. This can be partitioned into a component due to mortality in the prereproductive period, I_m, and variability in expressed fertility during the reproductive period, I_f, thus:

$$I_t = \frac{V_n}{(\bar{N})^2} = I_m + \frac{I_f}{l_{15}} \qquad (5)$$

where $I_m = V_m/(\bar{N})^2$, $I_f = V_f/(\bar{N}_{15})^2$, l_{15} is the survivorship probability to age 15, $\bar{N}$ the average number of offspring per person ever born, $\bar{N}_{15}$ the average number of offspring per person who survives to age 15 and V_n, V_m, V_f being the variances in offspring number for all people ever born, the variance due to prereproductive mortality, and the variance in offspring number among those who reach the age of reproduction.

As originally devised, the index was intended for use in modern populations where mortality during the reproductive years is essentially zero. Used in this manner the index will identify the cumulative effect of differential mortality and differential fertility in contributing to the opportunity for selection. However, in tribal and prehistoric populations where mortality during the reproductive period is likely to be appreciable, this no longer holds since the I_f component will also include the effects of differential adult mortality. In such cases some modification of the index is desirable to account for deaths during the reproductive period (e.g. Koyabashi, 1969), and to provide a more realistic estimate of the total contribution of differential mortality to the opportunity for selection.

For skeletal populations, computations of such an index must be approached differently. One attempt to circumvent the lack of observations of the fertility schedule has been made by Henneberg (this volume). Henneberg's results are derived from two previous works (Henneberg, 1976; Henneberg & Piontek, 1976) and are aimed at estimating the reproductive rate of a prehistoric population relative to its reproductive potential. The reproductive potential is a measure of the reproduction that would occur if the same fertility schedule obtained but adult mortality was essentially zero during the reproductive period. Hence, the problem can be conceived in terms of partitioning the I_f component as defined above into a fertility component and an adult mortality component.

In order to estimate the fertility schedule of prehistoric populations Henneberg makes use of the observation that the majority of culturally similar populations exhibit concordant age-specific distributions of relative fertility (i.e. although mean birth rate may vary considerably the proportion of births per woman in a given age class remains more or less constant for a given level of social organisation). Using a variety of data he develops an "archetype of fertility", $1 - s_x$, which represents the proportion of completed fertility, U_c, by age x, the values being 0·05, 0·23, 0·45, 0·65, 0·83, 0·95, 1·0 for the 7 age classes in the reproductive period (Henneberg, this volume). This similarity in age patterns of relative fertility has been noted by Talwar (1970) and also by Weiss (1973a,b) who used this fact to construct model life tables and indices of growth regulation. Using these values Henneberg calculates the reproduction actually achieved compared to that which would have obtained had there been no mortality in the reproductive period. The Net Reproductive Rate (R_0), representing the number of females produced per female born, is computed from the rate of juvenile mortality and presumed sex ratio at birth while a range of values is given for children born to women reaching menopause, U_c (equivalent to the Total Fertility Rate or TFR). Finally a Biological State Index (I_{bs}) is derived to reflect the amount of reproductive potential lost as a consequence of mortality before and during the reproductive period. This index can be construed as indicating the opportunity for selection to act through mortality differentials as perceived from skeletal data (in which we are restricted to an analysis of mortality only). Further, the total index, I_{bs}, is a function of juvenile mortality (indicated by survivorship to age 15) and mortality during the reproductive period (indicated by R_{pot}), viz: $I_{bs} = l_{15} \cdot R_{pot}$ (see below). The relationship between the various indices constructed by Henneberg is indicated by defining them in terms of age-specific birth and death rates.

First we note that U_c (or completed family size) is equivalent to the Total Fertility Rate (TFR) or sum of age-specific birth rates, b_x, i.e.

$$TFR = \sum_{x=15}^{\omega} b_x.$$

Similarly the archetype of fertility, $1 - s_x$, represents the proportion of the Total Fertility Rate achieved by age x, i.e.

$$1 - s_x = \sum_{i=15}^{x} b_i \Big/ \sum_{i=15}^{\omega} b_i. \tag{6}$$

Further, since the proportion of individuals who die at age x in the reproductive period, d_x, can be written in terms of survivorship to age x, l_x, i.e.

$$d_x = \frac{l_x - l_{x+1}}{l_{15}}; \quad \sum_{x=15}^{\omega} d_x = 1$$

we may derive R_{pot} as follows:

$$R_{pot} = \sum_{x=15}^{\omega} d_x(1 - s_x)$$

(from Henneberg—3), and substituting for d_x, and $1 - s_x$ we have:

$$R_{pot} = \sum_{x=15}^{\omega} \left(\frac{l_x - l_{x+1}}{l_{15}} \right) \cdot \left(\frac{\sum_{i=15}^{x} b_i}{\sum_{i=15}^{\omega} b_i} \right) \tag{7}$$

$$= \frac{1}{l_{15} \sum_{i=15}^{\omega} b_i} \cdot \sum_{x=15}^{\omega} l_x - l_{x+1} \cdot \sum_{x=15}^{x} b_i$$

$$= \frac{1}{l_{15} TFR} \cdot \sum_{x=15}^{\omega} l_x b_x. \tag{8}$$

Further, if we let $\bar{F}$ represent the average family size of all women who survive to the beginning of the reproductive period, then

$$\bar{F} = \sum_{x=15}^{\omega} l_x b_x / l_{15}$$

giving

$$R_{pot} = \frac{\bar{F}}{TFR}. \tag{9}$$

Hence, R_{pot} is simply the ratio of the average family size of all women who reach the beginning of reproductive period to the average family size of all women who successfully survive throughout the reproductive period.

Similarly, since R_0, the Net Reproductive Rate, is the average number of females born to all females born this can be expressed as:

$$R_0 = 1/2 \sum_{x=15}^{\omega} l_x b_x \cdot l_{15}$$

assuming an equal sex ratio at birth.

By substitution we have:

$$R_{pot} = \frac{2R_0}{l_{15} TFR}$$

as in Henneberg (equation (3)).

Lastly, I_{bs}, which represents the loss in reproduction due to all causes or mortality, can be defined by:

$$I_{bs} = \frac{\displaystyle\sum_{x=15}^{\omega} l_x b_x}{\displaystyle\sum_{x=15}^{\omega} b_x} = l_{15} R_{pot} = \frac{2R_0}{TFR}. \tag{10}$$

It should be noted at this point that the values of R_{pot} and I_{bs} are only average values drawn from a distribution where the range in values is determined by the variability in fertility schedules among the population studied.

Taken in conjunction with the inevitable data inaccuracies that will occur in such studies, this implies that different values for estimates of R_{pot} may not have much biological significance. Since the "archetype" values given by Henneberg are based on only 4 data sets they may be less representative than the values given by Talwar and by Weiss (op. cit.) which derive from significantly larger data sets. Their values which show a more peaked distribution ($1 - s_x = 0.10, 0.35, 0.59, 0.79, 0.93, 0.99, 1.00$) would yield somewhat higher estimates of R_{pot} than given by Henneberg. Given this inherent uncertainty in deriving representative estimates from a single population it might be more appropriate to attach biological significance to average values for a set of culturally similar populations. In that case, differences in average values of the state indices might well reflect the biological consequences of different levels of cultural organisation. However in the data given by Henneberg there does not appear to be any consistent pattern to the distribution of I_{bs} among the populations as a function of cultural organisation. Hence, it is difficult to assess the observed variability in biological terms.

In a similar vein, it should be pointed out that the fact that populations in Medieval Europe were capable of growth (Henneberg & Piontek, 1976) does not necessarily mean that such growth actually occurred. To the extent that all populations have a degree of birth regulation, the average U_e (TFR) values presented in Henneberg are probably rather high estimates. Irrespective of the constraints imposed by the mortality schedule, virtually all human populations show some potential for growth (i.e. some degree of fertility limitation) and Henneberg's data concur with this.

Lastly, it must be stressed that these various indices (founded on Fisher's Fundamental Theorem) indicate only the opportunity for selection to act rather than the actual intensity of selection. Changes in allele frequencies due to selective pressure will only occur if the variability of mortality and fertility is heritable and genotype specific. Since demographic data give no information concerning these relationships, we can only consider the relative opportunities for selection to act at specific points in the demographic history of one population compared to another. The actual selective intensities at various stages of the life cycle will be dictated by the magnitude of soft selection compared to the regime of hard selection at that point. With our present state of knowledge these remain matters that we can only speculate upon.

4. Inter-relationship Between Cultural Changes and Demographic Structure

The approaches to relating the opportunity for selection to the age schedules of mortality and fertility so far discussed rely on the assumption that these schedules are fixed. If these rates change, then selective opportunities will change as well. Should the changes be of the density dependent type (reflecting short-lived responses to stochastic disturbances from the underlying vital rate schedule), then only slight fluctuations in the opportunity for natural selection are to be expected. However, in addition to these small feedback effects, human evolution has experienced marked changes in demographic structure as a function of cultural evolution. This has been especially true in the evolution of civilisations and in the more recent industrial revolution. This marked change in the social and ecological structure of human populations has had ramifications in three main areas of demographic concern: (a) the extent to which population growth is regulated and by what mechanisms; (b) the density, spatial distribution and degree of aggregation of individuals; and (c) distribution of vital rate schedules as a function of socio-cultural practices.

(a) In the first case, regulation of population growth must have initially occurred primarily through the operation of biological processes with mortality differentials predominating. As the evolution of human societies proceeded, population regulation became mediated more by cultural practices than by physiological processes (as a consequence we must also assume that the components of selection have likewise changed throughout the ages). While the increasing influence of cultural factors on altering mortality rates is well understood (and adequately documented for the past centuries), the relative influence of cultural and physiological factors on altering fertility rates through time is less well understood. It is clear that changing cultural practices during the past 200 years have had a marked and pervasive effect on fertility schedules of many human populations (e.g. see Jacquard & Ward, this volume). It is less clear to what extent physiological processes have contributed to the regulation of fertility and whether these effects vary from one level of cultural organisation to the next.

The view that in the past, physiological processes rather than cultural patterns pre-dominated in the regulation of population size by affecting fertility schedules, is exemplified by Howell (this volume). Based on the belief that physiological factors leading to birth spacing in present day hunter-gatherers were important in the prehistoric period, she develops an intriguing hypothesis. Instead of viewing lactation directly or indirectly as the overriding factor contributing to the suppression of ovulation following a birth, as has been commonly argued for such societies (Skolnick & Cannings, 1973; Lee, 1972; Newman, 1972), she postulates an additional mechanism. By developing the critical fatness hypothesis advanced by Frisch (1973, 1976) she presents a persuasive case for the automatic regulation of fertility in hunter-gatherers as a consequence of their nutritional status and cultural organisation. This can be compared to hypotheses put forth to explain regulation in certain animal populations by a combination of resource limitations and crowding (e.g. Williams, 1971). While it has yet to be demonstrated that this is a widespread phenomenon in other human groups of similar culture, the possibility that ovulatory periods controlled by nutritional status could have been an important regulatory mechanism in prehistoric times deserves serious consideration. It is likely that many factors operated. The relative importance of critical fat levlels as a fertility regulator compared to the effect of lactation or cultural constraints (e.g. abortion and infanticide) will vary as a function of the degree of nutritional stress experienced by the prehistoric populations. This remains to be determined, as does the relative efficacy of other physiological mechanisms in a variety of extant tribal cultures under different regimes of age-specific vital rates, and differing degrees of environmental stress.

(b) The second way in which demographic structure is affected by changes in levels of cultural complexity is in the manner in which these changes alter (i) the density and spatial dispersion of individuals within subpopulations and (ii) the size of subpopulations and the spatial relationships between them. This in turn has a feedback effect on the patterns of mating and communication between (and also within) subpopulations. Hence the characteristics of the spatial distribution of a population are placed in a demographic context by viewing them as a function of the socio-cultural parameters expressed by a population in its ecological setting, modulated by the specific regime of population regulation practiced by the group. The changing relationship between the parameters of this feedback system are discussed more fully in the papers by Jorde Harpending (this volume), and will be discussed below. Here we wish to concentrate on the relationship between demographic structure and the spatial distribution of sub-populations as these can be inferred for prehistoric populations. Different spatial distributions in a given socio-cultural setting have some evolutionary importance since they will regulate the flow of genes from one segment of the population to another. This pattern of gene flow is a function not only of the migration rates between subpopulations but also of the degree of genetic differentiation among them. It cannot be measured merely as a function of geographic distances between them (e.g. Ward & Neel, 1970).

Using data from living primitive populations, anthropologists have discovered many regular patterns of mating which are fundamental aspects of the structure of living primitive groups. The extent to which these patterns are a function of the availability of individuals of a given relationship, and hence a function of the demographic character-istics of the population is not well understood. The availability of various kinds of relatives as a function of vital rates has been determined for large nationstates (Goodman et al., 1974). It is less clear how these parameters might be inter-related in the generally small populations characteristic of the prehistoric past (but see Hajnal, 1963; Williams, 1975). Simulation studies have provided the greatest degree of information to date. They indicate that in small populations with some degree of growth regulation, certain marriage systems may be inherently more stable than others (Skolnick & Cannings, 1974), but the rates of long term genetic drift are not extensively affected by differences in mating structure (Cannings & Skolnick, 1975).

With respect to the degree of mating between subpopulations, there are some preliminary indications that the principle of uniformitarianism may be inappropriate. This is exemplified by the conclusion of Wobst (this volume), who derives patterns of spatial organisation in Paleolithic hunter-gatherers from the spatial variability observed among lithic artifacts, using methods of locational analysis. He argues that the models of tribal structure generally used by anthropologists may not apply to these early band societies. The models based on analogy with extant tribes assume a population that consists of a mating network of hexagonally packed subpopulations with a relative barrier to mating across tribal boundaries (Birdsell, 1958, 1968; Williams, 1974). Wobst argues that the clinal variability in lithic assemblages implies that each subpopulation is the center of its own mating network and that tribes with their hierarchically structured barriers to mating did not exist. Instead Wobst derives a processual model by which artifact assemblages of Pleistocene man are assessed in terms of the presumed pattern of subdivision among mating populations. The conclusions have important ramifications for models of gene flow over large geographic areas and the maintenance of genetic heterozygosity over long time periods. If Wobst's model is correct, it implies that in Paleolithic times genetic microdifferentiation did not occur to the extent it is observed in present day tribal populations. In addition to providing a new model for the basic social structure of early human populations, and illustrating the care with which the assumption of uniformitarianism must be applied, his paper illustrates the necessity of critically examining demographic inferences made from indirect archaeological data.

Much more work is required to assess whether the artifactual remains of groups such as the Bushmen or Australian aborigines would reflect tribal closure to archaeologists. While some work has been attempted along these lines (e.g. Peterson, 1975), it is too early to decide whether we should modify our ideas regarding the permanence of tribal closure or merely revise our concepts of how this is expressed in terms of artifactual assemblages. For instance, it is entirely possible that tribally closed bands might display clines in artifact and stylistic components. One such example is the demonstration that genetic, linguistic, and anthropometric clines can be discerned in Australia (Birdsell, 1949; Abbie, 1951, 1968; Simmons, 1973), despite the presence of relative mating barriers due to the existence of local tribes. Since clinal variability in genetic and anthropometric characters can be discerned within tribal populations displaying a high degree of genetic microdifferentiation (Morgan & Holmes, in press; Ward & Neel, 1976) the existence of clines in less extensively subdivided populations is not conclusive evidence against tribal closure.

The existence of uniform hexagonal mating networks becomes important in assessing the probability that human races could be significantly different subpopulations of *Homo sapiens* that have evolved in relative isolation (Cavalli–Sforza & Bodmer, 1971; Nei & Rouchoudhury, 1974; many others). Wobst's views which imply a large amount of gene flow between subpopulations, would support the conclusion that "races" are merely abstractions of a continuum of variability throughout a widespread human species (Lewontin, 1972; Birdsell, 1972; Brues, 1972; Weiss & Maruyama, 1976).

(c) The third area of demographic structure that is affected by cultural change is the changing pattern of mortality and fertility schedules. As we discussed above, the age-specific distribution of mortality rates appears to have undergone a radical change as populations have evolved through different levels of cultural complexity. It is entirely possible that the age-specific pattern of fertility rates has undergone similar changes during the course of man's evolution. While there is an obvious lack of data to this point, some generalisations follow from inspection of the distribution of fertility parameters by cultural level in data used by Talwar (1970) and Weiss (1973a,b). Their distributions can also be compared with those obtaining from large industralised populations and some tentative conclusions may be drawn. It seems likely that the more ancient prehistoric populations, which were less buffered from the environment, may have exhibited smaller contributions to fertility in the later age categories. Hence fertility would tend to be concentrated in the earlier age classes with the peak fertility regime moving forward in age, as the populations go back in time. If this assertion is correct, then Henneberg's "archetype of fertility" differs in precisely the wrong direction from the values given by Talwar and Weiss (his distribution being lower and flatter, see above). More work is obviously required to resolve this point.

The overall effect of cultural changes has been to reduce the variability of both mortality and fertility as shown by Jacquard & Ward (this volume). This in turn will have profound effects on the opportunity for natural selection to act in modern populations compared with populations of a few centuries ago. As we have noted above, this does not imply that natural selection has necessarily changed in overall magnitude. However, it may mean that the distribution of selective effects has changed markedly. With different patterns of the opportunity for selection, it seems likely that various components of selection will have changed in importance as a consequence of the cultural evolution of man. For example, the dramatic change in infant mortality in recent times indicates that the component of selection due to infectious diseases in infancy has been greatly reduced in importance (e.g. Jacquard and Ward, this volume). In contrast, other components of selection may have increased in importance (e.g. selection for genetically mediated aspects of family size limitation).

5. Temporal Trends in Demographic Parameters

Having discussed the implications of changing demographic parameters for the rates and type of biological evolution in man, we now cite some specific examples where an analysis of the historical record indicates the change in demographic structures. Three basic processes can be considered. First, there is the demographic transition consequent upon initial coloniziation and subsequent growth. Secondly, there are the secular changes in demographic structures that may be observed in a small subdivided population during the past two centuries. Thirdly, there is the situation where a colonising population competes with an already established population.

The first case is exemplified by the report on the colonisation of the Connecticut Valley from 1650 to 1850 (Swedlund et al., this volume). This study not only illustrates some of the basic approaches that can be applied to studying changing demographic parameters in a historical context but also raises some points of theoretical interest. The most characteristic attributes of successful colonising populations once they have become dispersed into the new environment are: (a) their capacity to undergo periods of rapid growth during their inception, and (b) the capacity to stabilise their growth parameters and become established once a certain population density is reached. While either aspect may predominate in a given colonising situation (various ecological contexts may select for a heavy reliance on only one aspect of these different strategies (Diamond, 1974)) both have to be present to some degree. These attributes can be conceived of in terms of density regulated growth with damping occurring as a function of carrying capacity.

Swedlund's study gives specific documentation of density regulated growth and the imposition of a carrying capacity in a human population. The carrying capacity is culturally based and as it changes there are noticeable changes in the population size. This is a clear illustration of the behaviour of a human population in a colonising situation, and it can be compared to other studies of similar situations. The problem has been investigated by several anthropologists, but the recent history of the New World may yield the clearest descriptions of this process. The rapid rates of growth early in the colonising period have also been noted in other colonising situations, e.g. Pitcairn, Tristan de Cunha, Australia (Birdsell, 1957), and thus corroborate the existence of ecologically derived principles in human populations.

The extreme importance that should be attached to the inherent growth rates of the local population is shown by the negligible effect of migration. Even in the relatively early stages when immigration might be expected to have a considerable effect, the growth processes are dictated by the internal growth rates. In genetic terms this implies that in colonising situations the extent of genetic microdifferentiation will be largely a function of the relative growth rates of the constituent subpopulations than the degree of genetic exchange among them. As the carrying capacity is reached, migration will play a more important role; as long as each subpopulation displays an equally homogeneous response in achieving decreased (or zero) growth rates.

One question raised by this work which could be given more attention in the future is: what are the relative effects of declining fertility and mortality in this type of demographic transition? It will be interesting to see how these two vital forces change in relation to each other, as this gives information regarding selective pressures. The operation of natural selection in ecologically controlled human populations will depend on whether alterations in either differential mortality or in differential fertility give the greatest opportunity for selective processes to operate.

The study by Skolnick et al. (this volume) which investigates the effect of secular changes in demographic parameters is distinctive in that the analysis can be specifically couched in genetic terms. This is made possible by virtue of the fact that the basic historical parameters of birth, death and marriage rates have first been converted into genealogical parameters. By so doing, the historical registers containing basic demographic parameters can now yield not merely expectations of the opportunity for selection, but rather estimates of the intensity of selection and also of which stages of the life cycle are actually under selective pressures at a given historical instant. As noted above, these are the very qualities required of analyses investigating the evolutionary consequences of specific changes in demographic parameters. Hence the study by Skolnick et al. warrants careful attention as a model for definitive work in this area.

There is an urgent requirement for such studies combining genetic analyses (based on genealogical information) with analyses of demographic changes through time. They need to be carried out in a variety of human populations at different levels of cultural organisation. Such studies may very well provide the key to our interpretation of the genetic consequences of the various demographic structures of prehistoric populations. Some preliminary studies have already been initiated on some populations at the tribal level (e.g. Chaventré, 1972; Langaney & Gomila, 1972; Ward, 1975). However, they have all been beset by the problems mentioned by Skolnick *et al.*, namely the difficulty of constructing a record linking alogrithm and extending the record links sufficiently far back in time to be useful. Thus, their results, like those presently obtaining from the Parma Valley, tend to be both tentative and tantalising, rather than definitive. With more attention given to such studies in the future, we should be able to define evolutionary parameters in human populations more effectively.

Besides demonstrating a remarkably effective approach to the construction of linked pedigrees, Skolnick *et al.* demonstrate the secular changes that have occurred in three demographic parameters in this isolated community. First, the change in the age-specific distribution of fertility rates throughout the 350 years of the analysis is indicated by the changing pattern of age at marriage and age differences between spouses. The analysis of secular change in these parameters indicates the attainment of a higher average fertility per couple through time. As the variability in these parameters drops through time the opportunity for selection to act through fertility differences will also be lessened. Completed family size is shown to have risen through time (as expected from the first analysis) largely as a consequence of declining mortality rates through the reproductive period. This result stresses yet again the importance of recognising the contribution of differential adult mortality to variability in expressed fertility in all non-industrialised human populations. Also, the effective immigration rate is constantly depressed throughout this period of secular change due to the relatively lower reproductive performance of migrants. This result parallels that found by Swedlund *et al.* (this volume) and Ward & Raspe (1973) in instances of colonising populations. It thus appears that in stable populations as well as colonising populations with a high growth rate, the rate of gene flow may be considerably below that predicted by the proportion of immigrants entering the population (Ward & Neel, 1970).

Thus the overall, preliminary, findings for the isolated communities in the Parma Valley tend to parallel the secular changes observed over much of Europe in this period. Hence the opportunity for selection to act through differential fertility has decreased with time. However, the rather greater changes that can be expected in the distribution of mortality rates will probably indicate that in the Parma Valley, as elsewhere, the *relative* contribution of fertility differentials to selective potential has increased over the past 350 years. The difference will be that in the case of the Parma Valley the genea-logical structure extending back to the 17th century will allow us to estimate selective components of demographic processes more precisely than previously.

Finally, we consider the situation of a colonising population competing with an established population. Using Fiji as an example, Roberts Mohan (this volume) indicate the rapidity with which an invading population can outcompete an existing population solely due to differential demographic parameters. They also clearly point out that the differences in demographic parameters need not have any genetic (or adaptive) basis but instead can arise as a series of historical quirks. This raises the possibility that the overall population size of our species may have been approximately stable during many millenia while component subpopulations continuously underwent periods of growth and extinction as a function of fluctuation in vital rates. If so, this would allow the somewhat greater stability of underlying vital rates in small populations with nonzero growth rates (viz. Weiss Smouse, this volume) without any necessary imposition of a severe genetic load since the differences in growth rates are due to historical accidents. However, this concept also implies a rather more transitory nature of prehistoric populations than is generally deduced from the archaeological data (on the other hand, it would not be too discordant with ethnographic data: perhaps the temporal continuity of artifactual assemblages should not be too strictly interpreted in terms of the temporal stability of the underlying populations).

In overview, it appears that the demographic parameters of the three situations colonisation, stabilisation and competition are largely mediated by cultural processes. While the regulation of populations growth appears divorced from immediate environmental constraints, the populations in all three situations behave in a manner analogous to that predicted by ecological models of resource utilisation, carrying capacity and competition. If growth parameters in various settings are largely a function of historical quirks and cultural practices, then the genetic consequences of these patterns of response are minimal. What is still largely unknown, and what may ultimately be most important in determining evolutionary rates, is the degree of demographic heterogeneity within subpopulations. Here there is much scope for further work, particularly in assessing whether levels of cultural organisation have any effect on the extent of such within-group demographic heterogeneity.

6. Demographic and Genetic Consequences of Increased Buffering from Environmental Variables through Cultural Evolution

The above discussion indicates that many of the demographic changes during human evolution are intimately related to cultural parameters. Certainly in the realm of population limitation both cultural parameters (e.g. infanticide, evolution, sex taboos, etc.) and environmental factors contribute to the regulation of fertility schedules. Other factors affecting the fertility-controlling behaviour of tribal populations have been discussed by Carr–Saunders (1922) and Krzywicki (1934). As cultural organisation becomes more complex, a greater degree of buffering from environmental factors is to be expected. Thus, during cultural evolution the response of fertility schedules to environmental variability is expected to become lessened as cultural parameters play an increasingly important role in regulating patterns of reproduction. This changing relationship can be observed in the patterns of correlation between population size and environmental parameters such as rainfall (e.g. Birdsell, 1957). The increasing importance of cultural factors in determining patterns of growth is discussed by Spooner (1972). However, more definitive evidence calls for an investigation between fertility schedules (or birth rates) and varying environmental parameters.

This problem of relating variability in birth rates to environmental variability can be approached by utilising methods borrowed from engineering sciences (Harpending & Bertram, 1975· Jorde & Harpending, this volume). Variation in environmental parameters such as rainfall, which affect food supplies, can be quantified. Fluctuations in birth rates can then be analysed in terms of environmental fluctuations by the technique of *spectral analysis*. By analysing these time series, Jorde and Harpending show that there seems to be a relationship between a population's ability to stabilise its food supplies against environmental fluctuations, and the pattern of birth rate fluctuations. More advanced cultures are able to buffer their population parameters effectively against short term rainfall cycles and hence display greater (short term) demographic stability than simpler societies. However, more advanced populations may be more demographically sensitive to long term trends.

Investigations into stability relations between population parameters and environmental variables are a relatively new venture for archaeologists as well as for demographic and physical anthropologists. In developing models of analysis for this problem, attention should also be paid to the effects of population size itself on birth and death rates as well as purely environmental factors. Clearly, the vital rates of any human population are a complex function of many factors (cultural and biological) and the simple models which now exist are little able to cope with their interrelations. The findings of Jorde & Harpending imply that the varied effects of human culture on the biodemography of the human species will not form a consistent pattern. Some changes, such as the evolution of large states with intensive agriculture will produce conditions under which epidemics of infection can occur, unlike their relative absence in smaller, simpler societies (e.g. Black, 1975). Likewise, more intensive agricultural efforts may have been responsible for the malaria patterns of West Africa (Livingstone, 1958; Wiesenfeld, 1967). Thus cultural advances can give rise to patterns of increased mortality. Compensation may occur due to increased fertility rates and a greater degree of environmental buffering. Increased stability in food supplies implies that short term climatic fluctuations will pose less serious a threat than for hunter-gatherers since nutrition will be more dependable (especially for infants). However, this reliability in food resources as a function of dependence on agriculture can also leave such populations more vulnerable to climatic disasters, drought, and so on, and thus give rise to quite severe long term fluctuations. Hence the argument can be made that in the long term, primitive societies are those in which conditions for survival are maximised (e.g. Sahlins, 1972).

In considering the genetic effect of increased buffering of the environment, we can consider the genetic consequences of recent cultural changes that have ameliorated health problems. As Jacquard & Ward (this volume) indicate, there are several factors to be considered. First, medical improvements have clearly advanced life expectancy especially by reducing childhood deaths. However, medical advances have also moved many of the pressures of disease and death to later ages to the extent that certain aspects of our total life's health may be worse than before. Since many of these later diseases are more prolonged, expensive and crippling, the cost to both individual and society has been raised (Wright, 1960). In addition, one viewpoint has it that medical advances have increased the number of "defective" alleles in our gene pool by allowing the survival and reproduction of those who would otherwise have died. Finally, the resulting changes in mortality and fertility patterns can be conceived in terms of changing the opportunity for natural selection. However, there is little evidence for changes in the relative importance of fertility and mortality factors in opportunities for selection (Weiss, 1972, 1973a; Henneberg, this volume). The major component in changing opportunities for selection arose as an outcome of the industrial revolution, which has been responsible for the most dramatic change in human demography.

In discussing these points, Jacquard & Ward note that cost of genetic disorders is hard to evaluate and that concepts of "good" and "bad" genes are both difficult to define and culturally subjective. These issues also arise in the evaluation of changing fertility patterns. In part this is a consequence of the reproductive response to the birth of defective children. Until the nature of reproductive compensation is known for a given disease the effect of medical treatment of that disease on the gene pool cannot be gauged. Depending on the nature of the genetic control for particular ailments, reproductive compensation may be eugenic or dysgenic. Generalisations about the evolutionary affect of fertility response to disease cannot be made. However, as Fraser (1972) indicates, medical treatments will tend to be less important than fertility responses to long term eugenic/dysgenic effects.

The extensive changes in fertility patterns during recent years, resulting in a greater reduction in the mean and variance of family size than ever before (as far as we can determine), may have had profound genetic effects. Fertility has been very drastically reduced in many large industrial states. Not only has completed family size decreased, but a large proportion of the population produce no offspring whatever. The variance in family size is reducing rapidly, as is the variance in age of childbearing. This suggests that the opportunity for selection to act (predominantly through fertility differences) is confined to a small body of adults and a short time span compared to previous populations. Under these circumstances, reproductive compensation may have a disproportionately larger effect than in populations with large mean family sizes. However, as stressed above, these culturally controlled aspects of human reproductive behaviour are variable in their response. The extent to which selection operates, whether culturally mediated or biologically derived, is still unknown. We can only guess at the genetic consequences of this last great demographic change brought about by cultural forces. The evolutionary consequences of such changes in demographic structure need to be explored much more fully. So too does the interaction between cultural and biological parameters in creating a favourable milieu for the operation of selection. Similarly, it is of considerable relevance to investigate more fully the extent of the genetic component contributing to variability in fertility. The evolutionary consequences of the recent great changes in demographic structure will remain unknown until we can answer these questions. By the same token, the genetic future of our species as a function of our changing demographic profile remains a mystery. In the absence of information regarding either mechanisms or processes we should be wary lest we cast ourselves precipitously into the void.

References

Abbie, A. A. (1951). The Australian aborigine. *Oceania* **22,** 91.
Abbie, A. A. (1968). The homogeneity of Australian aborigines. *Archeological and Physical Anthropology in Oceania* **3,** 223.
Acsádi, G. & Nemeskéri, J. (1970). *History of Human Life Span and Mortality.* Budapest: Akademiai Kaido.
Anderson, W. W. & King, C. E. (1970). Age-specific selection. *Proceedings, National Academy of Sciences* **66,** 780–786.
Angel, J. L. (1969). The bases of paleodemography. *American Journal of Physical Anthropology* **30,** 427–438.
Birdsell, J. B. (1949). The racial origins of the extinct Tasmanians. *Record of the Queen Victoria Museum,* Launceston **2,** 105.
Birdsell, J. B. (1957). Some population problems involving Pleistocene man. *Cold Spring Harbour Symposium on Quantitative Biology* **22,** 47–70.
Birdsell, J. B. (1958). On population structure in generalized hunting and collecting populations. *Evolution* **12,** 189–205.
Birdsell, J. B. (1968). Some predictions for the Pleistocene based on equilibrium systems among recent hunter gatherers. In (R. B. Lee & I. De Vore, Eds.) *Man the Hunter.* Chicago: Aldine.
Birdsell, J. B. (1972). The problem of evolution of human races: classification or clines? *Social Biology* **19,** 136–162.

Black, F. L. (1975). Infectious diseases in primitive societies. *Science* **187,** 515–518.

Brues, A. M. (1972). Models of clines and races. *American Journal of Physical Anthropology* **37,** 389–399.

Cannings, C. & Skolnick, M. H. (1975). Genetic drift in exogamous marriage systems. *Theoretical Population Biology* **7,** 39–54.

Carr–Saunders, A. M. (1922). *The Population Problem: A Study in Human Evolution.* Oxford: Clarendon Press.

Cavalli–Sforza, L. L. & Bodmer, W. F. (1971). *The Genetics of Human Populations.* San Francisco: Freeman.

Charlesworth, B. (1970). Selection in populations with overlapping generations. I. The use of Malthusian parameters in population genetics. *Theoretical Population Biology* **1,** 352–370.

Charlesworth, B. (1972). Selection in populations with overlapping generations. III. Conditions for genetic equilibrium. *Theoretical Population Biology* **3,** 377–395.

Charlesworth, B. (1973). Selection in populations with overlapping generations. V. Natural selection and life histories. *American Naturalist* **107,** 303–311.

Charlesworth, B. (1974). Selection in populations with overlapping generations. VI. Rates of change of gene frequency and population growth rate. *Theoretical Population Biology* **6,** 108–133.

Charlesworth, B. & Giesel, J. T. (1972a). Selection in populations with overlapping generations. II. The relations between gene frequency and demographic variables. *American Naturalist* **106,** 388–401.

Charlesworth, B. & Giesel, J. T. (1972b). Selection in populations with overlapping generations. IV. Fluctuations in gene frequency with density-dependent selection. *American Naturalist* **106,** 402–411.

Chavantre, A. (1972). Les Kel-Kummer, Isolat social. *Population* **27,** 771–783.

Coale, A. J. & Demeny, P. (1966). *Regional Model Life Tables and Stable Populations.* Princeton: Princeton University Press.

Crow, J. F. (1958). Some possibilities for measuring selection intensities in man. *Human Biology* **30,** 1–13.

Crow, J. F. (1966). The quality of people: Human evolutionary changes. *Bioscience* **16,** 863–867.

Diamond, J. M. (1974). Colonization of exploded volcanic islands by birds: the supertramp strategy. *Science* **184,** 803–805.

Edwards, A. W. F. (1967). Fundamental theorem of natural selection. *Nature* **215,** 537–538.

Euler, L. (1760). Recherches generales sur la mortalite et la multiplication du genne humain. *Histoire de l'Accademie Royale des Sciences et Belles-Lettres,* annee 1760, pp. 144–164, Berlin, 1767.

Fisher, R. A. (1929). *The Genetical Theory of Natural Selection.* Oxford: Clarendon Press.

Fraser, G. R. (1972). The implication of prevention and treatment of inherited disease for the genetic future of mankind. *American Journal of Human Genetics* **20,** 185–205.

Frisch, R. E. (1973). The critical weight at menarche and the initiation of the adolescent growth spurt and the control of puberty. In (M. Grumback et al., Eds.) *The Control of the Onset of Puberty.* New York: John Wiley.

Frisch, R. E. (1976). Demographic implications for the biological determinants of female fecundity. *Social Biology,* in press.

Ginsberg, R. B. (1973). The effect of lactation on the length of the post partium anovulatory period: An application of a bivariate stochastic model. *Theoretical Population Biology* **4,** 276–299.

Goodman, L. A. (1971). On the sensitivity of the intrinsic growth rate to changes in the age-specific birth and death rates. *Theoretical Population Biology* **2,** 339–354.

Goodman, L. A., Keyfitz, N. & Pullman, T. W. (1974). Family formation and the frequency of various kinship relationships. *Theoretical Population Biology* **5,** 1–27.

Hajnal, J. (1963). Concepts of random mating and the frequency of consanguineous marriages. *Proceedings of the Royal Society* (B) **159,** 125–177.

Haldane, J. B. S. (1927). A mathematical theory of natural and artificial selection, Part IV. *Proceedings of the Cambridge Philosophical Society* **23,** 607–615.

Harpending, H. C. & Bertram, J. B. (1975). Human population dynamics in archeological time: Some simple models. In (A. C. Swedlund, Ed.), *Population Studies in Archaeology and Biological Anthropology: A Symposium.* Memoirs of the Society for American Archaeology, No. 30, Washington, D.C.

Henneberg, M. (1976). Notes on the reproduction possibilities of human prehistorical populations. *Przeglad Antropologiczny,* in press.

Henneberg, M. & Piontek, J. (1976). Biological state index of human groups. *Przeglad Antropologiczny,* in press.

Jacquard, A. (1974). *The Genetic Structure of Populations.* Heidelberg: Springer–Verlag.

Kobayashi, K. (1969). Changing patterns of differential fertility in Japan. *Proceedings of the XII International Congress of Anthropological and Ethnological Sciences* **1,** 345–347.

Krzywicki, L. (1934). *Primitive Society and its Vital Statistics.* London: Macmillan.

Langaney, A. & Gomila, J. (1973). Bedik and Niokholonko, intra- and inter-ethnic migration. *Human Biology* **45,** 137–150.

Lee, R. B. (1972). Population growth and the beginnings of sedentary life among the Kung bushmen. In (B. Spooner, Ed.) *Population Growth: Anthropological Implications.* Cambridge: Massachusetts Institute of Technology Press.

Lewontin, R. C. (1972). The apportionment of human diversity. *Evolutionary Biology* **6,** 381–398.

Li, C. C. (1967). Fundamental theorem of natural selection. *Nature* **214**, 505–506.

Livingstone, F. B. (1958). Anthropological implications of sickle cell gene distribution. *American Anthropologist* **60**, 13–22.

McLaren, I. H. (Ed.) (1971). *Natural Regulation of Animal Populations*. Chicago: Atherton Press.

Moore, J. A., Swedlund, A. C. & Armelagos, G. J. (1975). The use of life tables in paleodemography. In (A. C. Swedlund, Ed.) *Population Studies in Archaeology and Biological Anthropology: A Symposium*. Memoirs of the Society for American Archaeology, No. 30, Washington, D.C.

Morgan, K. & Holmes, T. M. (n.d.). On an attempt to estimate heritable traits from intervillage distances among the Yanomama Indians. *American Journal of Physical Anthropology* (in press).

Neel, J. V. & Weiss, K. M. (1975). The genetic structure of a tribal population, the Yanomama Indians. XII. Biodemographic studies. *American Journal of Physical Anthropology* **42**, 25–52.

Nei, M. & Rouchoudhury, A. K. (1974). Genic variation within and between the three major races of man, Caucasoids, Negroids and Mongoloids. *American Journal of Human Genetics* **26**, 421–443.

Newman, L. (1972). *Birth Control: An Anthropological View*. Addison-Wesley Modular Publication, Module 27, pp. 1–21.

Norton, H. T. J. (1926). Natural selection and Mendelian variation. *Proceedings of the London Mathematical Society*, Series 2, **28**, 1–45.

Petersen, W. (1975). A demographer's view of prehistoric demography. *Current Anthropology* **16**, 227–245.

Peterson, N. (1975). Hunter–gatherer territoriality: The perspective from Australia. *American Anthropologist* **77**, 53–68.

Pollak, E. & Kempthorne, O. (1970). Malthusian parameters in genetic populations. I. Haploid and selfing models. *Theoretical Population Biology* **1**, 315–345.

Pollak, E. & Kempthorne, O. (1971). Malthusian parameters in genetic populations. II. Random mating populations in infinite habitats. *Theoretical Population Biology* **2**, 357–390.

Poole, W. K. (1973). Fertility measures based on birth interval data. *Theoretical Population Biology* **4**, 357–387.

Potter, R. G. (1970). Births averted by contraception: An approach through renewal theory. *Theoretical Population Biology* **1**, 251–272.

Price, G. R. (1972). Fisher's fundamental theorem made clear. *Annals of Human Genetics* **36**, 129–140.

Price, G. R. & Smith, C. A. B. (1972). Fisher's Malthusian parameter and reproductive value. *Annals of Human Genetics* **36**, 1–7.

Sahlins, M. (1972). *Stone Age Economics*. Chicago: Aldine.

Simmons, R. T. (1972). Blood group genetic studies in the Cape York area. In (R. L. Kirk, Ed.) *The Human Biology of Aborigines in Cape York*. Australian Aboriginal Studies, No. 44, Canberra.

Skolnick, M. H. & Cannings, C. (1972). The natural regulation of population size for primitive man. *Nature* **239**, 287–288.

Skolnick, N. H. & Cannings, C. (1974). Simulation of small human populations. In (B. Dyke & J. W. MacCluer, Eds.) *Computer Simulation in Human Population Studies*. New York: Academic Press.

Spooner, B. (Ed.) (1972). *Population Growth: Anthropological Implications*. Cambridge: Massachusetts Institute of Technology Press.

Swedlund, A. C. & Sessions, S. E. (n.d.). A developmental model of prehistoric population growth in Black Mesa, northeast Arizona. In (G. J. Gummerman & R. D. Euler, Eds.) *Papers on the Archeology of Black Mesa*. Carbondale: Southern Illinois University Press (in press).

Talwar, P. P. (1970). *Age Patterns of Fertility*. University of North Carolina, Institute of Statistics, Mimeo Series No. 656.

Turner, J. R. G. (1970). Changes in mean fitness under selection. In (K. Kojima, Ed.) *Mathematical Topics in Population Genetics*. New York: Springer–Verlag.

Wallace, B. (1970). *Genetic Load, its Biological and Conceptual Aspects*. Englewood Cliffs, N. J.: Prentice-Hall.

Ward, R. H. (1975). Fertility patterns and inbreeding levels in a small genetic isolate. *American Journal of Physical Anthropology* **42**, 337.

Ward, R. H. & Neel, J. V. (1970). Gene frequencies and microdifferentiation among the Makiritare Indians. IV. A comparison of a genetic network with ethnohistory and migration matrices. A new index of genetic isolation. *American Journal of Human Genetics* **22**, 355–365.

Ward, R. H. & Neel, J. V. (1976). The genetic structure of a tribal population, the Yanomama Indians. XIV. Clines and their interpretation. *Genetics* (in press).

Ward, R. H. & Raspe, P. D. (1973). Inbreeding levels stabilized by flexible breeding structure. *Proceedings of the XII International Congress of Genetics* **74**, 291–292.

Weiss, K. M. (1972). A general measure of human population growth regulation. *American Journal of Physical Anthropology* **37**, 337–344.

Weiss, K. M. (1973a). *Demographic Models for Anthropology*. Memoirs of the Society for American Archaeology, No. 27, Washington, D.C.

Weiss, K. M. (1973b). A method for approximating fertility in the construction of life tables for anthropological populations. *Human Biology* **45**, 195–210.

Weiss, K. M. (1975). Demographic disturbance and the use of life tables in anthropology. In (A. C. Swedlund, Ed.) *Population Studies in Archaeology and Biological Anthropology: A Symposium*. Memoirs of the Society for American Archaeology, No. 30, Washington, D.C.

Weiss, K. M. & Maruyama, T. (1976). Archeology, population genetics and studies of human racial ancestry. *American Journal of Physical Anthropology* (in press).

Wiesenfeld, S. L. (1967). Sickle-cell trait in human biological and cultural evolution. *Science* 157, 1134–1140.

Williams, B. J. (1974). *A Model of Band Society*. Memoirs of the Society for American Archaeology, No. 29, Washington, D.C.

Williams, B. J. (1975). Age differentials between spouses and Australian marriage systems. In (A. C. Swedlund, Ed.) *Population Studies in Archaeology and Biological Anthropology: A Symposium*. Memoirs of the Society for American Archaeology, No. 30, Washington, D.C.

Williams, G. C. (Ed.) (1971). *Group Selection*. Chicago: Aldine-Atherton.

Wright, S. (1948). On the role of directed and random changes in gene frequency in the genetics of populations. *Evolution* 2, 279–294.

Wright, S. (1960). On the appraisal of genetic effects of radiation in man. In *The Biological Effect of Atomic Radiation, Summary Reports*. Washington: National Academy of Sciences, pp. 18–24.

Wynne–Edwards, V. C. (1962). *Animal Dispersion in Relation to Social Behaviour*. New York: Hafner.

Yellen, J. & Harpending, H. C. (1972). Hunter gatherer populations and archaeological inference. *World Archaeology* 4, 244–253.

Zubrow, E. B. W. (1971). Carrying capacity and dynamic equilibrium in the prehistoric Southwest. *American Antiquity* 36, 127–138.

Nancy Howell

Scarborough College, University of
Toronto, West Hill, Ontario,
Canada

Toward a Uniformitarian Theory of
Human Paleodemography

1. Introduction

Paleodemography is a subject which is simultaneously intensely interesting and devilishly difficult. It is intensely interesting because its subject matter is the life and deaths of our ancestors. We cannot have a clear idea of the history of our species without knowing quite a lot about the risks of mortality to which they were subject, and about their ability to bear children to keep the groups alive. The subject is difficult because of the nearly complete loss of the data needed for the analysis. Archeological finds indicate that some people lived at a site over a certain time range, and if we are lucky they may tell us something about the numbers of people who lived there (by house or hearth counts for instance) and those who died there (by skeletal remains in burial sites). But they can never provide the range of data that the demographer of contemporary people has come to expect, the census, the vital statistics, the cooperative informants who can tell us when and where and why they did (or didn't do) things relevant to their reproduction and survival. In the historical period the situation is not quite so bad, as the skeletal collections are sometimes large and may be nearly complete, and we may find written records to help to interpret what is found. But in the prehistoric period, when most of the people we are interested in were living by hunting and gathering, in groups that were both nomadic and relatively small, we cannot realistically expect to ever find archeological evidence that will permit us to solve the problems of paleodemography in a completely empirical manner, even for one group.

Since 1967, I have been working on a detailed study of the demography of the !Kung-speaking San (or "Bushmen") of the Kalahari Desert, a hunting and gathering nomadic people who live in small groups (or who did until the very recent past). To make this study, I found it necessary to use the results of modern demographic studies on other people who are easier to study, using model life tables, for instance, to smooth out and fill in gaps in fragmentary data based on small numbers of deaths, and model stable populations to estimate the age structure of the population and the ages of individuals (Howell, 1973). I was able to use these stable models without confidence that the San had the same basic biological make-up upon which the models were based because if they had been grossly different, internal inconsistencies would have appeared in the analysis. In effect, I used the models as a null hypothesis of the processes of fertility and mortality in the San population, and since the anticipated internal inconsistencies did not appear, the null hypothesis could be accepted as a reasonably close description of the population.

In the area of paleodemography many researchers are doing something similar, that is, applying the known demographic patterns of the present to the past. We might label this strategy as uniformitarianism, to borrow a term from geology. This simply means that the events of the past are caused by the same processes which are at work at the present time. In geology, it means interpreting mountains and valleys and oceans as the result of the same processes of uplifting, deposition and erosion that occur at the present time, in contrast to the position of catastrophism that looks for dramatic single events or changes in the nature or scope of the processes themselves as causes. A uniformitarian position in paleodemography implies that the human animal has not basically changed in its direct biological response to the environment in processes of ovulation, spermatogenesis, length of pregnancy, degree of helplessness of the young and rates of maturation and senility over time. This does not imply that humans have not changed in the rates of *performance* of these processes, but only that the processes still respond in the same way to variations in environment, including the cultural and technological aspects of human society as part of the external environment. Another way of stating this is to assert that the demographically relevant biological processes of our species are constant in our genetic composition, subject only to variation in response to environmental forces, and that the species has not undergone any significant intra-species evolution since its first appearance as *Homo sapiens*. The limitation of this argument to *Homo sapiens* should be underlined. Earlier species of hominids may have matured at a different rate, may have had shorter pregnancies, had multiple births or more mature offspring at birth, or whatever. This argument does not apply to them. For the 40,000+ years of *Homo sapiens* existence, however, it is at least useful to postulate that there has been no evolution of the demographically revelant biological processes, while other genetically controlled physical characteristics such as skin color, body size, or any feature which is variable in contemporary populations may have undergone considerable change under selective pressures.

The uniformitarian view is not new. G. G. Simpson stated the basic idea clearly in 1949 in the following passage.

> "Each normal individual organism has a life pattern which is characteristic of its species and which it follows without strong deviation, barring accident or pathology. Growth continues for a typical period of time to a typical size as limit. Sexual fertility begins at a characteristic time, continues over a period variable within rather definite limits, and then ceases. Degeneration begins to get the upper hand at some time during the period of maturity and leads to decline, senility, and inevitable death. The potential span of life seems to be very rigidly set by the nature of the organism. All of the great strides of medicine do not seem to have raised the potential life span of man by one minute; they have only made it possible for more men to come nearer to realizing their potential spans without being cut off earlier by disease or by avoidably rapid degeneration." (p. 71)

More recently, Acsádi and Nemeskéri have come to a similar formulation, in their *History of Human Life Span and Mortality* (1972) in which they explicitly treat the central problem as one involving the history of performance in mortality rather than one involving the evolution of capacity to live to advanced ages. In one section, they compare the estimates of survivorship derived from their Maghreb skeletal series with the U.N.

model life table (level 0, expectation of life at birth 20 years). They note that they coincide almost completely, and make the following observation about this similarity.

"... the conformity of facts and models suggests further-reaching conclusions. ... The relationship of ancient mortality with the "level 0" model—which, after all, has been constructed by analysing the mortality of modern man—suggests that the biological rules of mortality of *Archanthropus* and *Palaeanthropus* were not basically different from those of modern man. Putting it another way this would mean that the biological possibilities, realized in our day, were "contained" in ancient man as well." (p. 173)

Other scholars use the uniformitarian assumption, too, implicitly or explicitly. When a collection of skeletons is aged on the assumption that observable biological markers of maturity correspond to certain chronological ages, the procedure is either uniformitarian or it amounts to measuring with what I have called elsewhere "a rubber yard stick." (C. A., 1974). When Weiss (1973) constructs model populations combining life tables derived from anthropological population studies with age-specific fertility schedules, he must assume that the population in question distributes its childbearing over the lifespan in about the same way as modern populations do (i.e. between 15–50, with the maximum between the ages of 20–30). In this way, he is taking a uniformitarian position. Other examples could be cited. But if the uniformitarian position on human populations is not new, neither is it completely accepted. Investigators sometimes report features of the populations they studied which are completely outside of the known range of the well-studied portion of contemporary peoples, and these reports seem to go unchallenged. To take an example which I have carefully considered because it refers to the Naron-speaking San people who live only a few hundred miles away from the !Kung-speaking San people that I have studied, Silberbauer (1965) stated:

"Bushmen age rapidly in their appearance and an individual who, one is quite certain, could not possibly be a day less than seventy years old, proves to be no more than 40. (p. 15) ... Life expectancy among Reserve Bushmen is difficult to calculate, but I do not believe that many live beyond 45." (p. 17)

Silberbauer clearly implies here that the Naron have a radically different biological process of maturation, senility and death from the human populations whose experience is summarized in the sets of model life tables. They do not, according to his description, simply have a higher probability of death at each age but the whole age-specific pattern is foreshortened, so that old age occurs at 40. I have not studied the people he describes, but I can assert confidently that what he says is not true of the !Kung people that I have studied. Exhaustive studies of the age composition of the current population clearly show that the biological milestones of puberty, the beginning and end of the childbearing period and the onset of old age occur within the expected ranges for the !Kung population.

Another case of reasoning based on biological parameters that are not known among contemporary peoples can be seen in Sussman's comparison of gorilla and human population processes during the Neolithic (1972), in which he says

"Evidence indicates ... that most preagricultural peoples died before 30 years of age (Deevey, 1960; Vallois, 1961). Thus the reproductive span of the preagricultural female might be estimated liberally as from 16 or 17 to 33 or 34 years of age, a period of 16 to 18 years." (pp. 258–259)

Sussman seems to be asserting that most preagricultural women die just before or after the age of thirty, thereby ending their reproductive years, a situation which is unknown among contemporary peoples. The life expectancy of thirty, which seems reasonable for a preagricultural population, is achieved as an average of considerable infant and childhood mortality, a certain amount of adult mortality, and a rapidly rising rate of mortality after the age of fifty. Life expectancy, then, offers no guide to the age at which women complete their childbearing under uniformitarian assumptions. Sussman is describing a totally different biological arrangement than the one we know.

Even if the Silberbauer and Sussman examples are exceptional, and the acceptance of the uniformitarian position via its incorporation in model life tables and stable population models is fairly general, the uniformitarian basis for a theory of paleodemography needs to be more fully and explicitly stated so that its implications can be exploited.

Some of these implications are methodological. Tools like the series of model life tables (U.N., 1955; Coale & Demeny, 1967; Weiss, 1973) are convenient reminders of what the common contemporary human population processes are, and can be seen as null hypotheses of what we should expect to find in an unknown situation, leading to interest, surprise or disbelief in accounts which do not fit the models. Without a uniformitarian assumption, one has no basis to check the internal consistency of the various statements made in a research report, and the investigator has no basis to estimate parameters about which no information is available from the data which do exist. For paleodemography, the Coale and Demeny models which provide the age composition of the graveyard as well as the living populations associated with various levels of mortality and fertility should be invaluable.

It is the theoretical implications of uniformitarianism, however, which seem to be particularly valuable and almost entirely unexplored. If, in fact, the fertility and mortality processes which shape populations are either invariant or fluctuate with aspects of the environment in predictable ways through a definable range of variation, these facts permit us to increase our understanding of the adaptations of prehistoric populations greatly, not only for understanding the demographic process itself but also for aspects of those societies which are necessarily related to their demography, such as kinship studies, age and sex role studies, transmissions of information over time, the organization of work, and the pressure on resources caused by population growth. To the extent to which the uniformitarian position is acceptable, we have a basis for the construction of theoretical models of paleodemography, even in the absence of a firm empirical body of evidence. To the extent to which a uniformitarian position is not acceptable, interpretations of evidence which require it, such as the aging of skeletons or the construction of model populations should be reexamined.

What is required, then, is a specification of the uniformitarian position on human fertility and mortality, concentrating on the invariance and causes of variation between populations on different aspects. The balance of this paper is addressed to this task. First for fertility and then for mortality, I attempt to describe a uniformitarian position and then to estimate some reasonable bounds on the levels of performance that prehistoric populations might produce, along with the environmental factors that may be associated with the high and low boundaries of this restricted range. The range of population structures implied by the limits of fertility and mortality performance are described, and some of the theoretical implications of the types of demographic adaptations suggested are explored briefly.

2. Setting Limits on Fertility in Prehistoric Human Populations

When attempting to understand the limitations of human fertility, one is forced to concentrate almost entirely upon the biological processes of women rather than men. The reasons for this are simple: men are capable, in principle, of producing enormous numbers of offspring simultaneously or in sequence. Women's reproductive biology, however, is sufficiently constrained that it can be readily understood as a sequence of time-consuming states through which the individual woman moves, some of which result in a birth. During any given month a woman either ovulates or she does not. When she ovulates, she may conceive or not. Since the total number of months available is limited, periods of time occupied by anovulatory and infertile states limit the number of babies that can be borne per woman. Whatever reductions in fertility are caused by aspects of men's essential role in the reproductive process must have their effects on the woman's state during particular months, so the same result is produced by concentrating entirely on the women as would be produced by studying both the men and the women. The following discussion of fertility, therefore, is almost entirely female-centered.

The upper limit of fertility is set by the proportion of all women who are engaged in childbearing, the length of the fertile period in women's lives, and the speed at which they produce babies during the fertile period. A population which is maximizing fertility will have all of the women married all of the time during their reproductive years, will have early menarche and late menopause, and will have the shortest possible intervals between births. The contemporary Hutterites of Western Canada and the U.S. (Eaton & Mayer, 1953) come closest to these conditions among contemporary populations. They are a well nourished, healthy group of people who desire maximally large families for religious and practical reasons. The married women achieve a Total Fertility Rate* of 10·4, the world record. The Hutterite record might be slightly higher if more of their children died in infancy, since the interval to the next birth tends to be shortened when a baby dies. The maximum fertility that we can posit for prehistoric populations under the uniformitarian assumption, then, must be close to eleven children per woman who survives to the end of the childbearing period, if the population resembles the Hutterites in all relevant ways. The key to narrowing the range of fertility levels that could be attained by prehistoric populations is contained in the phrase "all relevant ways". Exactly which ways prehistoric populations might resemble the Hutterites (desire for children, health and nutrition, etc.) may be clarified by a look at the reproductive customs and patterns of the !Kung-speaking San, and the recent work of Frisch (1974, 1976) which seems to explain the San material.

The !Kung arrange marriage for all of their young women before the beginning of the

---

* The Total Fertility Rate is the sum of the age-specific fertility rates, and represents the number of children who would be born to the average woman who survives through the child-bearing years. The Total Fertility Rate is almost the same as the number of children born to women at age 50 in populations like the Hutterites in which there is little mortality between 15–50, while the two measures may differ greatly in high mortality populations. The Total Fertility Rate is free of the influence of the age structure of the population (unlike birth rates) and will be the only measure of fertility used in this paper.

reproductive period, and permit remarriage for all women who divorce or are widowed, usually within a year of the end of the earlier marriage. The !Kung do not practice contraception or abortion. On the contrary, they complain that their god is stingy with children and say they would like to have more. From these bare facts, one might expect to find fertility very close to the Hutterite levels, but one does not. The Total Fertility Rate is close to 5, less than half of the record. One of the central questions of the !Kung research, therefore, has been to gain some understanding of how this relatively low fertility rate is produced.

Part of the answer lies in the restriction of the childbearing period. Although women are having intercourse regularly from an early age, menarche (first menstruation) comes relatively late, about sixteen and a half years on the average, and the first pregnancy occurs about three years later, again on the average. Menopause (cessation of menstruation) occurs in the early forties, some years earlier than is known from other populations. Since the first and last years of the childbearing period are the portions when age-specific fertility is lowest, the reduction in fertility is not proportional to the years reduced. Late menarche and early menopause may be reducing the San's fertility by one or two children, not more.

The major factor in reduction of fertility involves the length of the interval between births. The women do not report an unusually high rate of spontaneous abortion or miscarriage which would explain the long intervals between live births. Nor do they seem to have an unusually low level of fecundability (capacity to conceive) as they usually get pregnant again promptly following an infant death. When a child is born that survives infancy, however, the interval to the next pregnancy is almost uniformly at least 35 months. Lee (1971), Sussman (1972) and others have argued that hunters and gatherers need to have such long birth intervals, given the need to invest considerable effort in each child through long lactation and the need to carry small children on group moves. The argument is persuasive, but stating that a result is needed does not explain how the result is obtained. Many people in the world today could be said to "need" to have fewer children than they have, but the reduction in fertility does not automatically follow. To understand the mechanism, we have to look at the reproductive process itself.

Prolonged and heavy lactation as a suppressant of ovulation was considered as the explanation of the long birth intervals, but studies in other parts of the world suggest that while lactation does suppress ovulation for a period of up to 18 months, it has not been known to produce intervals on the order of 36 months (Menken, 1975). The San women report that menstruation resumes in 8 to 12 months after birth, in most cases, further undercutting the lactation hypothesis. Other hypotheses entertained involved the changes in social relations that might be caused by the baby's existence: perhaps marital coitus was made difficult or impossible by the omnipresence of the baby, by the systematic refusal of other members of the group to give sufficient privacy to the parents or perhaps by the hovering attentions of the baby's grandmothers. While these explanations have a certain appeal, recent research on the biological control of ovulations, the "critical fatness" hypothesis (Frisch, 1973, 1974, 1976) suggests a simpler and more systematic basis for explanation.

Frisch developed the "critical fatness" hypothesis in the course of research on the significance of critical weights at menarche. She found that the mean weight at menarche is the same for early and late maturing females within a population, although it differs within each group by height, and that the mean critical weight has remained the same over time for particular populations or ethnic groups, even though the age at menarche has declined rather sharply as nutritional status has improved. On the basis of these observations, she formulated the hypothesis that females reach menarche whenever they acquire a critical volume of fat on their bodies in proportion to their lean body weight. Large women would require a greater amount of fat to reach menarche than short slight women, according to this hypothesis, but since they are likely to be larger, to some degree, due to access to better and more regular food supplies during childhood, they are able to build up the necessary fat deposits from their abundant food supply, while young women who are less well nourished or who had to cope with environmental stresses (such as high altitude) tend to be both smaller in final stature and to reach the critical fatness level, and therefore menarche, at later ages.

Frisch finds that menarche is associated with one critical fatness level and actual ovulation (or stable reproductive capacity) is associated with another, higher level. Adolescent sterility, then, can be defined as the period when a young woman has passed the menarche level but has not yet reached the ovulatory level of fatness. The length of this period, then, will depend upon the young woman's ability to deposit fat on her body. Frisch finds that these critical levels are not limited to the initiation of each phase, but that maintenance of the fatness is essential to the continuation of the process. Women who lose their fat deposits later in life become first anovulatory and, if the weight loss continues, later amenorrheic, which continues until the necessary fat deposits are regained.

The Frisch hypothesis seems to go a long way toward explaining the findings of my study of the San. The San are extreme by contemporary standards in their small stature and thinness, especially those who still subsist by hunting and gathering rather than in dependency to their cattle-raising neighbors, the Tswana and Herero peoples. Birth weights are normal but children fall behind European and African standards for height and weight by the age of two, remaining smaller throughout life. Children are uniformly thin, but lively and apparently well nourished (Trusswell & Hanson, 1968). Cross-sectional height and weight curves indicate that growth continues until the late teens for women and the early twenties for men. No substantial work effort in the area of food production is expected from young people before the ages at which growth is complete. The girls conspicuously build up fat deposits, especially in breasts and buttocks, during their teens, reach menarche at a mean age of 16.5 and bear their first child, on the average, around the age of 20. If the child survives, the young woman is necessarily engaged in an activity schedule which demands extra fuel: between lactation, carrying the baby, and providing a substantial share of the increased food requirements of the family, she may need an extra 1000 calories per day in addition to her maintenance requirements. To the extent to which she fails to obtain additional food, she will lose her fat deposits. After two or three years, when the baby's lactational demands decrease, she will be able to rebuild her own fat deposits gradually, resuming ovulation when she reaches the critical level and re-entering the risk of pregnancy. The baby will be totally weaned from the breast during the next pregnancy, if not before. If the second child is one of the approximately 25% who fail to survive, the mother will soon be at risk of pregnancy again, having already established the necessary fatness level. In fact, most mothers who have an infant death are pregnant again within a year. If the second baby survives, the cycle of fat loss below the critical level for ovulation and gradual recovery of fat deposits will reoccur, continuing until menopause.

The critical fatness levels for San women are not known, so the preceding description must be clearly labelled as hypothetical. The research needed to test this hypothesis will obviously be difficult. Data on weight at all phases of the cycle does not exist for any one woman (the data collection extended over only two years), but the cumulative data from some twenty women for whom we have weights over some parts of the cycle seem to support this interpretation. The major factor in reducing San fertility below the levels of the Hutterite women, then, is the suppression of ovulation through loss of fat deposits caused by the increased activity inherent in caring for a baby.

Failure to achieve and maintain critical fatness levels is probably a small factor in loss of fertility in the modern populations we know best. Most women are well over the critical fatness levels throughout their adult life when food is abundant. Even women who "diet" in industrialized societies are unlikely to become so slim that they cross the critical fatness threshold. Where food is not so readily available, the critical fatness levels may be crossed and recrossed by women during their life. The Total Fertility Rate of India, to take a well known example, was about six in the period 1951–60, which is not high for a non-contracepting population which practices early and widespread marriage (Visarian, 1969). India's fertility is high only in conjunction with relatively low mortality rates, which together cause a rapid rate of population growth. Clearly delay in adolescent growth and lowering of fecundability for the people currently experiencing famine are implied by this hypothesis (Frisch, 1976). In hunting and gathering societies, however, where food is ordinarily not stored, the critical fatness factor may be the crucial one in understanding the phenomena of long birth intervals and consequent low fertility. Indeed, the "Venus of Willendorf" and the many other obese female figures found in prehistoric deposits may be interpreted as an indication that the hunters and gatherers have known about the crucial role of fatness in fertility all along.

The critical fatness hypothesis seems to help explain the San case, but now we want to return to the question of the factors which will determine to what extent a given prehistoric population can approach the maximum fertility achieved by the Hutterites. The Frisch work implies that the maximum fertility level that can be achieved by a people is a function of the environment in which they live. We do not want to argue here that all prehistoric hunters and gatherers were limited in their maximum fertility as the San are, but only that those who lived in environments which offer the kind of food supplies that the San have would have this kind of limitation. It is an oversimplification to see the cause of the critical fatness problem in a scarcity of food. The absolute amount of food in an environment depends in large part upon what the people define as their proper food. Many observers of hunters and gatherers have commented on the large portion of even that which is defined as desirable food that goes uneaten (Lee & DeVore, 1969). The feature of the environment that determines whether or not the critical fatness mechanism will be operative is not the scarcity of food but its caloric cost to the people. Groups like the San for whom food is always available out in the bush but who have to use a large proportion of what they can collect and carry back in the effort to obtain it may be relatively limited in their capacity to build fat deposits, while those who live where food supplies are relatively more concentrated and easier to obtain may have an easier time maintaining or rebuilding fat deposits and therefore shorter birth intervals.

A second important point about the effects of the critical fatness mechanism on maximum fertility achievable in prehistoric populations is that the mechanism may be imposed directly by the environment, as discussed above, and no doubt it often is, but the same mechanism can be imposed or modified by the social organization, through the distribution of work in the society. This point will be discussed in more detail in the concluding section of this paper: it is mentioned here to indicate that we cannot simply look at the environment to determine whether the critical fatness mechanism would restrict fertility.

With these considerations in mind, we can suggest some numerical values for the range of Total Fertility Rates to be expected in prehistoric populations. A consideration of the way of life of even the most prosperous prehistoric hunters and gatherers suggests that the Hutterite example is not applicable: The Hutterites have super-abundant food resources and modern medical care. A well nourished hunting and gathering group might be modelled on the Yanomama (Neel & Weiss, 1975), who have enriched their diet with the banana in the last century and who currently have a Total Fertility Rate of 8. A Total Fertility Rate of 8, then, is proposed as being a maximum for prehistoric populations. The San offer a model of groups which have a lower ceiling of maximum fertility, a Total Fertility Rate of 5. I would expect that this range would bracket the most commonly achievable levels of maximum fertility for prehistoric populations. Fertility below maximum levels could be achieved by any group that found it in their interest to do so, using the kinds of mechanisms that we commonly see in the world today, restricted marriage, abstinence or non-coital sexual relations, and probably contraception and abortion. The floor under minimum levels of fertility must be set by the mortality conditions with which the population has to cope, and these are likely to be sufficiently high so that fertility cannot be greatly reduced, while individual couples may reduce their fertility for their own family reasons. In general a model of early and near-universal marriage along with practices which tend to maximize fertility is probably realistic for these small scale, undifferentiated societies.

3. Setting Limits on Mortality in Prehistoric Human Populations

The uniformitarian view of mortality is based upon the idea that the human species has a fixed life span. The aging process leads to bodily breakdown after a period of time, even in the absence of sickness and accidents. This view is consistent with recent research on the aging process, which concentrate on the cellular level of senescence (Marx, 1974). The maximal life span of humans cannot be known exactly, since all populations are subject to accidents and illness, but it is striking that the oldest living person in a number of countries that keep accurate records of age are close to 110. Maximum life span then, is at least 110 and is a constant according to the uniformitarian view.

When we speak of levels of mortality, we mean the proportion of the maximal life span that is achieved by members of the population. When mortality is high, the average age of death is low; when mortality is low, the average age at death may be more than 75 years. The level of mortality, then, is variable and the causes of the variability lie in the environment, both the natural environment of hazards, stresses and populations of microbes and in the human social environment (shelter, nutrition, nurturance for the sick and weak, antibiotics and medical care). The age distribution of whatever level of mortality exists has a characteristic pattern, which is predictable within rather narrow limits. The average age pattern of mortality under various levels of mortality is expressed in model life tables (U.N., 1955; Coale & Demeny, 1965; Weiss, 1973). The age distribution of mortality does not lend itself to a simple mathematical description, but can be understood by dividing the life span into three segments: (a) infancy and childhood, in which the probability of dying starts at a high level at birth and declines swiftly in the first year, more slowly to the age of about ten, when the probability of death in the next year reaches the minimum for the life span; (b) adolescence and adulthood, ages 10–50, in which the probability of dying in each year rises steadily but not sharply; and (c) old age, from 50 until there are no more people left to die, in which the probability of death rises steadily and sharply each year. The relative importance of the three segments and the slope of the curve in each segment depends on the overall level of mortality in the population. When mortality is high, the infant and childhood segment accounts for a large proportion of all deaths, and when mortality is lower the old age segment accounts for more, as mortality can only be pushed to higher ages, not eliminated. The age pattern is remarkably similar for the two sexes, but the probability of death for females is somewhat lower at all ages. The regularities in the age and sex distribution of death may be seen as the result of differential biological ability to withstand stress when the stresses are impinging upon all members of the population equally. The variable aspects of life tables, and no particular population ever matches the model life tables exactly, can be attributed to variations in the causes of death, some of which have age-specific patterns (Preston et al., 1972) and in variations in the societies' provision of defenses against pathogens for certain groups.

When a population conforms to model life tables for a particular level of mortality, then, one concludes that the stress factors and defenses are impinging evenly on all age and sex groups and the underlying differences in biological capacity to resist stress are operating. When deviations from the model life tables are found, they require an explanation in terms of special disease or stress patterns or differential care taken of particular age and/or sex groups in the population. In Neel & Weiss' recent report on the demographic processes of the Yanomama (1975), for instance, they provide a life table calculated from actual mortality experience, with an expectation of life at birth of 20 years. Comparing that life table with the models, one immediately sees that the age and sex pattern differs considerably from the model life table with the same expectation of life at birth. When compared with the model for expectation of life at birth of 30 years, however, one sees a close fit over the total life span, with two striking deviations: there is much more infant mortality in the Yanomama life table than predicted by the model, especially for females, and there is much more mortality in the young adult years than would be expected from the model. Neel & Weiss discuss the prevalence of infanticide and especially female infantacide in great detail in their report, while the conditions that lead to excess young adult mortality are not so clear. The use of uniformitarian assumptions allows one to interpret the Yanomama material as displaying the constant biological susceptibility to death, environmental stresses which would permit them to achieve an expectation of life at birth not exceeding 30 years, and special stresses impinging upon infants and young adults which reduces the expectation of life at birth to 20 years in an atypical pattern.

The !Kung-speaking San of my study have proven to have an expectation of life at birth of about thirty years, with no striking deviations from the model life tables for that level of mortality, as determined not only from vital statistics of the past decade but from the retrospective accounts of the children born to each woman. Looking at a cohort of new-born infants, one would expect about 23 % to die in the first year of life, 40 % to be dead before reaching the age of 15, 60 % before the age of 45, while 15 % can be expected to live to 60 and beyond.

In order to try to set some limits on the expected range of mortality conditions in prehistoric hunting and gathering societies, we can not do better than to turn to Acsádi & Nemeskéri's *History of Human Life Span and Mortality* (1970). They organize a vast amount of scholarship around the question of trends in the average and maximum age at death in prehistoric populations. Overall, one is impressed with the evidence they present to suggest that nearly all of the change in the typical mortality of human populations has occurred in the recent past, rather than being a gradual and continual development of improvements in mortality. Their meticulous analysis of what is often fragmentary data suggests a slow advance in expectation of life at birth with an expectation of life at birth of less than twenty for the (pre-human) *Sinanthropus*, to life expectancy in the low twenties for the "Maghreb-type" of the Neolithic, to the high twenties for Copper Age populations, reaching 30 years with consistency only under civilizations. Mortality of less than 20 years life expectancy is possible and indeed must have occurred to many populations. Limited human fertility cannot compensate for the losses due to death at much below 20, but no doubt many populations experienced higher mortality for at least short periods of time. When the mortality conditions persisted, they must have either moved to a more favorable environment or simply died out. Certainly the possibility of extinction of particular populations must be considered for the prehistoric period. We may tentatively conclude that prehistoric hunting and gathering populations fell into the range of mortality of expectation of life at birth of 20 to 30 years when they were thriving, and lower levels only when they were declining and failing to replace themselves.

Sexual differences in mortality at each age may have been variable or actually reversed from the contemporary pattern, in which females show a higher probability of survival at each age and for many specific causes of death (Preston *et al.*, 1972). Acsádi & Nemeskéri found that seven out of eight skeletal series for very ancient populations showed higher life expectancy for males than for females. In interpreting this finding, they note that in contemporary populations, too, males have higher life expectancy in a number of populations with very high mortality. They suggest that:

> "In the course of history it was not the biological differences between the sexes that underwent modification, but rather the respective status of the sexes, and mortality conditions changed accordingly. In countries where adult women are practically engrossed with pregnancy, childbirth, suckling, and in addition have to do all the work that falls on them by ancestral division of labour, often more exacting and wearing than the men's work, female mortality continues to be higher even today."

The biological tendency seems to be in the direction of lower mortality for females than for males at every age. Where we find exceptions to this rule, such as the Yanomama (Neel & Weiss, 1975), at least some Eskimo groups (Steiger & Schrier, 1972) and Australian aboriginal groups (Birdsell, 1972), we look for the special causes, infanticide or other, that are involved.

4. Environment and Population Dynamics

The environments in which prehistoric populations of hunting and gathering peoples live can be classified in two ways which are relevant to their demographic performance, by the relative absence or presence of food supplies and of pathogens. When food supplies are scarce or dispersed so that they are calorically expensive to acquire, the population may find its fertility limited by the critical fatness process. It has been suggested above, that a range of five to eight births per woman who survives to the end of the childbearing period may be attainable, depending upon the degree of fatness, which in turn is at least in part a function of the environment.

An independent but probably correlated dimension of the environment is the presence of pathogenic agents that cause death to the population. Harpending (in press) has found that mortality rates sharply increase on the northern boundaries of the San range, a well watered area that appears to be an ideal environment but which seems to harbour malaria. To clarify the interrelations between these two aspects of all environments, the four-fold Table 1 below considers the extremes of the ranges of fertility and mortality, along with the characteristics of the environment that should produce the extremes. Most populations, of course, would be somewhere in the middle of the ranges, and of course the environments will vary somewhat from one year to another, a factor which is being neglected here for simplicity.

Table 1   **Extreme environments for prehistoric populations**

		Presence of pathogens	
		Low	High
	Expectation of life at birth:	30 years	20 years
Food Supply	Rich, total fertility = 8	Type 1	Type 3
	Poor, total fertility = 5	Type 2	Type 4

The four-fold Table 1 classifies environments and populations together, on the assumption that the demographic processes are a direct response to the environment. The potential for population growth is of course implied for each type: type 1 populations will be growing rapidly, as they are both rich and healthy, conditions that are ideal for a population which has room for expansion, but which poses certain problems for those who do not. Types 2 and 3 are both in balance with their environments. Type 4 societies are simply impossible, that is, the combination of high levels of pathogens with the sort of food supply that leads to the critical fatness problem cannot be a suitable environment for humans. When this occurred, and we must assume that environments fluctuated to some extent from one year (or decade, or century) to another, the people probably moved when they could, and diminished or extinguished as a population when they could not.

Classifying populations into these types is of limited usefulness unless we have some ways of knowing which type a particular population would have been. Skeletal remains may provide information on the age composition at death in a prehistoric population, but it cannot provide the level of mortality unless we know the growth rate of the population during the period of time when the people died. Assuming that the growth rate was zero automatically classifies the population as a type 2 or 3, since a positive growth rate is a defining characteristic of type 1 and a negative one for type 4. Perhaps it will be possible to measure features of the environment as well as the population to classify societies.

To estimate fertility levels, if one accepts the critical fatness hypothesis, one would concentrate on analysis of the food supply, attempting to identify the species eaten from camp debris and plotting the likely distribution of those species in the environment. The more plentiful and concentrated the food resources, the higher the estimated fertility would be. In addition, we might consider the possibility that the stature of the people is an indication of the relative availability of food. When food supplies are scarce for adult women they are likely to be scarce for children too, and caloric deficiency in childhood will produce adults that are small in stature. Following this line of reasoning, the smaller the people, the more likely it is that the critical fatness mechanism produced fertility in the low end of the range. Small stature caused by genetic factors rather than caloric deficiency may be interpreted in the same way, in as much as the selection for small stature may come from the adaptative advantages of needing to accumulate a smaller absolute amount of fat to restart ovulation.

To estimate mortality levels, the analysis of skeletal materials is obviously the first line of attack. Population density is probably the best environmental indicator of level of mortality, since so many causes of death are contagious, but other factors such as purity of the drinking water or climatic shifts during the year may also be important. Population density, of course, is almost certain to be correlated with the rich food supplies that are suggested as the cause of high fertility, which is consistent with my view of the two rather different ways of being in balance with the groups's resources. Type 2 societies, like the !Kung San of my study, should be identifiable as small thin people living at low densities with low fertility and mortality, while type 3 groups will consist of larger people more densely settled, living with higher fertility and mortality. The type 2 population would have an easier life and more leisure than the type 3, because they would produce the same number of survivors by fewer births and would thus spend less energy providing for people who would not ultimately become producers. Neither group has any demographic motivation to practice female infanticide or to exaggerate the sexual division of labour.

For all of the people who have demographic problems, i.e. fertility or mortality higher or lower than they wish it would be, there are a number of ways of influencing these processes though dramatic or subtle differences in the treatment of the sexes. A brake can be applied to high fertility by customs which require the mothers of young children to engage in strenuous fat-depleting work activities: conversely high fertility can be encouraged by a division of labour that provides abundant food to these women without exertion. The social arrangement of the nuclear family as a food production and consumption unit should have a depressing effect on fertility, because the mother's efforts must increase directly with her family's needs, while societies that produce and consume food over a larger unit may spread out the work load so that it does not coincide exactly with a woman's pregnancies. The San have the custom that the woman produces directly for her own family while the men's meat contributions must be shared out among all those in the living group, thus insuring that the woman's difficulties with maintaining her fat deposits cannot readily be solved by her husband's increase in hunting success. Such customs should be analyzed for their pro-natal and anti-natal implications.

The type 1 situation, which appears so attractive, is unstable unless there is opportunity for expansion to new lands. No doubt many prehistoric populations lived under these conditions (although the type 1 is the extreme of the two distributions) since we know that the human population expanded enough to occupy the whole world before the origin of agriculture and those expanding populations are particularly important ones since all the others are descended from them. But it must also have been a frequent occurrence in prehistory that the limits of expansion were reached. Nature will solve the problem, as Malthus long ago pointed out, in a brutal and undiscriminating way: the mortality of all will increase, or all will go hungry which will have the effect of reducing fertility. Customs of infanticide, and particularly female infanticide, on the one hand, and the unequal division of labor which assigns heavy work loads to women and not to men may be interpreted as rational responses to a type 1 situation in which further expansion is blocked.

If all adults had the capacity to make an equal contribution to the food supply, one might expect to find the reverse situation, of male infanticide and/or an unequal demand for work from males in adulthood, in societies that are attempting to cope with the type 4 situation of high pathogens and a poor food supply. No doubt the food contributions of males though hunting are critical in this regard. With hunting, and the type 4 situation, indiscriminate infanticide and senilicide are more likely to be seen.

5. Conclusion

The present paper has been an attempt to argue that it is theoretically profitable to conceptualize the problem of paleodemography as one involving a constant biological capacity to respond to various environmental situations. Aside from the behavior directly involved in birth and death, what are the theoretical implications of the conclusion that prehistoric populations must have been characterized by relatively high fertility and mortality, distributed by age like that of contemporary populations?

One important implication is the expected presence of old people in the population: between five and ten percent of those born will survive to the age of 65 and beyond under the limited mortality conditions suggested. Since these old people have to be drawn from those who survive the rigors of childhood and adult life, they are likely to be precisely the people who have produced large families. Family structure in which three generations or even four generations are alive at the same time is likely to have been a general feature of prehistoric populations, even though only a minority of those alive at any one time would be involved in such families. Maintenance of information through the memory of living people over a period of fifty years or more could routinely be expected.

One important feature of prehistoric populations that we cannot infer from the uniformitarian view is the size of such societies. Although there is undoubtedly a lower limit below which a population finds it impossible to provide a stable number of people for the division of labour and for mate selection, that size will depend upon the rigidity of rules for allocation. The upper limit of population size is set by the group's ability to communicate sufficiently to maintain the endogamous group. This does not depend upon the levels of fertility and mortality in any direct way.

The number of kin that people will have, on the average, at various stages of their life is determined by the fertility that generates them and the mortality that eliminates them. If we look at kinship as the generating process of links between people that permit or inhibit the formation of subgroups that may organize for concerted joint action, then the frequency distributions of numbers of kin generated under various demographic regimes provides some insight into the internal social structure of such groups. With uniformitarian assumptions, such analyses can be made for prehistoric populations as well as for contemporary ones.

Finally, as suggested above, features of social structure and culture such a the organization of food producing and consuming units, sex role differentiation and infanticide may be explicable as efforts of the population to exercise some communal control over the demographic constraints under which they live. While consideration of the adaptive significance of such customs is frequently made, use of uniformitarian assumptions about the fertility and mortality of groups permits a sharper analysis about the amount of demographic control possible through the use of various alternatives.

The uniformitarian perspective on prehistoric populations is certainly useful, although of course our need for it does not guarantee that it is an accurate description of the demographic processes of perhistoric populations. This paper has argued that uniformitarian assumptions are already widely used in paleodemographic studies. Explicit rejection of those assumptions will undermine the foundations of much of the work already done in the field. Explicit acceptance of those assumptions will permit considerable advances in the construction of models of population dynamics of prehistoric hunters and gatherers.

References

Acsádi, G. & Nemeskéri, J. (1970). *History of Human Life Span and Mortality*. Budapest: Akadémiai Kiadó.

Birdsell, J. B. (1972). *Human Evolution: An Introduction to the New Physical Anthropology*, Chicago: Rand McNally & Company.

Coale, A. J. (1974). The history of human population. *Scientific American* **231**, 41–51.

Coale, A. J. & Demeny, P. (1966). *Regional Model Life Tables and Stable Populations*, Princeton, N.J.: Princeton University Press.

Current Anthropology (1974). C. A. Book Review of *History of Human Life Span and Mortality* by G. Acsádi and J. Nemeskéri, *Current Anthropology* **15**, No. 4, December 1974.

Dumond, D. E. (1975). The limitation of human population: a natural history, *Science* **187**, 713–721.

Eaton, J. W. & Mayer, A. J. The social biology of very high fertility among the Hutterites. *Human Biology* **25**, (3), 206–264.

Frisch, R. E. (1973). The critical weight at menarche and the initiation of the adolescent growth spurt, and the control of puberty. In (M. Grumback *et al.*, eds.) *The Control of the Onset of Puberty*. New York: Wiley-Interscience.

Frisch, R. E. & McArthur, J. W. (1974). Menstrual cycles: fatness as a determinant of minimum weight for height necessary for their maintenance or onset. *Science* **185** (13), September 1974.

Frisch, R. E. (1976). Demographic implications of the biological determinants of female fecundity. *Social Biology*, (in press).

Harpending, H. (in press). Genetic and demographic variations in Kung populations. In (R. B. Lee and I. DeVore, Eds.) *Kalahari Hunter–Gatherers*. Cambridge, Mass.: Harvard University Press.

Howell, N. (1973). The feasibility of demographic studies in anthropological populations. In (M. H. Crawford and P. L. Workman) *Methods and Theories of Anthropolegical Genetics*. Albuquerque: University of New Mexico Press.

Howell, N. (in press). The population of the Dobe Area Kung. In (R. B. Lee and I. DeVore, Eds.) *Kalahari Hunter–Gatherers*. Cambridge, Mass.: Harvard University Press.

Lee, R. B. & DeVore, I. (Eds.) (1968). *Man the Hunter*. Chicago-Aldine Publishing Company.

Lee, R. B. (1972). Population growth and the beginnings of seden-life among the Kung Bushmen. In (B. Spooner, Ed.) *Population Growth: Anthropological Implications*. Cambridge, Mass.: M.I.T. Press.

Marx, J. (1974). Aging research (1): Cellular theories of senescence. *Science* **186**, 1105–1106.

Menken, J. A. (1975). *Estimating Fecundability*. Unpublished Ph.D. dissertation, Princeton University.

Neel, J. V. & Weiss, K. M. (1975). The genetic structure of a tribal population, the Yanomama Indians. *American Journal of Physical Anthropology*, **42**, 25–52.

Preston, S. H., Keyfitz, N. & Schoen, R. (1972). *Causes of Death Life Tables for National Populations*. New York: Seminar Press.

Silberbauer, G. (1965). *Bushman Survey Report*. Gaberones: Bechuanaland Government.

Simpson, G. G. (1949). *The Meaning of Evolution*. New Haven Conn.: Yale University Press.

Steiger, W. L. & Schrier, C. (1974). A matter of life and death: an investigation of the practice of female infanticide in the Arctic. *Man* **9** (2).

Sussman, R. W. (1972). Child transport, family size and increase in human population during the Neolithic. *Current Anthropology* **13** (2), 258–259.

Trusswell, A. S. & Hanson, J. D. (in press). "Bio-medical Research Among the Bushmen." In (R. B. Lee and I. DeVore, Eds.) *Kalahari Hunter–Gatherers*. Cambridge, Mass.: Harvard University Press.

United Nations. (1955). *Age and Sex Patterns of Mortality. Model Life Tables for Under-Developed Countries. ST/SOA/Series A/22*. New York: United Nation. Sales No.: 55.XIII.9.

Visaria, P. M. (1969). Mortality and fertility in India, 1951–61. *Milbank Memorial Fund Quarterly* (January 1969) **XLVII** (1), Part 1.

Weiss, K. M. (1973). *Demographic Models for Anthropology*. Memoirs of the Society for Archaeology, Number 27.

Maciej Henneberg

Reproductive Possibilities and Estimations of the Biological Dynamics of Earlier Human Populations

Department of Physical Anthropology,
Adam Michiewicz University,
10, *ul Fredry, 61-701 Poznan,*
Poland

1. Introduction

The interrelations between man as a biological species and all the determinants of his condition are of a very complex nature. In order to understand them we must extensively study not only the present state of mankind but also historical trends. In the studies of earlier human populations one of the crucial points is the question of their numerical growth. By solving this question one is able to shed some light on the problems of the eco-cultural state of prehistoric groups, their powers of territorial expansion, social mechanisms regulating population size, the rate and direction of changes in genetic composition, and so on.

Omitting migration, the biological and social dynamics of human groups have very strong feedback relations with fertility and mortality. For prehistoric and early historic times we have many data concerning mortality; although there is still a need for further methodological improvement and for new materials, in general our knowledge about this phenomenon is in a far better state than is our knowledge about fertility.

Attempts undertaken by physical anthropologists and demographers to estimate the fertility of earlier human populations lead to varied and sometimes even contradictory results. If one tries to estimate the natural increase of a given population, represented by a skeletal series with a known mortality pattern, the use of different methods for fertility estimations may lead to extremely different conclusions, as the author has shown previously (Henneberg, 1976). Disregarding methods which are purely speculative, based on general regularities only, and making no references to skeletal evidence, there are three different ways to estimate the fertility level of prehistoric groups. First, the number of births in a group may be reconstructed from the average duration of the reproductive period (calculated on the basis of mortality data), divided by an hypothetical duration of the birth interval (Angel, 1969; Nemeskéri, 1970, 1972; papers in *Current Anthropology* **13**, 203–267, 1972). Usually it is assumed that the average birth spacing in each population is about 30 months and that this is constant during the entire life of an adult woman up to the age of menopause. The second method is based on the reconstructed age structure of living females and hypothetical, age-specific fertility rates (*Wstęp do Demografii*, 1967; Acsádi & Nemeskéri, 1970). Finally, one can estimate the number of deliveries from female pelvic bones. Changes in the pelvic bone, especially in the region of the pubic symphysis, are induced by pregnancies and deliveries, and they are more marked in individuals of higher parity (Putschar, 1931; Stewart, 1957; Angel, 1969). Unfortunately, accurate corroboration of the number of children born to a female with given degrees of change in her pelvic bone is impossible since the degree of change after the same number of deliveries is quite variable among different individuals. Moreover, we do not have many good examples of pelves from females with registered numbers of childbirths.

These methods do not permit us to establish the actual number of births in a prehistoric population, and we must therefore rely on assumptions or very rough approximations only. Therefore, the most reasonable approach to the problem of reproduction in earlier human populations is to measure the impact of mortality on the reproductive capacity of populations. In order to construct a method suited to this purpose, we must take into consideration the mortality data combined with known regularities in procreation found in common to all populations not practicing modern forms of birth control ("non-Malthusian" populations, in the sense that Malthus showed that populations would all eventually have to control their own growth in some manner).

2. Regular Patterns of Procreation in Non-Malthusian Populations

Various non-Malthusian populations with well known fertility and natality have considerably different fertility rates (Lorimer, 1954; Pressat, 1966; Henry, 1972). Differentiation of fertility levels in non-Malthusian populations is determined mainly by the variable duration of the intervals between births. Minor roles are played by the differences in the ages of beginning and cessation of reproductive activity, and in the cultural factors leading to the absolute sexual inactivity of particular individuals. The duration of the intervals between births is influenced by many ecocultural factors; these factors are population-specific with many interrelations of very complex structure. The numerous factors influencing fertility levels in non-Malthusian populations do not permit us to outline a common model for all of them concerning the set of age-specific fertility rates and/or intervals between births.

Table 1   **Relative cumulative number of births in the non-Malthusian populations with different fertility**

Age (x) / Population	Age-specific fertility rates (after Pressat, 1961)				Cumulative number of births per woman (U_x)				Relative cumulative number of births ($1 - s$)			
	1	2	3	4	1	2	3	4	1	2	3	4
20–24 years	323	389	419	550	0·8	1·0	1·1	1·4	0·13	0·13	0·13	0·13
25–29 years	288	362	429	502	2·3	2·9	3·2	4·0	0·38	0·38	0·39	0·37
30–34 years	282	372	355	447	3·8	4·6	5·1	6·4	0·61	0·62	0·63	0·58
35–39 years	212	275	292	406	5·0	6·1	6·8	8·5	0·81	0·82	0·82	0·78
40–44 years	100	123	142	222	5·8	7·1	7·8	10·1	0·94	0·95	0·95	0·93
45–49 years	33	9	10	61	6·1	7·4	8·2	10·8	0·99	1·00	1·00	0·99
50–					6·2	7·4	8·2	10·9	1·00	1·00	1·00	1·00

1 = Bengal, Hindu villages, 1945–46.
2 = Geneva, husband born before 1600.
3 = Crulai, 1674–1742.
4 = Hutterites, marriages contracted between 1921–1930.

However, the increase of the *relative*, cumulative proportion of births with the age of adults is almost the same for all non-Malthusian populations. This regularity is illustrated in Table 1, for some groups. The regulation of birth spacing does not greatly influence these birth distributions during the reproductive period of parents. This characteristic distribution in general reflects changes with age in fecundability, the tendency for spontaneous abortions, etc., that is, in basic biological phenomena related to reproduction.

Based on this regularity in relative cumulated fertility, we may construct an "archetype of fertility" as follows: Let the total fertility of individuals living through their entire reproductive period (i.e. at least 50 years old), or the completed fertility, be given as U_c. Then for individuals dying at any age x, prior to age 50, the number of offspring they will be expected to have reproduced (U_x) will be some fraction of U_c, based on the age and the reproductive pattern. Thus,

$$1 - s_x = U_x/U_c \tag{1}$$

where s_x is the expected proportion of completed fertility lost due to pre-menopausal death. The value of s_x will be called the "proportion of reproductive loss", and it gives information about reproductive loss of an individual dying at age x.

On the basis of fertility data from various non-Malthusian populations (Lorimer, 1954; Pressat, 1961; *Wstęp do Demografii*, 1967; Acsádi & Nemeskéri, 1970; Henry, 1972) the present author has established the following set of average s_x values which constitutes a good approximation for those groups taken into account, and which may be called our "archetype of fertility":

Age (x)	15–19	20–24	25–29	30–34	35–39	40–44	45–w
s_x	0·95	0·77	0·55	0·35	0·17	0·05	0·00
$1 - s_x$	0·05	0·23	0·45	0·65	0·83	0·95	1·00

3. Estimation of Reproductive Rates in Earlier Human Populations

Making use of the archetype of fertility when the mortality structure of a given group is known, one can compute the "potential gross reproductive rate", R_{pot}. This parameter is the sum of the reproductive potential remaining after the premenopausal deaths of adults. If reproduction begins at age b (generally taken to be age 15) and its cessation is at age c (generally taken to be 45–50), and if the proportion of those dying at age x, above age b, among all deaths of those over age b is d_x ($= D_x/D_{15-w}$), then we will have

$$R_{pot} = \sum_{x=b}^{x=c} d_x(1 - s_x) = \sum d_x - \sum d_x s_x = 1 - \sum d_x s_x. \tag{2}$$

To be exact, d_x should be the proportion of those dying in age class x among all persons beginning reproductive period; however, skeletal material does not permit us to make this calculation directly without additional assumptions, and the differences between values of d_x calculated in both ways seem unimportant in relation to our problem.

R_{pot} thus gives information on what proportion of total reproductive potential is realized under the given mortality conditions relative to that which would be realized if there were no adult mortality before age c. It may be used directly for interpopulational comparisons without any assumptions about the actual fertility rates or the duration of the birth intervals, so long as the cumulative fertility schedule, $1 - s_x$, may be assumed to be the same.

It is sometimes useful to estimate the average family size in a particular group. In such a case, the number of children in the family can be estimated from R_{pot} times some hypothetical value of U_c, the completed family size. Obviously, corrections for infant and juvenile mortality have to be made. Acsádi & Nemeskéri (1970) have suggested that the most reasonable value of U_c for earlier human populations is 8·0, while according to Lorimer $U_c = 7·45$. Surely U_c varied within a broad range in earlier populations, so these values may be treated as rough approximations only.

For estimates of the Net Reproduction Rate (R_0) in populations it is necessary to take into account the mortality of subadults. From the following expression, one can estimate R_0 for a prehistoric group:

$$R_0 = R_{pot}(0·5)(U_c) \frac{100 - d_{0-15}}{100}, \qquad (3)$$

where d_{0-15} is the proportion of liveborn children who die before their fifteenth birthday (taken from the life table), and 0·5 corrects approximately for the sex ratio at birth. Such a definition of R_0 is somewhat different from that used in demography where only females are taken into account. However, there are two reasons for our definition in paleobiological studies. Firstly, we have no way to estimate, with sufficient accuracy, the sex of individuals below adult ages. Secondly, from genetical and evolutionary viewpoints both sexes have equal importance and must be taken into consideration. Inaccuracies resulting from the state of preservation, sex and age estimations of skeletal finds, and the differences between both definitions of R_0 suggest that comparison between our results and standard demographic data ought to be made very carefully. However on the approximate level our estimates are comparable with purely demographic data since in demography $R_0 = 1$ when succeeding female generations are of the same size and age structure, while in our definition $R_0 = 1$ when generations of parents and their adult descendents, disregarding sex, are of equal size and the same age structure. When $R_0 < 1$, population declines, and when $R_0 > 1$ it increases.

For accurate R_0 estimates, very reliable data on mortality are required, but it is also possible to make some statements on minimal and maximal R_0 values for skeletal series with incomplete juvenile remains on the basis of extreme d_{0-15} and U_c values which may be presumed for non-Malthusian populations. Limitations of such estimates and their usefulness are described in a previous paper (Henneberg, 1976).

One of the most important problems for studies in paleodemography is the question of population models. Human paleobiologists are forced to work with models of stable or stationary populations, since almost all skeletal series do not have detailed data on fluctuations in population size or mortality conditions, etc. during the time span in which a given cemetery was used. All life tables for skeletal populations known to the author were constructed according to the stationary population model, so when we compute R_{pot} and R_0 values for them we are dealing with acute mortality conditions disadvantageous for reproduction. Hence estimates on the capacity for natural increase among earlier human populations, computed with low assumed values for U_c, are rather minimal estimations. In Table 2 are listed data on reproduction of some groups with well established life tables. It is obvious that in prehistoric and early historic times many populations with a great reproductive capacity were present.

Table 2 R_o and I_{bs} estimations in some earlier human populations, data for modern Poland are given for comparison

Population	R_o estimation when $U_o =$			I_{bs}	R_{pos}	d_{0-14}	Source of mortality data
	7	8	10				
Neanderthal				0·26–0·32	0·56	0·38–0·40	Vallois (1937); Acsádi & Nemeskéri (1970)
Upper Paleolithic	1·06	1·21	1·51	0·30	0·49	0·38	Vallois (1937)
Mesolithic	1·04	1·19	1·48	0·30	0·42	0·30	Vallois (1937)
Maghreb type (Epipaleolithic)	1·23	1·40	1·75	0·35	0·75	0·53	Acsádi & Nemeskéri (1970)
Nea Nikomedeia (Early Neolithic)	0·81	0·92	1·15	0·23	0·58	0·58	Angel (1969)
Volni (Neolithic)	1·54	1·76	2·20	0·44	0·69	0·36	Acsádi & Nemeskéri (1970)
Germany, Neolithic	1·68	1·92	2·40	0·48	0·66	0·27	Ullrich (1972)
Alsonemedi (Copper Age)	1·79	2·04	2·55	0·51	0·80	0·36	Acsádi & Nemeskéri (1970)
Grossbrembach (Early Bronze Age)	1·12	1·28	1·60	0·32	0·53	0·42	Ullrich (1972)
Lerna (Middle Bronze Age)	1·05	1·20	1·50	0·30	0·66	0·56	Angel (1969)
Sulcin (Late Bronze Age)	1·47	1·68	2·10	0·42	0·64	0·34	Piontek (1976)
Intercisa Brigetio (I–IV c.A.D.)	1·50	1·72	2·15	0·43	0·68	0·36	Acsádi & Nemeskéri (1970)
Valachians (IV c.A.D.)	1·40	1·60	2·00	0·40	0·56	0·29	Nicolaescu & Wolski (1972)
Keszthely-Dobogo (Late Roman Era)	2·10	2·40	3·00	0·60	0·83	0·28	Acsádi & Nemeskéri (1970)
Sopronkohida (IX c.A.D.)	1·76	2·01	2·52	0·50	0·93	0·46	Acsádi & Nemeskéri (1970)
Artand (IX c.A.D.)	2·03	2·32	2·90	0·58	0·78	0·26	Ery (1967)
Espenfeld (XI–XII c.A.D.)	1·09	1·24	1·55	0·31	0·60	0·49	Bach & Bach (1971)
Czarna Wielka (XI–XII c.A.D.)	1·54	1·76	2·20	0·44	0·65	0·32	Modrzewska (1958)
Hungarian model (XI–XII c.A.D.)	1·72	1·96	2·45	0·49	0·80	0·39	Acsádi & Nemeskéri (1970)
Reckahn (XII–XIV c.A.D.)	1·64	1·88	2·35	0·47	0·66	0·28	Schott (1964)
Villages in parish Szczepanowo (Poland, middle of XIX c.A.D.)				0·32	0·79	0·59	Author's unpublished data
Poland 1960–1966				0·94	0·99	0·05	*Rocznik Demograficzny* (1968)

One may suspect that in the series considered in the present paper the number of dead subadults is underestimated due to the loss of adequate skeletal material in the cemeteries. However, when we take values of R_{pot} computed for these groups and assume for all of them that $d_{0-15} = 60\%$ (which is the upper limit for long periods of about 100 years) and $R_0 = 1 \cdot 1$, we compute a range of birth rates between 200–370 per thousand per year (the average fertility rate for fertile-age females) and of birth spacing of from 26·8 to 51 months, excluding the Mesolithic group. These values are within limits found by demographers in contemporary non-Malthusian populations (Pressat, 1961; Henry, 1972).

The results obtained here strongly suggest that many prehistoric populations were capable of at least moderate natural increase, so that reconstructions of age structure and size of living populations from skeletal data ought to be based on a stable, rather than a stationary, population model. When we compare our results with very slow increase of the total Eurpoean population during these times, it may be suggested that such a slow increase of total numbers of people in great regions was due to the rapid extinction of some groups (or large segments of them) perhaps due to cultural factors (e.g., intergroup competition) and/or epidemics, natural disasters, and so on. Significant influence from birth control seems impossible at least in sedentary groups. Questions touched on above can be solved ultimately only in close collaboration between physical and cultural anthropology.

4. Application of R_{pot} in Investigations of Natural Selection in Man

In 1958 J. F. Crow developed his Index of Total Selection. One part of this Index is the parameter I_m, a measure of the intensity of natural selection due to differential mortality. It seems that this measure is not precise, because fitness (or selective value) of individuals dying during their reproductive period is not estimated as a function of their age at death. The death of an individual before the end of the reproductive period, but after the birth of some of his (or her) children, has a selective significance which is not equivalent to the death of an immature or senile person. The second part of Crow's Index is I_f, a measure of selective intensity due to differential fertility, does not allow us directly to estimate fertility differentials due to genetic diversity only and having an essential influence on the operation of natural selection: I_f is strongly influenced by results of birth control and other cultural factors regulating the number of births which are almost entirely independent of the genetic endowment of the parents. Moreover, the fertility standards in the form required for I_f calculation are applicable solely with regard to contemporaneous living populations. Hence I have proposed the "Biological State Index" for the investigation of natural selection in man (Henneberg & Piontek, 1976), applicable with no significant modifications to prehistoric as well as to modern populations.

We have formulated the concept of the Biological State of populations and its measure as follows (Henneberg & Piontek, 1976).

"The Biological State of a population is a measure of the general level of selection pressures, acting through mortality on all its individuals. A measure of the Biological State thus understood is provided by a quantity expressing what fraction of a given generation has a chance to participate fully in producing the next generation under the given mortality conditions. This is a measure of the reproductive possibility of the population as a whole or, equivalently, its average individual. The Biological State is thus an expression of adaptation, taken as the totality of biological and cultural characteristics making the reproductive success of a population possible though not necessarily causing it."

The Biological State Index according to this definition is constructed on the basis of the mortality structure and the probability of not producing the completed family size, due to the deaths of individuals in reproductive years (s_x):

$$I_{bs} = 1 - \sum_{x=0}^{x=w} d_x s_x, \tag{4}$$

where w is the oldest possible age for survival in the population. Since s_x for immature individuals is 1·0, the formula may be modified and written in the form:

$$I_{bs} = R_{pot} \frac{100 - d_{0-15}}{100}. \tag{5}$$

It is clear that I_{bs} corresponds to $R_0/0\cdot5\ U_c$. The values of I_{bs} by definition can range from 0 to 1. Hence, on the basis of the I_{bs} we are able to evaluate the selective pressure in a given population without any data on other populations as points of reference.

Essential information as to the mode of action of selection through mortality is provided by separate consideration of subadult mortality (d_{0-15}) which completely excludes individuals from bearing children, and R_{pot} expressing relative differentiation of adult individuals' fitness. Analysis of these values allows us, jointly with other information, to interpret the regulation of natural selection by the changes in the protection of children and the living conditions of adults, etc.

In Table 2, I_{bs} values from several groups are given. It follows from these data that in the course of history the general biological state does not improve so much, but rather the upper limit of adaptive capacity changes, although groups with a low adaptation level are always present. It may also be seen that the improvement in the biological situation of adults (R_{pot}) occurs well in advance of the decline of childhood mortality. This last phenomenon is proved also by observations of the increase in life expectancy of newborns (e_0^0) and of adults (e_{20}^0). During the course of history of European populations the increase in e_{20}^0 is more marked and is greater than increases in e_0^0 (Henneberg et al., 1976; cf. data from the life tables in Acsádi & Nemeskéri, 1970).

The probable causes and the mechanism of these trends together with their implications for biological changes in our species are discussed in detail in another paper (Henneberg & Piontek, 1976). Here I would like to cite only our conclusions, which are in accordance with well known statements by many human biologists:

1. Historic increases in the divergence of biological states led to an increase in interpopulational differences with regard to the mechanisms and range of intragroup variability in morphophysiological characters.

2. In conditions of poor biological state, intraspecies variability is maintained mainly due to interpopulation differences, at a relatively low level of intragroup variability.

3. A considerable improvement in biological state causes an increase of intrapopulational variability and its significance for the variability of the species. Hence, the range of variability in modern populations will become closer to the variability range for the whole of our species even without intensive gene flow.

I wish to express my deepest gratitude to Dr Habil. J. Strzałko and Dr J. Piontek, with whom I work in the Biological History of Human Populations Program, for many useful remarks and their help in discussing the results of my work, and to Doc. Dr Habil. A. Malinowski, Head of the Department of Physical Anthropology at A. Mickiewicz University for his kind interest and help in solving our problems.

References

Acsádi, G. & Nemeskéri, J. (1970). *History of Human Life Span and Mortality*. Budapest: Academiai Kiadó.

Angel, J. L. (1969). The bases of paleodemography. *American Journal of Physical Anthropology* **30,** 427–438. Anthropology and population problems (1972). *Current Anthropology* **13,** 203–267.

Bach, H. & Bach, A. (1971). Anthropologische Untersuchungen. In (Bach, H. and Dušek, S.) *Slawen in Thüringen*. Weimar: H. Böhlaus Nachfolger.

Crow, J. F. (1958). Some possibilities for measuring selection intensities in man. *Human Biology* **30,** 1–13.

Ery, D. (1967). An anthropological study of the late Avar Period population of Ártánd. *Annales Historico-Naturales Musei Nationalis Hungarici* **59,** 466–484.

Henneberg, M. (1976). Notes on the reproduction possibilities of human prehistoric populations. *Przeglad Antropologiczny*, in press.

Henneberg, M. & Piontek, J. (1976). Biological state index of human groups. *Przeglad Antropologiczny*, in press.

Henneberg, M., Ostoja-Zagórski, J., Piontek, J. & Strzałko, J. (1976). Głoene załozenia teoretyczno-metodyczne badań biologii populacji pradziejowych w Europie środkowej. *Przeglad Archeologiczny*, in press.

Henry, L. (1972). *On the Measurement of Human Fertility*. Amsterdam: Elsevier Publishing Company.

Lorimer, F. (Ed.) (1954). *Culture and Human Fertility*. Paris: UNESCO.

Modrezewska, K. (1958). Długość trwania życia wczesnośredniowiecznych mieszkańcó Podlasia. *Czlowiek w Czasie i Przestrzeni* **1,** 65–72.

Nicolaescu–Plopsor, D. & Wolski, W. (1972). Necropole de Secol IV e.n. Din Muntenia, Elemente De Analiza Demografica Comparata. *Studii Si Cercetari de Antropologie* **9,** 109–117.

Nemeskéri, J. (1970). Die paläodemographischen Probleme des Mittel-Donau-Beckens in der Bronzezeit. *Homo* **21,** 80.

Nemeskéri, J. (1970). Die archäologischen und anthropologischen Voraussetzungen paläodemographischen Forschungen. *Praehistorische Zeitschrift* **47,** 5–46.

Piontek, J. (1976). Badania paleobiologiczne populacji z III–IV okresu epiki brąsu z Sulęcina woj. Zielonogórskie. *Przeglad Antropologiczny*, in press.

Pressat, R. (1961). *L'analyse démographique, méthodes, résultats, applications*. Paris: Presses Univ. de France.

Putschar, W. (1931). *Entwicklung, Wachstum und Pathologie der Beckenverbindungen des Menschen*. Jena: Fischer Verlag.

Rocznik Demograficzny 1945–66. (1968). Warsaw: Główny Urząd Statystyczny.

Schott, L. (1964). Zur Paläodemographie der hohmittelalterlichen Sidelung von Reckahn. *Etnographische-Archäologische Zeitschift* **4,** 132–142.

Stewart, T. D. (1957). Distortion of the pubic symphyseal surface in females and its effect on age determination. *American Journal of Physical Anthropology* **15,** 9.

Ullrich, H. (1972). *Das Aunjetitzer Graberfeld von Grossbrembach*. Weimar: H. Böhlaus Nachfolger.

Vallois, H. (1937). La durée de la vie chez l'homme fossile. *Anthropologie* **47,** 499–532.

Wstęp do Demografii. (1967). Warsaw: Państwowe Wydawnictwo Ekonomiczne.

H. Martin Wobst

Department of Anthropology,
University of Massachusetts,
Amherst, U.S.A.

Locational Relationships in Paleolithic Society

1. Introduction

Paleolithic data are more fragmentary and more systematically biased than those of more recent prehistoric periods. It is interesting to see that Paleolithic archaeologists, in their traditional methodology and theoretical outlook, have quite well adapted to this data base: since "sites" are the most inclusive products of sociocultural systems which can be completely recovered archaeologically, sites have traditionally served as the largest units for research, analysis, and interpretation which are in any way culturally realistic. Even though Paleolithic archaeologists have distilled archaeological "cultures", "assemblage types", and "traditions" from shared site inventories and given them social meaning, these entities do not have counterparts with social meaning among modern hunter-gatherers. Paleolithic archaeology lacks an analytical concept compatible with the "society" or "culture" of ethnology, or with the "population" of general ecology. This lack of concern with cultural behaviors which transcend the confines of isolated settlements but nevertheless significantly influence their archaeological form and structure condemns Paleolithic archaeology to a worm-eye's view of socio-cultural evolution and to increasing isolation within the social and behavioral sciences. If Paleolithic archaeologists want to maintain a more fruitful discourse with the remainder of science, they have to attack prehistoric cultural behavior at a level of integration and analysis which is more encompassing than the individual settlement and which is more sensitive to socio-cultural processes between interacting settlement populations than the traditional archaeological "cultures", "traditions", and "assemblage types".

In a previous paper I have introduced the mating network as a behavioral concept which may allow us to organize and integrate socio-cultural processes which relate adjacent settlement populations and which, at the same time, significantly shape the form and structure of cultural behavior at individual settlements (Wobst, 1974). Among recent hunter–gatherers, the mating network is identical in personnel to such ethnologically established entities as the maximum band (Steward, 1969: 290), the dialectical tribe (Birdsell, 1953; 1968: 231–233, 246), or the connubium (Williams, 1974), that is, it defines the largest social entity beyond the local group which has behavioral concomitants. The mating network among hunter–gatherers also circumscribes the standard unit of ethnographic field work (Murdock, 1967); and theories of hunter–gatherer behavior have been designed for, and tested against, a universe of these entities (see for example

Damas, 1969; Williams, 1974; or Yengoyan, 1968). I have attempted to demonstrate that the mating network is archaeologically graspable, and the the size, longevity, and location of prehistoric mating networks are predictable (Wobst, ibid.). Since all animals have mating networks, the concept is more general and more flexible than maximum band, dialectical tribe, or connubium. Thus, it should have heuristic value even in the absence of Band Society—a useful feature if one wants to investigate the origins of Band Society.

I have approximated the minimal size of hunter–gatherer mating networks in a series of computer simulations, by answering the following question: given a series of different life tables which reflects the range of observed hunter–gatherer demographic structure, and given a series of different sets of mating rules which reflects the likely range of hunter–gatherer mating behavior, how large does a mating network have to be to assure that any member, upon reaching maturity, will find a suitable mate? The answer ranged from 175 to 475 individuals (of all ages), the majority of the assumptions yielding values in the upper part of this range (ibid.; 161–170). As these are minimal size estimates, 475 people may be considered a practicable lower limit.

In this paper I want to discuss some of the locational implications of the concept of mating network for Paleolithic archaeology.

2. Paleolithic "Cultures" and "Assemblage Types" *Versus* the Mating Network

The ethnographic present found the inland hunter–gatherers of Alaska, Canada, and Siberia at population densities from 0·5 to 0·005 persons/km². This range estimate is based on a large number of sources, among them the following general works (with bibliographies): Bicchieri (1972), Damas (1969), Kroeber (1939), Lee & DeVore (1968), Levin & Potapov (1964), Vanstone (1974). Even if the influence of contact period decimation is removed, most groups would still show densities below 0·05 persons/km². Exploiting a broadly similar range of fauna, and being as strongly dependent on meat as recent northern hunters, Eurasian hunters during glacial intervals may be expected to show population densities in a comparable range. The absence of bow-and-arrow hunting, harpoons, domestic draft animals, and exploitation of fish runs in glacial northern Eurasia during much or all of the Pleistocene may even have confined populations to the lower end of the range for modern northern hunters. Certainly nothing in the archaeological record suggests higher population densities than 0·05/km² during glacial intervals, not even in those areas of Eurasia which have received most attention from Paleolithic archaeologists (see, for example, David, 1973).

Hunter–gatherer societies studied by ethnographers are, on the average, surrounded by 6 neighbors (Birdsell, 1958; Wilmsen, 1973; Wobst, 1974: 154). In this way they approximate the most efficient spatial packing pattern of regular hexagonal territories. Assuming that their population size coincides with the minimal size of mating networks (475 individuals) and assuming for simplicity's sake hexagonal areas for the societies or mating networks, Table 1 shows the area occupied by societies in the given population density range under the given assumptions.

A territory of 95,000 km² (at 0·005 persons/km²) includes *all* of the Paleolithic of southwestern France and stretches from the Mediterranean Sea to the Atlantic Ocean. Even a territory of 9500 km² (at 0·05 persons/km²) encompasses the entire Périgord with all of

Table 1   **Area and diameter of mating networks at different population densities**

Population density (persons/km^2)	Area (km^2)	Diameter (km)
0·05	9500	120
0·04	11875	135
0·03	15833	156
0·02	23750	191
0·01	47500	270
0·009	52777	285
0·008	59375	302
0·007	67857	323
0·006	79166	349
0·005	95000	382

its Paleolithic sites (Sonneville–Bordes, 1960). It also circumscribes all of the Moravian Paleolithic sites (Klima, 1957), or the entire Crimean Paleolithic (Klein, 1965). Mate exchange requires the maintenance of a dense communication network and is frequently symbolically supported by food sharing, exchange, and ritual. If the people in the area of la Quina were regularly exchanging mates with the people around le Moustier, la Ferrassie, la Micoque, and Combe Grenal, the contemporaneous occurrence of distinct assemblage types at these or other sites in and around the Périgord cannot be explained in terms of different ethnic affiliations, and this does not apply to Middle Paleolithic assemblage types only. It is similarly obvious that formally similar lithic assemblages cannot document any ethnic affinities between their makers if they are located thousands of kilometers apart from one another, as in the case of some French and Near Eastern assemblages (Brodes, 1955). Symboling of social affiliation cannot be maintained for millenia in the absence of communication. Thus, as a first and very gross locational implication, the concept of the mating network supports those Paleolithic archaeologists who look for more processual explanations for the variability between contemporaneous lithic assemblages.

3. Limiting Conditions for the Origins of Band Society

The mating network becomes a more rewarding explanatory device if it is segmented into its functional subunits—the local groups or minimum bands. The personnel of local groups among hunter-gatherers usually consists of several related families which at least during part of the year share a settlement and a given range of cultural activities. This unit tends to maintain a territory through habitual use, delimited by the proximity of other minimum bands, by natural obstacles, and by factors of distance and exploitative efficiency. Ethnographically, minimum bands range in size from 15 to 75 people if specialized marine, lacustrine, and riverine populations are excluded (Birdsell, 1957; Damas, 1969; see also Wobst, 1974: 170). The mode in this distribution appears to be in the neighborhood of 25 people. Presently, there is no evidence from Paleolithic settlements in northern Eurasia to indicate higher modes in local group size during any time in the Pleistocene.

Assume, for simplicity's sake, that mating networks in Pleistocene Eurasia consisted of local groups of mean size 25. To assure a compatible mate for any member upon reaching maturity, therefore, a given local group would normally have to engage in mate exchange

Table 2   **Relationship between population density and intra-mating network distances (km)**

Population density	Distance between nearest neighbors	Distance between most distant local groups	Distant between central and most distant group
0·05	24·0	96·0	48·0
0·04	26·0	107·4	53·7
0·03	31·0	124·0	62·0
0·02	37·9	151·9	75·9
0·01	53·7	214·8	107·4
0·009	56·6	226·5	113·2
0·008	60·0	240·2	120·1
0·007	64·2	256·8	128·4
0·006	69·3	277·4	138·7
0·005	75·9	303·9	151·9

with 18 other local groups (for a total of 475 people). If we place these local groups, again for simplicity's sake, into a hexagonally packed arrangement so that each group has 6 nearest neighbors, some interesting questions are raised (see Table 2 and Figure 1).

The first of these is related to the origin of Band Societies, that is, mating networks which are closed to such an extent that the participating local groups derive virtually all of their mates from the same set of personnel. In this case, the mating networks of the 19 different local groups would be essentially congruous. As population density decreases along column 1 in Table 2, the marginal groups (numbers 8 to 19 in Figure 1) are placed into a more and more unfavorable distance relationship relative to the groups in the center of the network. At population density 0·005, members of marginally located groups would have to move more than 300 km to reach the more distant members of their mating network (column 3, Table 2). At low population density, it is questionable whether local groups could maintain sufficiently dense communication to assure a peaceful exchange of mates over the distances required in the closed situation. Food sharing, joint ritual, and exchange—of sufficient intensity to facilitate mate exchange—are unlikely over some of the implied distances. As population density in our idealized distribution pattern decreases, it becomes more and more profitable for local groups to develop their own mating network, that is a mating network which does not coincide with those of any of their neighbors. In this way all local groups would achieve identical spatial relationships to their

Figure 1. Hexagonally packed mating network (each number represents a local group).

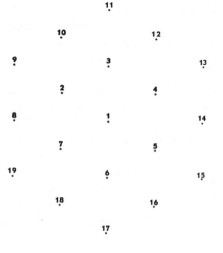

Figure 2. Example of overlapping mating networks. Each dot represents a local group. Only 2 of the many possible mating networks are shown. Note how the locational advantage of the marked group changes depending on the mating network it participates in.

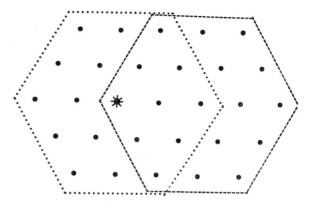

pool of potential mates (Figure 2). The communication network required of any given group would be of minimal size. In a closed mating network, the summed distances from a group at the margin to all other groups are almost 60% larger than the sum of the same distances from a centrally located group (Table 3). All of the groups can achieve identical and optimal location in their respective pool of mates only, if they select mates among those 475 people nearest to them.

The latter situation produces continuously distributed, partially overlapping mating networks. Genetically closed local breeding isolates could not materialize under these conditions since the chain of mate exchange would lack clear breaks and boundaries. This also prevents the maintenance of distinct cultural isolates. As local groups would have to exchange mates, and maintain conditions suitable for mate exchange equally in all directions, sharp social boundaries cannot develop and cannot be maintained. As a result, we would not expect to find evidence for social boundary processes in the archaeological record. Such evidence would originate from a need to signal or symbolize ethnicity or group affiliation, distinctiveness from neighbors, and aggression (or suppression of aggression) in interaction contexts involving members of distinct mating networks. The result would be a clinal distribution of stylistic variability without any marked discontinuities. Further, in the absence of breaks in communication quality or quantity, the different archaeologically graspable elements of extractive and productive endeavors should produce mutually non-congruous, spatially distinct distributions. These distributions should coincide only with the mutually non-congruous, spatially distinct, and temporally changing distribution of the variables which articulate with these elements. Thus, we can conclude that band societies with distinct dialects, ritual, and other behaviorally maintained clusters of idiosyncracy, like those in the ethnographic present or in some general models of hunter–gatherer behavior (for example Birdsell, 1968;

Table 3   **Summed distances from a given local group to all other local groups in mating network (at 0·01 persons/km²)**

(1) Summed distances from central group in closed mating system to all other groups	2157 km
(2) Summed distances from marginal group in closed mating system to all other groups	3337 km
(3) Summed distances from *any* local group in open mating system to the other groups it exchanges mates with	2157 km

Williams, 1974), cannot have arisen before a certain population density threshold was reached over wide areas. The maintenance of reasonably closed communication systems and reasonably closed mating networks becomes possible only when the participating local groups are in reasonable proximity, quite independent of any socio-cultural variables. As indicated, the hypothesized absence of Band Society among hunter–gatherers under conditions of low population density has test implications for the distribution of archaeological form and structure.

A further, mechanical threshold for the origin of Band Society as we know it today is related to the demographic impact of mating system closure. The smaller the effective breeding population, the greater are the annual (stochastic) fluctuations in fertility, mortality, and sex ratio. I have demonstrated in a previous paper (Wobst, 1975) that, to make up for the reproductive loss resulting from these fluctuations, mated females in relatively closed populations have to be considerably more fertile than in populations which draw their mates from partially overlapping and thus open mating networks. To get culturally idiosyncratic, reasonably closed mating networks started requires not only a sufficient population density, but population vital rates which are comfortably removed from zero growth so that closure does not lead to extinction.

It is suggestive in this respect that the Lower, Middle, and early Upper Paleolithic distribution of Paleolithic form and structure which may be called stylistic follows clines without any clear boundaries or breaks. For example, Middle Paleolithic burial rites (Binford, 1968) have a far wider continuous distribution than the area which would be occupied by a single closed mating network. In addition, stylistic elements that may be taken to symbolize boundary processes between ethnic groups and social group affiliation are altogether rare up to the middle of the last glaciation. These considerations indicate that Band Society—and the closed mating system as one of its operational expressions— may not even extend back to early *Homo sapiens*.

The previous line of argument can be reversed to see what happens if, indeed, the mating network is closed. Assume again an ideal hexagonal pattern (for simplicity's sake only, since any other pattern would only amplify the trends illustrated here). Table 4 shows the relationships among the local groups that participate in the mating network if we use a population density of 0·01 persons/km² as our example.

The inequalities in terms of access to the participants of the mating pool are glaring. The central group has a clear locational advantage over the others who in turn are mutually differentiated from one another. The egalitarian society has become internally differentiated, if only in terms of the accessibility of its component local groups. If not counteracted by social mechanisms, the band society contains the seeds of central placism within its boundaries. For it would save the people at the margins considerable energy

Table 4   **Mean distance from a given group to all other groups in the mating network (at 0·01 persons/km²)**

Group number in Figure 1	Location within network	Mean distance	Percentage of line 1
1	Center	84 km	—
2 to 7	Surrounding center	97 km	115%
8, 10, 12, 14, 16, 18	Inner periphery	120 km	142%
9, 11, 13, 15, 17, 19	Outer periphery	131 km	155%

to move toward the center: in this way they could increase their accessibility to potential mates, they could decrease their own efforts to obtain mates, and they could lower their social effort in having to maintain the boundaries with neighboring societies. Similar rewards could be achieved if they themselves could usurp the central position in a mating network, by attracting mates from the marginal local groups of the adjoining society, thus forming their own mating network.

To counteract these disruptive tendencies, several social mechanisms are available to the society in question: ritual can be made more society-specific to increase social solidarity within the mating network and make desertion to another mating network more difficult; the number of occasions can be increased during which several local bands get together for ritual and other reasons, thus reducing the differential in communication efficiency between the participating groups; territorial symbolism and ritual can be intensified to increase the affiliation of local groups with the area they habitually exploit; stable patterns of intra-societal mate exchange can be encouraged (such as the Australian section systems) to make an individual's mate choice more predictable; and, since marginal local groups are closer to resources exotic to the area, they can improve their locational lot by intensifying inter-societal exchange.

Any one of these processes has test implications for the archaeological record. Unfortunately, however, they cannot be measured with the Indices of Grattoirs, Burins, or Composite Tools, nor, at present, through any other gross formal characteristic of lithic assemblages. Rather, they find their most direct expression in items that are archaeologically rare: portable art, burial rites, cave painting, dress, and items which measure the intensity of inter- and intra-societal exchange. Not only do these items increase considerably in elaboration and in number after the early Upper Paleolithic, but they also increase considerably in areal specificity. This is exemplified, for example, by Pavlovian portable art in Moravia (Klíma, 1963), Hungarian fossil-shell-for-ornament gathering stations (Gábori, 1969), French and Cantabrian cave paintings, and German Magdalenian ritual sites (Bosinski, 1969).

Given the disadvantages of mating system closure compared to open mating systems, such as increased social cost for ritual and communication and decreased reproductive success, and assuming that the population density threshold had been passed repeatedly before, one might ask why band societies should have developed at this particular time in human evolution. While this question is somewhat outside the scope of this paper, one is tempted to suggest that it was at this time that work groups, requiring more personnel than a single local group could provide, had achieved a sufficient pay-off to have become a predictable part of the seasonal round of activities. Further, that additional pay-off could be gained by minimizing the turn-over in this personnel. Such pay-offs may well have derived from large scale game drives that effectively exploited the windfall of the spring and fall migrations of large herbivores. Structural poses of this size may have been instrumental to the subsistence and persistence of later Upper Paleolithic populations in tundra environments. It is in this type of ecosystem in particular, that we should look for the origins of reasonably closed mating networks.

4. Irregularly Shaped Mating Networks

In the previous discussion we have assumed that the local groups are arranged in an infinite pattern of packed hexagons. This assured that the resulting mating networks

Figure 3. Irregularly arranged mating networks. The lower group numbers indicate the more centrally located local groups.

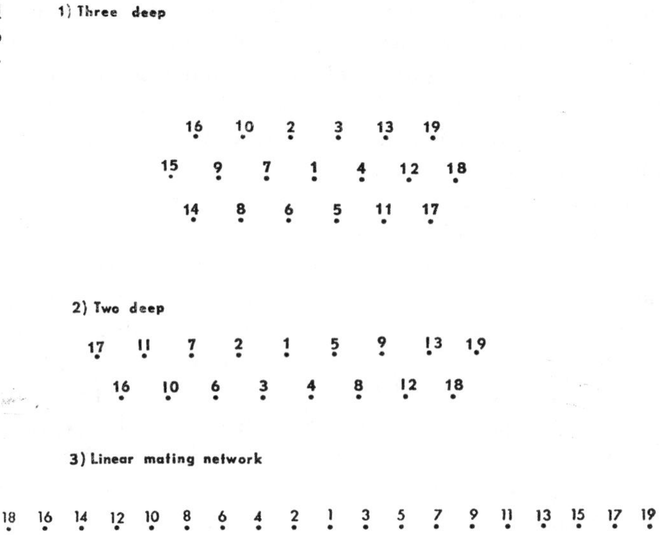

1) Three deep

```
      16   10   2    3   13   19

   15    9    7    1    4   12   18

      14   8    6    5   11   17
```

2) Two deep

```
   17   11   7    2    1    5    9   13   19

      16   10   6    3    4    8   12   18
```

3) Linear mating network

```
18  16  14  12  10  8  6  4  2  1  3  5  7  9  11  13  15  17  19
```

themselves were of ideal hexagonal shape. In Table 5 this condition is relaxed. The mating network is allowed to become more and more linear, while the local groups maintain their hexagonal areas (see also Figure 3). Table 5 contrasts the mean distance from the central local group, and from the marginally located groups, to all other local groups in the mating network.

Table 5 may explain why linear environments such as seacoasts were not exploited by specialists until quite late in the course of human evolution, while specialized exploitation of various sets of land resources seems to have a longer history. Not only does full-time specialization on a linear environment require extreme population densities to begin with, but it also creates such a strong locational dichotomy between the more centrally located and the more marginally placed groups that it may well overburden the social mechanisms available to egalitarian band societies.

This becomes even more apparent when the nearest neighbor distances in the mating network are compared with the maximal distances between local groups. In the linear case, the extreme distance is 18 times larger than the minimal distance. In an optimal,

Table 5   **The effect of mating network linearization (population density 0·01 persons/km²)**

Arrangement	Mean distance from the most centrally located group to the other groups in the mating network	Mean distance from the most marginally located group to the other local groups
(1) Ideal hexagonal packing	84 km	131 km
(2) 3 deep, see Figure 3	100 km	176 km
(3) 2 deep, see Figure 3	140 km	258 km
(4) Linear arrangement, see Figure 3	268 km	510 km

hexagonally packed arrangement the extreme is less than 7 times the minimum distance. Further, in the linear case, only 10 % of all inter-group distances are nearest neighbor distances while in the hexagonally packed case 24 % are nearest neighbor distances. Thus, a full-time specialization on marine resources (or any other lineally spaced resources) becomes possible only when the population density is sufficient so that distances between settlements can be minimized. Even with sufficient population density, the contrasts in locational efficiency are so strong that it is doubtful whether a society could long remain egalitarian if its populations are lineally arranged.

The same factors are bound to affect the locational behaviors of hunter-gatherers in other respects. Besides providing food, drink, and shelter, a society has to be able to provide its members with a reasonable chance to obtain mates. If there are areas which would discriminate against their occupants by their marginal location to a mating network, they will be occupied only if all other possibilities are exhausted. Such *a priori* marginal locations include coastal islands, peninsulas, oases, mountain valleys, and tail ends of watersheds. It is probable that many of these areas were not exploited during much of the Pleistocene, even though each by itself may have been able to support a local group in relative luxury. The resulting underexploitation of productive areas may be one of the many reasons why the population density of most egalitarian societies tends to stay far below regional carrying capacities (see for example Sahlins, 1972).

5. Conclusions

The demographic processes which link the settlements of a given society and the socio-cultural mechanisms which integrate adjacent settlement populations have to be taken into account if the behavior of hunter-gatherers at a given prehistoric settlement is to be fully explicated. The natural environment in which a given Paleolithic settlement is located and the articulation of its prehistoric occupants with each other and with their habitat can account only for a part of the settlement's archaeological form and structure. At least as important are variables which cannot be inferred from a settlement's archaeological and paleoenvironmental remains because they relate to its articulation with a supra-site entity–the site's social surroundings.

In this paper I have suggested that the mating network may be a suitable device for dealing with questions of the social environment during the Paleolithic, and for integrating Paleolithic research more fully into the related social and behavioral sciences. It allows us to generate, refine, and evaluate hypotheses about cultural processes for which we had previously few, if any, test implications.

References

Bicchieri, M. G. (Ed.) (1972). *Hunters and Gatherers Today*. New York: Holt, Rinehart, and Winston.
Binford, S. R.(1968). A structural comparison of disposal of the dead in the Mousterian and Upper Paleolithic. *Southwestern Journal of Anthropology* **24**, 139–154.
Birdsell, J. B. (1953). Some environmental and cultural factors influencing the structure of Australian aboriginal populations. *American Naturalist* **87**, 171–207.
Birdsell, J. B. (1957). Some population problems involving Pleistocene man. In *Population Studies: Animal Ecology and Demography*, (Katherine B. Warren, Ed.), pp. 47–70. Cold Spring Harbor Symposia on Quantitative Biology 22.
Birdsell, J. B. (1958). On population structure in generalized hunting and collecting populations. *Evolution* **12**, 189–205.
Birdsell, J. B. (1968). Some predictions for the Pleistocene based on equilibrium systems among recent hunter-gatherers. In *Man the Hunter*, (R. B. Lee and I. DeVore, Eds.) pp. 229–240, 246. Chicago: Aldine.

Bordes, F. H. (1955). Le Paléolithique inférieur et moyen de Jabrud (Syrie) et la question du pré-Aurignacien. *L'Anthropologie* **59,** 486–507.

Bosinski, G. (1969). Der Magdalénien-Fundplatz Feldkirchen-Gönnersdorf, Kr. Neuwied. Vorbericht über die Ausgrabungen 1968. *Germania* **47,** 1–38.

Damas, D. (Ed.) (1969). Contributions to anthropology: band societies. *National Museums of Canada Bulletin* 228. Ottawa.

David, N. (1973). On upper paleolithic society, ecology, and technological change: the Noaillian case. In *The Explanation of Culture Change: Models in Prehistory* (Colin Renfrew, Ed.), pp. 276–303. London, The Old Piano Factory: Duckworth.

Gábori, M. (1969). Paläolithische Schnecken-Depots von Szob. *Acta Archaeologica* Budapest) **21,** 3–11.

Klíma, B. (1957). Übersicht über die jüngsten paläolithischen Forschungen in Mähren. *Quartär* **9,** 85–130.

Klíma, B. (1963). *Dolní Věstonice*. Praha: Akademie Vied.

Klein, R. G. (1965). The Middle Paleolithic of the Crimea. *Arctic Anthropology* **3,** 34–68.

Kroeber, A. L. (1939). *Cultural and natural areas of native North America*. University of California Publications in American Archaeology and Ethnology 38.

Lee, R. B. & DeVore, I. (Eds) (1968). *Man the Hunter*. Chicago: Aldine.

Levin, M. G. & Potapov, L. P. (Eds) (1964). *The Peoples of Siberia*. Chicago: University of Chicago Press.

Murdock, G. P. (1967). *Ethnographic Atlas*. Pittsburgh: University of Pittsburgh Press.

Sahlins, M. (1972). *Stone Age Economics*. Chicago: Aldine.

Sonneville–Bordes, D. de (1960). *Le Paléolithique Supéreur en Périgord*. Bordeaux: Delmas.

Steward, J. H. (1969). Postscript to bands: on taxonomy, processes, and causes. In *Contributions to Anthropology: Band Societies*, (D. Damas, Ed.), pp. 288–295. National Museums of Canada Bulletin 228.

Vanstone, J. W. (1974). *Athapaskan Adaptations*. Chicago: Aldine.

Williams, B. J. (1974). *A model of Band Society*. Memoir of the Society for American Archaeology 29.

Wilmsen, E. N. (1973). Interaction, spacing behavior, and the organization of hunting bands. *Journal of Anthropological Research* **29,** 1–31.

Wobst, H. M. (1974). Boundary conditions for Paleolithic social systems: a simulation approach. *American Antiquity* **39,** 147–178.

Wobst, H. M. (1975) The demography of finite populations and the origins of the incest taboo. *Memoirs of the Society for American Archaeology* **30,** 75–81.

Yengoyan, A. A. (1968). Demographic and ecological influences on aboriginal Australian marriage sections. In *Man the Hunter* (R. B. Lee & I. DeVore, Eds.), pp. 185–199. Chicago: Aldine.

Kenneth M. Weiss

Center for Demographic and
Population Genetics,
University of Texas, Houston, U.S.A.

Peter E. Smouse

Department of Human Genetics,
University of Michigan,
Ann Arbor, U.S.A.

The Demographic Stability of Small Human Populations

1. Introduction

To an anthropologist, questions of historical demography are more than inquiries into particular temporal events; they are investigations into basic human biology and the evolution of human culture. It is important that we be able not only to describe the births and deaths of a specific set of observed individuals, but that we describe the rates of birth and death which prevail in the population over a long time period.

We have two basic kinds of data. There are aged skeletal series from large burial sites, and there are censuses from living primitive populations. The former give us direct information from past populations, and the latter give us information from living populations generally assumed to be representative of cultures during the long period of human evolution. Hence, both sources are used to reconstruct human demographic evolution.

Most populations of these types are small ones which are not literate and do not keep records sufficient for demographic analysis. We generally have but a single census (or aged skeletal series) and only minor scraps of other information. There is almost never any actual data on age-specific rates of mortality, yet these rates are the fundamental parameters of demography and must be known.

With standard theoretical approaches, it has been shown that the age distribution of small groups is unstable from year to year, and may be unreliable as a source from which to determine age-specific death rates (e.g., Moore, Swedlund & Armelagos, 1975; Angel, 1969). It is also known that populations are so subject to extinction, due to statistical fluctuations in births and deaths, that they are too transitory and unstable for useful study (this is based on statistical theory, which can be found in Bartlett, 1960; Pielou, 1969; Keyfitz, 1968). If this is true, then we must avoid the use of typical anthropological data, and are to a great extent prevented from gaining a reasonable knowledge of past demographic patterns.

The mathematical models on which these assertions are based use fixed age-specific birth and death rates. Yet there is a wealth of biological and anthropological information to show that these vital processes of a population vary according to population size or density in a negative-feedback way. A population which becomes crowded suffers higher mortality and lowered fertility, and one which is uncrowded enjoys higher fertility and lower mortality. These facts must be incorporated into a realistic demographic model.

In this paper we use a density-dependent demographic model to answer two questions: How much extinction pressure exists for small populations over moderate time periods? How representative of the underlying demographic patterns is a census from such a population? For populations which survive to be observed, we shall show that stochastic fluctuations in the vital rates generally do not disturb the census greatly from that produced by a comparable deterministic population.

As anthropology usually relies on a census rather than direct observation of the vital rates, we will be examining the relationship between stochastic fluctuations in the vital rates and their reflection in the census. A census close to its underlying deterministic form is one from which vital rates that are close to their underlying average values may be obtained.

2. Methods

We have used a stochastic (Monte Carlo) simulation of a density-dependent demographic process which is a modification of the standard fixed-rate projection derived first by Lewis (1942) and Leslie (1945, 1948). In the standard model, the age-specific birth and death rates are all constant over time; we have made them dependent on the size and composition of the population at any particular time; details of the method are given in the Appendix.

If the census at time t is divided into m age classes, we represent the number of individuals in age class i by $n(i, t)$, and treat the entire census as an m-element vector $N(t)$. We use the notation t for time, but really we are speaking of the number of iteration steps from some beginning population $N(0)$, each iteration representing the length of time included in each age class.

An individual at age i has a probability $P(i)$ of surviving to the next age class and a probability $F(i)$ of producing an offspring of the same sex. If these vital rates are fixed, then it has long been known that, no matter what the starting population, the population will approach a fixed age distribution (proportions in the m age classes) and a size which grows at a fixed rate, λ, determined by the set of vital rates $P(i)$ and $F(i)$. Although mathematically convenient, such a model allows fractions of individuals to survive or to be born and hence is somewhat approximate.

It is known (e.g. Keyfitz, 1968) that if λ is small, that is, if the population's intrinsic growth rate is close to zero, then most small populations will eventually become extinct, due solely to the statistical aspects of birth and death. At some time enough individuals will die, or will not reproduce, merely due to chance, that the population will diminish and disappear. The rate at which this occurs depends on the value of λ. An example will be given below.

Real vital rates are not constant. The wealth of studies on animal behavior which are now available show that territoriality, aggression, sexual selection, crowding and its nutritional and hormonal concomitants, and perhaps most of social behavior directly affect the vital rates of the population. These behavioral processes generally operate to keep the population close to some equilibrium composition. Primitive populations are no exception to this pattern, and while there are exceptional circumstances, it is more realistic to model them with negative-feedback in their vital rates than it is to use the standard fixed-rate model.

By assuming that the effect of other individuals in the population on the survival or fertility of a given individual is proportional to the frequency with which encounters between them occur (other assumptions will lead to similar results), we can specify a form for the age-specific vital rates which has the desired negative-feedback properties. The time dependent, age-specific vital rates are expressed as follows:

$$P(i, t) = P_i e^{-\Sigma b_{ij} n_j},$$

$$F(i, t) = F_i e^{-\Sigma a_{ij} n_j} \tag{1}$$

where b_{ij} and a_{ij} are the damping effects of encounters of individuals in age class i with those in age class j, and where P_i and F_i are the density-independent, or maximal, vital rates for age class i. The exponential term is a damping factor with a value between 0 and 1, and hence expresses the fraction of the maximal vital rate which applies to a population with composition $N(t)$. The damping coefficients a_{ij} and b_{ij} represent the pattern by which crowding is reflected on the vital rates, and for various types of feed-back we merely must specify the relative values of these coefficients. To produce a population with any specific total size, one merely needs to adjust all of the coefficients by an easily-computed constant factor.

These density-dependent vital rates will produce a deterministic equilibrium in which growth eventually comes to zero. The model contains too many parameters to be of empirical use, but it is easy to simplify things by assuming simple patterns in the damping coefficients, by which realistic ecologically-stable populations may be modeled.

The stochastic element in birth and death processes must now be included to make the model more realistic. We do this by Monte Carlo methods. At any time t, we know the population composition $N(t)$, and using equations (1), we compute $P(i, t)$ and $F(i, t)$. Then for each individual in the population, we determine the chance of repro-ducing by drawing a random number between 0 and 1. If less than $F(i, t)$, we place an infant in the first age class at the next time $(n(0, t + 1))$. By drawing another random number we determine from $P(i, t)$ if the same individual survives to be a member of age class $i + 1$ at time $t + 1$. We do this for all individuals alive at time t, and the entire process is carried out for 100 iterations (until $t = 100$). We have used 5 age classes for illustrative purposes, but any number can be used; if human fertility ceases at age 50, this simulation can be visualized as covering 1000 years.

The properties of this model are such that the results of any single run for a set of starting conditions $(N(0), P(i, 0), F(i, 0))$ depend on the specific random numbers drawn. To understand the general properties of the system the same starting conditions must be replicated several times with different random numbers. We tried many cases with 100 replicates and found that the essential demographic properties are revealed by as few as 25 replicates. Since the computing costs are considerable, the results which are given below are based on 25 replicates.

We are interested in the representativeness of a single census. To look at this, we must compare the results of our simulation with the population which would be produced deterministically, that is, with the population representing the underlying average vital rates, free of the statistical fluctuations whose magnitude we are investigating. For all of the demographic patterns to be examined, we have iterated the deterministic model 1000 times, so that we know the equilibrium population $N(*)$ (see Appendix) to many decimal places of accuracy.

We have devised two indices to gauge the degree to which a population $N(t)$ is a reflection of the equilibrium $N(*)$. We need these to determine how well a small population, experiencing statistical fluctuations, represents its underlying equilibrium structure. The first measure, the Index of Numerical Convergence, P, is merely the population size at equilibrium, minus that at time t, divided by the equilibrium size. It is simply the fractional deviation of the actual population from the equilibrium.

The second measure, the Index of Angular Convergence, ϕ, is the angle between the population vector (we treat $N(t)$ as an m-dimensional vector) at time t and that at equilibrium. This is computed from the standard formula for the cosine of the angle between two m-dimensional vectors (e.g. see Schwartz et al., 1960). An angle of 20 degrees or less is, we feel, a close similarity between two age distributions for the small populations in which anthropologists are interested.

We need to know not only the deviation from equilibrium at any time (and the average of these deviations over all replications of the stochastic model), but also some measure of the variability of these deviations. Since we know the population toward which the model tends, we have computed the variance of these error measures about the equilibrium. In the case of the angular measure, we compute only positive values. Since the population oscillates around the equilibrium $N(*)$ in m-space, negative values would have little meaning. Since all values of ϕ are positive (or absolute values), the mean value of ϕ is not expected to be zero. These two indices tell us the degree of representativeness of a census in terms of population size and age composition, which relates to the usefulness of censuses from living populations. Many of us are interested in working with skeletal series since these are our only source of direct knowledge of man's demographic past. We cannot expect to estimate population size directly from the total number of such skeletons, since the length of time of deposition is critical (other methods of inference may be used to deal with this under some circumstances; see Ubelaker, 1974), but we can use the age distribution to determine whether a skeletal series is a fair representation of the demographic processes which produced it. This is done by determining a stationary age distribution from the skeletons (see Weiss, 1973) and by computing of a Graves Index G, which is merely the angle between the actual and the expected age distribution vectors (a measure comparable to ϕ for cemetery populations). This gauges the degree of reliability with which survivorship rates and a life table can be reconstructed from the data. The "actual" age distribution results from our stochastic simulation and the expected distribution is $N(*)$. The graves index indicates the reliability *of the complete cemetery* at any time t, relative to the start of deposition. Errors caused by incomplete sampling must be considered as a separate question which generally must be answered separately for each case. Complete cemeteries may occasionally be available (e.g. Ubelaker, 1974).

3. Results

The demographic properties of a population with density-dependent vital rates are functions of the value of λ, the growth rate intrinsic to the *undamped* vital rates, and of the damping coefficients (a_{ij} and b_{ij}). The damping coefficients determine the magnitude of the feedback effects at any particular population size. The growth rate λ determines how fast the population would grow if the damping term were equal to 1 (zero damping coefficients), and hence the population were determined only by the maximal vital rates P_i and F_i. The undamped growth rate determines what can be thought of as the resiliency of the population. In a population where λ is close to 1, there is very little potential growth, even in an ideal, undamped environment. If the population becomes overcrowded, the damping coefficients can cause it to rapidly return to its equilibrium composition, but if it becomes rarefied for any reason, its maximum growth rate, by which it returns toward equilibrium, is small. Thus, a stochastic model of such a population should show the maximum degree to which extinction pressure exists. It is easy to show that for a population with a low undamped growth potential, the equilibrium age distribution is very close to that of a fixed-rate model, no matter what the relative values of the damping coefficients. On the other hand, a population with large λ has more marked response to perturbation from equilibrium and the particular pattern of the damping coefficients can have a profound effect on the equilibrium age distribution.

We model three types of population here, to illustrate the range of possibilities. Based on the value of undamped growth, λ, they are populations with high growth potential ($\lambda = 1 \cdot 95$), medium growth potential ($\lambda = 1 \cdot 51$), and low growth potential ($\lambda = 1 \cdot 002$). We have simplified things by setting all undamped vital rates (P_i and F_i) equal, but this does not affect the gist of our results.

To test the effect of equilibrium population size on stochastic stability of the census, we simulate populations with $N(*) = 50$ and 100 individuals. The degree of stability of any stochastic process will increase with larger size, so if these populations produce reliable censuses, so will larger ones.

We use three types of density feedback, to isolate effects which can occur. In the first, only fertility rates respond to crowding, with survival rates unaffected ($b_{ij} = 0$, $a_{ij} = c$). We use the same value for all of the fertility damping coefficients to simplify our results, but we can show that this causes no loss of generality of important information. This pattern may be thought of as a damping only on infant survival rates. It is similar to the feedback now found in industrial nations, which rely largely on fertility control. The second type of feedback is that in which fertility is not damped, but all survival rates are damped; here again, we use a constant damping coefficient ($a_{ij} = 0$, $b_{ij} = c$); crowding affects the survival rate of every segment in the population. The third damping regime we study is one in which only post-infant survivals are damped ($a_{ij} = b_{0j} = 0$; $b_{ij} = c$, $i \neq 0$). Damping of infant survival is a common and effective means of population regulation, but is covered by the first (fertility damping) case. This third pattern tests the effectiveness of damping on the rest of the population instead.

In all, we test 9 populations, using combinations of the types just enumerated; Table 1 gives the details of these models. In addition to these density-dependent cases, we have simulated case number 1b, with no density dependent damping. This is a fixed-rate model for a population of size 50 with virtually zero growth. Such a population should be as sensitive to demographic fluctuation as any we are testing with the density model, and further, since $\lambda \approx 1$, the expected age distribution is like that of cases 3, 6, and 9, and provides a standard of reference. Table 2 gives the equilibrium age distributions of all 9 cases.

The undamped case is shown on the last lines of Table 6. Twenty-five replicates of 100 iterations were run (unless extinction occurred before $t = 100$). The starting population, $N(0)$, was the equilibrium population, rounded to the nearest whole individuals in each class. The means of the three indices of convergence and their variance are given for 3 steps in the simulations to show the progress of the populations over time. The variance is computed for the first 25 populations which survived to the time given.

Table 1   **Cases run**

Case no.	$N(*)$	F_i, P_i all i	Damping type	Damping coefficients		
				a_{ij} all i, j	b_{0j} all j	b_{ij} $i \geq 1$; all j
1	50	0·99	all fertility	0·0316	0	0
2	50	0·75	all fertility	0·01655	0	0
3	50	0·51	all fertility	0·0001	0	0
4	50	0·99	all survivorship	0	0·01332	0·01332
5	50	0·75	all survivorship	0	0·0077654	0·0077654
6	50	0·51	all survivorship	0	0·0000546	0·0000546
7	50	0·99	post-infant survivorship	0	0	0·0919
8	50	0·75	post-infant survivorship	0	0	0·02192
9	50	0·51	post-infant survivorship	0	0	0·000118
1a	100	0·99	all fertility	0·0158	0	0
2a	100	0·75	all fertility	0·002875	0	0
3a	100	0·51	all fertility	$0·4895 \times 10^{-4}$	0	0
4a	100	0·99	all survivorship	0	0·00666	0·00666
5a	100	0·75	all survivorship	0	0·00388	0·00388
6a	100	0·51	all survivorship	0	$0·2627 \times 10^{-4}$	$0·2627 \times 10^{-4}$
7a	100	0·99	post-infant survivorship	0	0	0·04595
8a	100	0·75	post-infant survivorship	0	0	0·01096
9a	100	0·51	post-infant survivorship	0	0	$0·56945 \times 10^{-4}$
1b	50	0·51	no damping	0	0	0

$N(*)$ = equilibrium population size. Cases for $0·99 = F_{ij}P_i$ are *high growth* type ($\lambda = 1·95$), $0·75$ is *medium growth* ($\lambda = 1·51$), and $0·51$ is *low growth* potential ($\lambda = 1·002$). Case 1b has $\lambda = 1$.

a_{ij} are damping coefficients for fertility, b_{0j} are damping coefficients for infant survival, b_{ij} ($i \geq 1$) are post-infant survival damping coefficients.

It is clear that the threat of extinction, and demographic instability, are significant for a population of 50 with approximately zero growth. Seven of 25 populations reached extinction before 100 iterations. The population size is within 10 percent of its equilibrium value for about 30 iterations, although with high variability; by the end of 100 iterations, however, we can only expect numeric convergence to 80 percent, and a variation so large that any single population can have virtually any size deviation. We cannot have confidence in an observed census size. The age distribution is generally within 10° to 12° of the equilibrium, but its variance is considerable (see below). The graves

Table 2   **Equilibrium age distributions* of cases run**

Case no.	Age class				
	1	2	3	4	5
1	0·204	0·202	0·200	0·198	0·196
2	0·328	0·246	0·184	0·138	0·104
3	0·508	0·258	0·132	0·067	0·034
4	0·509	0·259	0·132	0·067	0·034
5	0·509	0·259	0·132	0·067	0·034
6	0·509	0·259	0·132	0·067	0·034
7	0·990	0·010	0·0001	0·000001	0·00000001
8	0·750	0·188	0·047	0·012	0·003
9	0·510	0·259	0·131	0·066	0·034

* This is independent of equilibrium population size; values rounded to nearest 0·1%.

index shows that the net results of stochastic fluctuations have very little effect on the age distribution which can be reconstructed from a complete burial series; compensating fluctuations are sufficient to guarantee virtually perfect accuracy. This shows that without density damping, one has cause for suspicion of a single census taken from a small anthropological population. Smaller populations than 50 will have considerably more problems, unless several tribal subpopulations can be aggregated.

The results for the fertility damping cases are listed in Table 3. The numeric indices become more variable as the growth rate (λ) decreases. For $\lambda = 1 \cdot 002$, the population size is highly variable among replicates. In all cases, the variance is less for $N(*) = 100$ than for $N(*) = 50$, as expected. The angular index ϕ presents the opposite tendency. As λ decreases, so does the average value of ϕ, as well as its variance. This is due to the fact that the equilibrium age distribution becomes progressively steeper as λ is decreased. This narrows the range of achievable age-distributions, and reduced $\phi(t)$. The graves index G follows the same pattern as the numeric index P. The reason for this is not entirely clear.

The results for general survival damping are shown in Table 4. The numeric index P is more variable for small λ, as before. Neither the angular index ϕ nor the graves index G is responsive to growth rate, since the equilibrium age distribution is the same in all cases. As before, the variance of all measures decreases as $N(*)$ increases from 50 to 100.

The results for post-infant survival damping are shown in Table 5. Again, the numeric index P varies more for low growth than for high growth populations. This time, both the angular index ϕ and the graves index G become more variable as λ is decreased, since the age distribution becomes progressively flatter as λ is decreased. Again, large populations are less variable than small ones, as precited.

In general, low growth-low damping populations are most variable. One may compare such cases with the zero growth (no damping) case, as is shown in Table 6. As can be seen, cases 3, 6, 9 and 1b are essentially interchangeable, as far as the indices are concerned. The zero growth case (1b) experiences more frequent extinctions, but for those populations surviving, there is little to choose among them, as predicted.

The important point is that density damping and high growth potential are counteracting pressures which maintain the population close to the equilibrium structure. For populations of size 100, this stability is quite pronounced, and only low growth cases are quite unstable. For populations of larger size, stability should be considerable.

Because we have only computed age distribution convergence in terms of positive angles, it being rather academic whether the angle between two m-dimensional vectors is positive or negative, it is somewhat difficult to appraise the variance of angular convergence. This is in most cases about equal to the square of the mean of $\bar{\phi}$. Since the populations average $\bar{\phi}$ degrees out of equilibrium and also have mean square deviations of $\bar{\phi}^2$, this implies that most angular deviations are very close to the mean error in magnitude. Although the direction of the angle would actually change as the population oscillates about its equilibrium (i.e. if we computed the sign of the angle, keeping $N(*)$ as the reference vector), the magnitude of the error changes little. The population's age distribution may be thought of as moving in a tightly-constrained cone about the equilibrium vector, generally being $\bar{\phi}$ degrees out of equilibrium. Most populations will be very close to that degree of error. This is as close as we can come to specifying confidence limits for the angular convergence measures.

6

Table 3   Simulation results, fertility damping

Case no.	N(*)	(λ)		Numeric index P			Angular index ϕ			Graves index G	
				20	50	100	20	50	100	20	50	100
1	50	(1·95)	mean	−0·008	0·0168	−0·0208	15·6	14·5	12·4	0·3	0·2	0·1
			variance	0·0161	0·0094	0·0094	264	216	165	0·1	0·05	0·02
1a	100	(1·95)	mean	0·0028	0·0400	0·0020	10·4	10·4	10·5	0·2	0·2	0·1
			variance	0·0043	0·0050	0·0048	117	126	123	0·08	0·03	0·01
2	50	(1·51)	mean	−0·0184	−0·0056	0·0096	11·2	13·8	11·8	1·4	0·9	0·8
			variance	0·0247	0·0232	0·0208	136	208	160	2·2	0·9	0·7
2a	100	(1·51)	mean	−0·0064	−0·0124	0·0084	8·9	8·9	7·5	0·8	0·6	0·5
			variance	0·0074	0·0076	0·0142	92	91	61	0·8	0·4	0·3
3**	50	(1·002)	mean	0·1032	0·1056	−0·0616	7·0	8·5	10·7	1·3	0·8	0·6
			variance	0·1667	0·3300	0·4346	61	95	158	1·9	0·7	0·5
3a	100	(1·002)	mean	−0·0352	−0·0324	−0·0492	5·2	6·7	7·1	0·9	0·7	0·4
			variance	0·1295	0·2251	0·4010	31	47	89	1·2	0·6	0·2

** Lost 4 replicates at iterates 51, 58, 84, 8.

Table 4

Simulation results, survival damping

Case no.	N(*)	(λ)		Numeric Index P			Angular index ϕ			Graves index G	
				20	50	100	20	50	100	20	50	100
4	50	(1·95)										
			mean	0·0144	−0·0072	0·0000	8·2	8·3	7·7	1·2	0·8	0·6
			variance	0·0072	0·0084	0·0140	82	80	68	1·6	0·7	0·4
4a	100	(1·95)										
			mean	−0·0016	−0·0124	−0·0448	5·6	5·8	6·0	0·9	0·5	0·4
			variance	0·0045	0·0059	0·0073	35	36	45	0·9	0·3	0·2
5	50	(1·51)										
			mean	0·0136	−0·0160	−0·0096	8·4	8·9	8·5	1·3	0·8	0·5
			variance	0·0087	0·0168	0·0153	81	87	84	2·0	0·7	0·3
5a	100	(1·51)										
			mean	−0·0232	0·0168	−0·0088	5·6	5·0	5·5	0·9	0·5	0·4
			variance	0·0075	0·0092	0·0058	36	28	35	1·1	0·3	0·2
6**	50	(1·002)										
			mean	0·0288	0·1488	0·2080	7·8	9·0	10·9	1·2	0·8	0·6
			variance	0·1540	0·4472	0·8296	75	101	182	1·5	0·6	0·4
6a†	100	(1·002)										
			mean	0·0536	0·0908	−0·1100	5·5	5·2	6·2	0·9	0·6	0·4
			variance	0·1145	0·1404	0·2357	35	31	46	1·2	0·4	0·2

** Lost 4 replicates at iterates 80, 74, 53.

† Lost 1 replicate at iterate 84.

Table 5 Simulation results, post-infant survival damping

Case no.	N(*)	(λ)		Numeric index P			Angular index φ			Graves index G	
			20	50	100	20	50	100	20	50	100
7	50	(1·95)									
		mean	−0·0032	0·0168	0·0144	0·7	0·8	0·7	0·1	0·1	0·1
		variance	0·0032	0·0021	0·0040	0·7	0·8	0·7	0·03	0·02	0·01
7a	100	(1·95)									
		mean	−0·0024	0·0204	−0·0088	0·4	0·4	0·5	0·1	0·1	0·1
		variance	0·0029	0·0032	0·0019	0·3	0·4	0·4	0·01	0·004	0·003
8	50	(1·51)									
		mean	−0·0248	0·0192	0·0328	4·8	4·3	4·2	0·9	0·5	0·4
		variance	0·0121	0·0198	0·0241	29	23	27	1·0	0·4	0·2
8a	100	(1·51)									
		mean	0·0036	−0·0108	−0·0152	3·1	3·3	3·1	0·6	0·3	0·3
		variance	0·0103	0·0053	0·0105	12	13	11	0·4	0·1	0·1
9**	50	(1·002)									
		mean	−0·0584	0·1864	−0·0744	8·4	7·7	10·7	1·4	0·8	0·6
		variance	0·0176	0·3420	0·3108	91	75	170	2·1	0·9	0·4
9a†	100	(1·002)									
		mean	−0·0051	−0·0139	−0·0871	5·8	5·8	7·9	0·9	0·6	0·4
		variance	0·0679	0·1303	0·2846	41	40	157	1·0	0·4	0·3

** Lost 1 replicate at iterate 48.
† Lost 1 replicate at iterate 93.

Table 6   **Simulation results, populations with little growth**

Case no.	N(*)	(λ)		Numeric index P			Angular index φ			Graves index G	
			20	50	100	20	50	100	20	50	100
3**	50	(1·002)									
		mean	0·1032	0·1056	−0·0616	7·0	8·5	10·7	1·3	0·8	0·6
		variance	0·1667	0·3300	0·4346	61	95	158	1·9	0·7	0·5
6†	100	(1·002)									
		mean	0·0288	0·1488	0·2080	7·8	9·0	10·9	1·2	0·8	0·6
		variance	0·1540	0·4472	0·8296	75	101	182	1·5	0·6	0·4
9‡	50	(1·002)									
		mean	−0·0584	0·1864	−0·0744	8·4	7·7	10·7	1·4	0·8	0·6
		variance	0·0176	0·3420	0·3108	91	75	170	2·1	0·9	0·4
1b§	100	(1·002)									
		mean	0·0496	0·2504	0·1864	8·8	9·0	11·9	1·3	0·7	0·6
		variance	0·2188	0·6677	1·1039	112	123	290	1·9	0·7	0·4

** Lost 4 replicates at iterates 51, 58, 84, 8.
† Lost 1 replicate at iterate 84.
‡ Lost 1 replicate at iterate 48.
§ Lost 7 replicates at iterates 86, 69, 78, 73, 59, 40, 74.

In general, feedback based on fertility damping is slower-acting than that based on mortality, since disequilibrium effects in production of new individuals can only be introduced by way of age class 1, whence they must "age" their way along the census vector. This is why, with zero-growth fertility rates at present, the United States must still grow for several decades to come. With mortality damping, the survivorship of those left alive can decrease to restore population faster toward equilibrium. Hence with fertility-damping feedback, reaction is slower and errors are somewhat larger. With post-infant survival damping, feedback is fast, since infants are produced in large numbers from undamped reproduction, per parent, and mortality can cull these parents at all age classes when the population is crowded, and can allow them to survive—and hence reproduce—better when population size is down. Real situations will have combinations of these density reactions, of course, and will generally converge very rapidly and maintain close equilibrium. The pure damping strategies we have used merely illustrate their different effects when applied in isolation.

4. Discussion

We have found that a population with low growth potential is an unreliable source for single-census-based demographic statistics, because stochastic aspects of vital processes cannot be overcome by density-dependence. Populations with greater growth potential are demographically reliable to levels of accuracy to which anthropologists can aspire. Extinction is rare over a period of many generations, and the age distribution is not likely to deviate too far from its equilibrium form. Complete burial series are almost totally unaffected by stochastic processes. All of these results confirm the preliminary nonstochastic study by Weiss (1975) along these lines, where it was shown that even epidemics, wars, and so on, do not necessarily distort the age distribution for very long tim e periods.

These conclusions must be qualified to stress that (a) one must not attempt to reconstruct equilibrium vital rates from a census when there is evidence that systematic disruptions have recently occurred, (b) the basic demographic patterns must have prevailed for several decades prior to census, (c) the group must be in a viable state at the time of observation and of size at least 50 and preferably closer to 100 or more, (d) the census must be complete, and (e) one must be willing to accept the occasional severely distorted population, or out-lier, in the usual statistical sense.

It is obvious that recently disturbed populations should not be used to estimate general prevailing demographic rates, and that an incomplete census or a census for which many peoples' ages are doubtful must be dealt with carefully. We have shown that stochastic processes *by themselves* do not constitute a prohibitive disturbing force. This finding is somewhat corroborated by the general similarity of censuses from widespread anthropological populations (e.g. see Acsádi & Nemeskéri, 1970; Salzano, 1972; Weiss, 1973). This is true of some subpopulation census data as well: age distributions appear very similar to each other; this has been observed, for example, among Yanomama and in Micronesian data (personally examined by K.M.W.).

It seems well-established from our results that stochastic processes of life and death do not provide any substantial problem to the analysis of skeletal demographic data, if deposition has accumulated over a few generations. The overwhelmingly more important problems with such data involve the proper exhumation of juveniles, correct aging of skeletons, and the representativeness of the cemetery. Often, with care, these can be overcome (e.g. see Ubelaker, 1974).

Many different sets of age-specific birth and death rates can produce the same age distribution. However, if growth has been zero, or at least constant, for several decades, one can reconstruct death rates from a census. If we can further assume (or determine) a pattern of relative age-specific fertilities (Talwar, 1970; Weiss, 1973), then we can estimate the actual fertility rates as well, and can compute most demographic measures which are of interest to us.

Although we can reconstruct the details of the equilibrium population, we cannot infer the density-dependent process by which it is brought about. This is because we reconstruct only the values of $P(i, *)$ and $F(i, *)$, but the density factors are combined inseparably within these rates. Reasonable assumptions on the pattern of feedback might be made in some ethnological cases, however.

This model has instantaneous density feedback. Real populations will experience some lag time in response, although this must be limited, since if it were too great the feedback system would not be adaptive. Lag times are unlikely to affect the results we have found in any important way, but should increase the magnitude of the variance in all measures. Our experimental work with this model has been extensive, and we have had difficulty even contriving deviant cases. Our results depend only to the extent of fine detail on the particular type of density feedback used, which may affect the age distribution at equilibrium greatly, but has little effect on stability or stochastic resilience,

We cannot deal here with the question of the existence of biological equilibria in the first place. If the time period is long enough for largescale disturbances to be smoothed out, and short enough not be be affected by major ecological changes (such as climate, food sources, etc.), then it seems clear that a population will be constrained to a great extent in terms of size and age distribution. The similarity of anthropological populations in this regard is strong support for this statement. We have sought to estimate prevailing equilibrium rates. From the standpoint of many questions about human populations, it is the approximating of these general prevailing rates which is important. Their fine detail, and specific aspects of their fluctuations, are useful questions in their own right, but we are here interested in the average rates rather than in the variances. If anthropological data do not supply adequate information on average underlying equilibrium conditions, then surely we have no hope of analyzing the fluctuations about these averages. We have found that the data may be sufficiently reliable for the equilibrium vital rates to be inferred.

Appendix

We let the census at time t, grouped into m age classes of equal length, be represented by the vector $N(t)$ with elements $n(i, t)$, the census count for the ith age class. The probability that an individual in age class i at time t survives to age class $i + 1$ at time $t + 1$ is $P(i, t)$, and similarly, the chance that individual produces an offspring of the same sex is $F(i, t)$.

If we represent the transition of the population from $N(t)$ to $N(t + 1)$ in the standard matrix way (e.g. see Keyfitz, 1968), then with $M(t)$ the density-dependent transition matrix, we have

$$N(t + 1) = \mathbf{M}(t)N(t) \tag{A1}$$

or

$$N(t + 1) = \begin{bmatrix} P(0, t)F(1, t) & P(0, t)F(2, t) & \cdots & P(0, t)F(m, t) \\ P(1, t) & 0 & & 0 \\ & & \ddots & \\ 0 & P(2, t) & & \\ & & 0 & \ddots \\ 0 & & \ddots & \ddots \\ & 0 & P(m-1, t) & 0 \end{bmatrix} N(t). \tag{A2}$$

$P(i, t)$ and $F(i, t)$ are the functions of $N(t)$ given in equations (1) of the text. Since $\mathbf{M}(t)$ varies with $N(t)$, it is *not* generally true that $N(t + k) = M(t)^k N(0)$, as is fundamental to the approach to equilibrium of the *fixed-rate* model. In that model, the fixed matrix $\mathbf{M}$ has dominant eigen value λ, and eventually the population approaches an age-distribution equilibrium and a growth rate of λ. Hence, eventually $N(t) = \lambda^t N(0)$, taking as the zero point, a time when the age distribution has converged close to its equilibrium.

At any time t, our model has dominant eigen value $\lambda(t)$, which converges to a stationary value of $\lambda(*) = 1$. Using (*) to represent the fact that the system is no longer changing we can say that

$$N(*) = \mathbf{M}*N(*), \tag{A3}$$

and then the equilibrium age-specific vital rates, $P(i, *)$ and $F(i, *)$, are fixed. The details of this model, including a discussion of its stability, are given in Smouse & Weiss (1975). We have slightly modified the indices of convergences here since we know $N(*)$.

References

Acsádi, G. & Nemeskéri, J. (1970). *History of Human Life Span and Mortality*. Budapest: Hungarian Academic Society Publishing House.

Angel, J. (1969). The bases of paleodemography. *American Journal of Physical Anthropology* **30**, 427–438.

Bartlett, M. (1960). *Stochastic Population Models in Ecology and Epidemiology*. London: Methuen and Co., Ltd.

Hammel, E. A. & Hutchinson, D. (1973). Two tests of computer microsimulation: The effect of an incest tabu on population viability, and the effect of age differences between spouses on the skewing of consanguineal relationships between them. In (B. Dyke & J. W. MacCluer, Eds) *Computer Simulation in Human Population Studies*. New York: Academic Press.

Howell, N. (1973). The feasibility of demographic studies in "anthropological" populations. In (M. Crawford & P. Workman, Eds) *Methods and Theories of Anthropological Genetics*. Albuquerque: University of New Mexico Press.

Keyfitz, N. (1968). *Introduction to the Mathematics of Population*. Reading, Mass.: Addison-Wesley.

Leslie, P. H. (1945). On the use of matrices in certain population mathematics. *Biometrika* **33**, 183–212.

Leslie, P. H. (1948). Some further notes on the use of matrices in population mathematics. *Biometrika* **35**, 213–245.

Lewis, E. G. (1942). On the generation and growth of a population. *Sankhya* **6,** 93–96.

Moore, J. A., Swedlund, A. C. & Armelagos, G. J. (1975). The Use of Life Tables in Paleodemography. Washington, D.C.: Society for American Archeology, Memoir 30.

Morgan, K. (1973). Computer simulation of incest prohibition and clan proscription rules in closed, finite populations. In (B. Dyke & J. W. MacCluer, Eds) *Computer Simulation in Human Population Studies.* New York: Academic Press.

Neel, J. V. & Salzano, F. M. (1967). Further studies on the Xavante Indians. X. Some hypotheses-generalizations resulting from these studies. *American Journal of Human Genetics* **19,** 554–574.

Pielou, E. C. (1969). *An Introduction to Mathematical Ecology.* New York: John Wiley and Sons.

Salzano, F. M. (1972). Genetic aspects of the demography of American Indians and Eskimos. In (G. A. Harrison & J. A. Boyce, Eds) *The Structure of Human Populations.* Oxford: Oxford University Press.

Schwartz, M., Green, S. & Rutledge, W. A. (1960). *Vector Analysis.* New York: Harper and Brothers.

Smouse, P. E. & Weiss, K. M. (1975). Discrete demographic models with density-dependent vital rates. *Oceologia* **21,** 205–218.

Talwar, P. P. (1970). *Age Patterns of Fertility.* Chapel Hill: University of North Carolina Institute of Statistics, Mimeo Series 656.

Ubelaker, D. H. (1973). *Reconstruction of Demographic Profiles from Ossuary Skeletal Samples: A Case Study from the Tidewater Potomoc.* Washington, D.C.: Smithsonian Institute, Contributions to Anthropology 18.

Weiss, K. M. (1973). Demographic Models for Anthropology. Washington, D.C.: Society for American Archeology, Memoir 27.

Weiss, K. M. (1975). Demographic Disturbance and the Use of Life Tables in Anthropology. Washington, D.C.: Society for American Archeology, Memoir 30.

Alan Swedlund
Helena Temkin
Richard Meindl

Population Studies in the Connecticut Valley: Prospectus

Department of Anthropology,
University of Massachusetts,
Amherst, Massachusetts 01002, *U.S.A.*

1. Introduction

An emerging body of historical-demographic literature suggests that historical data are, indeed, useful for biological inference as well as for their more common application in sociological research. Although demographic data have clearly been useful in the analysis of population structure as defined by geneticists (e.g. Morton, 1973), we are now beginning to recognize the value of historical data in the illumination of *processes* which bring about observed structure (Harrison & Boyce, 1972; Workman *et al.*, in press). The application of demographic data to population genetic studies was shown relatively early (Fisher, 1930); it has been emphasized in the past (e.g. Sutter & Tran-Ngoc-Toan, 1957; Sutter, 1963; Cavalli-Sforza & Bodmer, 1971) and recently has been reiterated in a review of current problems in human genetics (Cavalli–Sforza, 1973).

The number of historic-demographic studies which focus on human biological problems is relatively small in comparison with those emphasizing social process, but the results have been encouraging. The majority of the published studies have been based on European populations. Studies done in Oxfordshire, England (e.g. Küchemann, Harrison & Boyce, 1967; Boyce, Küchemann & Harrison, 1967), Northumberland, England (Dobson & Roberts, 1971; Roberts & Rawling, 1974), the Parma Valley, Italy (e.g. Cavalli–Sforza, 1969), Switzerland (e.g. Hussels, 1969; Morton & Hussels, 1970) and the Aland Islands, Finland (Mielke *et al.*, in press) provide examples of the effective use of historical data. In addition to these studies in Europe a rather substantial literature exists on historical patterns in Japan (e.g. Yanase, 1962; Yasuda & Furusho, 1971; Yasuda & Kimura, 1973), but very little of this type of work has been done in the United States (e.g. Swedlund, 1972). There have been very noteworthy community studies done in the United States (e.g. Demos, 1970; Lockridge, 1966; Greven, 1970; Norton, 1971; Smith, 1972), but their emphasis has been primarily on socioeconomic factors without regard to microevolutionary considerations.

The purpose of this paper is to briefly describe one demographic project that is currently in progress involving data from the Connecticut River Valley in the northeastern United States. We shall present initial results on trends in population distribution, growth and composition for the early settlement period (1650–1850), and outline projected research. Our approach emphasizes both the social and the biological significance of demographic data from the region.

2. The Study Region

The Connecticut River Valley is located between the states of New Hampshire and Vermont to the north and in the states of Massachusetts and Connecticut as the river moves south. The specific area of research for this project is the section of the Valley located in Franklin and Hampshire Counties of western Massachusetts (see Figure 1). Demographic and geographical data are being collected on this region and a more intensive survey is being made of twelve communities located near the confluence of the Deerfield and Connecticut Rivers (see Figure 1). This project was begun in 1974, but earlier research (e.g. Swedlund, 1971, 1972) has been done on the specific community of Deerfield, Massachusetts, which is centrally located in the study area. To date, the emphasis has been on collecting and processing data from the early settlement period (1650–1850) but initial observations on the settlement geography of the area have also been reported (Swedlund, 1975).

Initial settlement of the region tended to occur by way of the Connecticut River. Settlers came from communities to the east and south but the River Valley represents the primary direction of in-migration to the area. Much of the River was navigable at this time but the Valley also afforded a pedestrian access. Overland routes to eastern Massachusetts were few and not well traveled and the areas to the north and west were unsettled "frontier" occupied by Indians and some English and French-Canadian trappers and explorers. Although further to the north there was a considerable Canadian population with which occasional contact (and warfare) was made, the western frontier (i.e. New York) was not frequented by settlers of this area until the early 1800s.

This area, with its attendant pattern of settlement into nucleated farm villages, would appear to represent a very useful case study for the analysis of demographic trends of biological and cultural significance. The isolation from outlying regions was relatively great prior to 1850, the land was well suited to agriculture and conducive to population growth, and records exist for the entire period of settlement. This situation is in some ways unique as opposed to the previously reported European studies. In contrast to the study of communities where settlement has occurred for a long period prior to the time records are available, this project provides for the analysis of communities from their very inception. We believe that the opportunity to observe a colonizing, growing population from its earliest beginnings is one of the project's most interesting and significant features.

3. Resources

The scope of this research project is both empirical and analytical. We intend to provide a comprehensive, descriptive demographic study and to consider the theoretical implications raised. All types of records available are being utilized for these purposes but primary emphasis is now being placed on the vital records and censuses for the time period 1650–1850. At the present time, vital statistics for 12 of the communities (see Figure 1) are being processed. Marriage records for all 12 towns are punched in IBM computer cards and transferred to tape. The complete vital statistics (births, marriages and deaths) of 3 of these 12 towns are being recorded for use in family reconstitution (Wrigley, 1965) and for intensive study of variation in town pattern. Aggregative statistics from the 1765 to 1850 censuses are also being computerized.

This region of the Connecticut River Valley provides an excellent source of historical demographic data for the following reasons. (1) The Valley was first settled by Europeans

Figure 1. Principal study area, Connecticut Valley Project, Hampshire and Franklin Counties, Massachusetts. Larger circle represents core area of two-county area. Smaller circle represents 12 communities of intensive study.

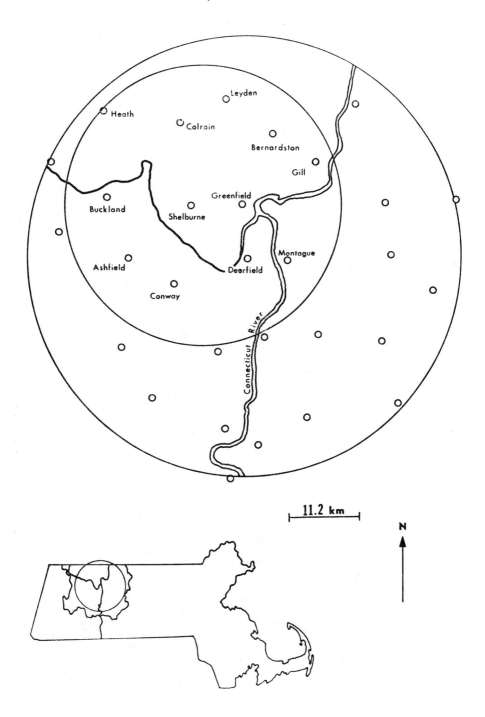

in the 1650s and, excepting the southern coastal settlements of New England, this area is one of the earliest occupied in the colonies of New England. The pattern of settlement was based on nucleated, agricultural villages constructed and inhabited by a small number of founding families. (2) Civil registration of births, deaths and marriages was made law in 1639 in the Massachusetts Bay Colony (Cassedy, 1969). In addition to these early civil records (many of which have been published by the New England Historical and Genealogical Society), census records are available from approximately 1765, with the official decennial U.S. Census beginning in 1790. There are also parish records and family genealogies available for several communities. Initial tests of the completeness and accuracy of the records indicate that they are well suited for the purposes outlined below and that they are at least comparable to many of the better European records used in historical studies.* (3) During this period, ethnic, social and religious diversity were at a minimum and an agricultural economy pervaded throughout the entire area. Apparently the indigenous Indian population was relatively small and, unfortunately, may have been decimated to some extent by the spread of European diseases prior to the time of any large scale population movement into the area. This is not to say, however, that the earliest settlers were able to avoid contact with the Indians, as significant hostility occurred in the late seventeenth century and into the early 1700s.

We envisage a wide range of problems which can be investigated within the study region. Demographic data are available from this earliest settlement period to the most recent national census. It is our intention to include recent population trends in our analysis, as well as the present focus on historic processes. The fact that a literate, agrarian society

---

* While most historical-demographic studies have employed data from England and continental Europe, data from the United States, and particularly New England, seem very promising. Under the provision of the General Court of Massachusetts, the civil registration of births, deaths and marriages was made law in 1639. This early data for civil, rather than ecclesiastical, registration means that actual recording of births and deaths, as opposed to baptisms and burials, occurred somewhat earlier than in many parts of Europe. The records from New England seem reliable, as evidenced from a number of community studies, and underenumeration does not seem to be a very serious problem with the possible exception of death registrations (see Norton, 1971).

Marital information in particular could be regarded as the best recorded vital event since all marriage records have been gathered and kept by civil officials exclusively. According to Cassedy (1969), this is because the Puritans and Pilgrims, as their Reformation leaders before them, considered marriage as a civil ceremony regardless of whether or not the act was actually performed by clergy.

Although there were inevitably many problems in recording and keeping these early vital statistics, the vital records for individual communities in Massachusetts represent some of the better data of this sort. According to Cassedy, England followed Massachusetts' example and in 1653, under the Civil Marriage Act, brought into effect a system of civil registration.

We have made a number of independent checks on our data by comparing the vital records within communities with the U.S. Census data for Heads of Households. We consistently find 70 to 80 percent identity in the comparisons, and for some communities the compatibility is even greater. There are certainly problems and errors to be dealt with, but with carefully designed sampling procedures we are confident that reliable observations on trends in distribution, growth and composition can be made.

can be studied as it proceeds through preindustrial and early manufacturing periods will provide many important areas of observation in regard to the cause and effect of demographic change. Our intention is to expand these observations into the areas of human microevolution, population planning, public health and related fields.

The materials for the present paper are derived from our initial efforts to gain a broad demographic profile of the area and time period under study. Before initiating sampling procedures, it is necessary to have preliminary inference on basic patterns of growth, fertility, migration, mortality and settlement distribution. From the indications collected, either from selected communities or from very general data, effective sampling methods could then be determined. The methods for obtaining these general measures and our preliminary results are presented below.

4. Demographic Features

Distribution: settlement pattern

The study area, as noted, was primarily settled by people moving up river in a south to north direction. Most of the earliest communities were founded by families who had contracted with the colonial government to establish a new community (or who purchased their land from these initial contractors) and who had secured permission to enter the frontier area. After initial settlements were formed and became somewhat stable, later communities were often settled by members from the earlier ones. Figure 2 shows the pattern of settlement in 25 year intervals between 1725 and 1800. Although the earliest community in this area was founded in 1656, only 8 communities were present in 1750. There was a tendency for settlement to occur along the river first, then to spread out into the higher and more hilly farmlands as time passed. The regularity of the most recent settlement distribution suggests the possibility of some form of optimum spacing relationship between agricultural communities of similar subsistence pattern, a process discussed elsewhere (Swedlund, 1975).

The "typical" founding pattern involved several families (*c.* 5–20) moving into an area and establishing adjacent house lots in a centralized area of the land purchased. Each house lot included a few acres with land for a family garden and barns. Much of the surrounding land, which was used for grazing livestock and for cultivation, was held in common, with most members of the community participating. Eventually this land would be deeded to established families. Individuals would purchase or gain rights to the land in accordance with their material wealth, house lot size and livestock holdings but responsibility for maintenance and use of the land was communal in the initial phase of settlement. This pattern provided close contact with neighbors and protection against the threat of Indian attacks, which in turn fostered the existing sense of community. Many of the basic settlement features were adopted from the English open-field system. The sex ratio tended to be more balanced than is the case in many colonizing situations and emphasis on family-oriented values is clearly evident in the historical literature of the area (e.g. Sheldon, 1895; Bacon, 1907). We do not find evidence of significant numbers of sojourners or servants during this early period.

For the time period 1650–1850 the entire study area can be characterized as being primarily agricultural in economy with nucleated rural settlements being the community type. Farming was primarily practiced for subsistence and for sale in local markets prior to the middle 1800s. In the middle to late 1800s commercial crops, particularly tobacco

Figure 2. The distribution of settlements in the area of the Connecticut and Deerfield Rivers, 1700–1850.

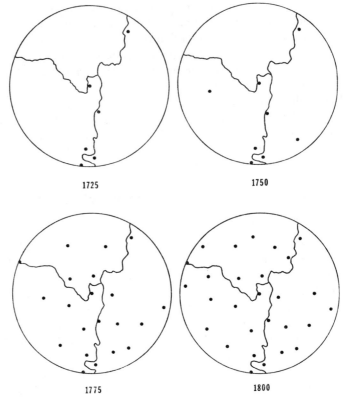

and onions, became important and earlier patterns of community farming began to change. Although some of the towns engaged in limited manufacturing (e.g., small mills or home industries) relatively early in time, the effects of this economic activity were not great until the 1840s when the railroads came to the area. Even as late as 1820 less than 4·8 percent of the population in Franklin, Hampshire and adjacent Hampden Counties was involved in manufacturing (Klimm, 1933). After the 1840s, increased manufacturing and commercial activity drastically affected demographic patterns. A second major wave of migration into the area occurred in the latter part of the nineteenth century and, whereas the early occupants of the region tended to be of English descent, this second wave included a large number of settlers from Central Europe. These people came to the area as a result of opportunities brought about by increasing manufacturing activity.

Patterns of growth

From 1765 on, it is possible to directly note population size in the counties and communities located in this area from the census records. More interesting in this case, however, is the relative growth that occurs over time in the study area. The general pattern of growth in Franklin and Hampshire Counties is presented in Figure 3. The values from 1765 are derived from the Royal Census of Massachusetts Commonwealth Census and all subsequent decennial values are from the U.S. Censuses. Adequate data are not available prior to 1765, except for a limited number of communities.

Figure 3. Population growth in Hampshire and Franklin Counties, Massachusetts, 1765–1900.

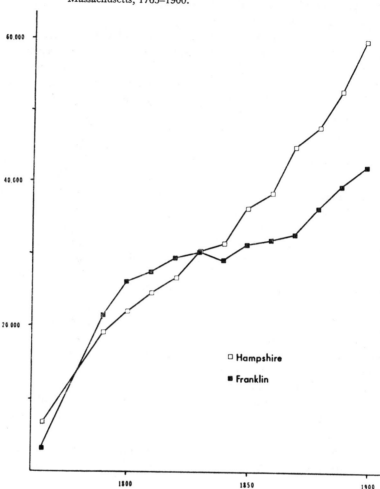

The growth rates occurring in the two-county area were determined overall and for various subdivisions of the curves by the formula (Barclay, 1958):

$$\frac{P_2}{P_1} = e^{rn}$$

where P_2 = population size at time 2, P_1 = population size at time 1, r = rate of growth per year and n = number of years between P_1 and P_2.

Growth for the entire area between 1765 and 1900 was relatively rapid ($r = 1\cdot69\%$), but more important are the rates during certain segments of this 135 year period. Growth between 1765 and 1800 in Franklin County was extremely high ($r = 5\cdot78\%$), with a leveling period between 1800 and 1850 ($r = 0\cdot30\%$). Franklin County again achieved a moderate growth rate between 1850 and 1900 ($r = 0\cdot59\%$). Hampshire County, by contrast, shows more consistent growth throughout the period considered, but rates in the early ($r = 3\cdot58\%$ for 1765–1800), middle ($r = 0\cdot91\%$ for 1800–1850) and late

7

($r = 0.99\%$ in 1850–1900) periods do roughly correspond to those observed in Franklin County. It may be observed that the peak period of growth (1750–1800) is also the time of most marked community establishment.

While growth rates in historical New England have received considerable attention (e.g. Potter, 1965; Norton, 1971; Smith, 1972) and the trends are well documented, the patterns in this specific region and the demographic components contributing to them are not. Our initial efforts to understand the nature of population growth as it occurred in this region prompted our investigation of three questions: (1) what major socioeconomic trends might account for the periodic change in growth rates? (2) how was the observed growth differentially represented in communities over space and time? and (3) what are the relative contributions of fertility, mortality and migration to this growth pattern? Fortunately, the social and economic data are sufficiently well documented so that observed trends could be related to dated events in Connecticut Valley history. Observations by Klimm (1933), Fitzpatrick (1949), King (1965), LeBlanc (1969) and Wilson (n.d.) provide the following summary of major shifts in economic activity.

From the original settlement period (*c*. 1660) until approximately 1800, the basic agricultural pattern described above predominated. Because of the relatively good farmlands and lack of competition from surrounding areas, the agricultural communities did very well and this success promoted rapid growth and settlement over the entire area. By about 1800 or slightly earlier, however, soils in the higher elevations (500 feet and above) were becoming seriously depleted and agriculture was consequently becoming a less viable economic strategy. In the lower elevations, agriculture was still being effectively practiced, but the initial effects of newer, successful settlements further west were being felt. The years between 1800 and 1850 represent a "no growth" period for Franklin County primarily because the traditional farm economy had fallen off and because manufacturing was just beginning to become an important alternative. During this same time period, Hampshire County sustained a higher growth as a result of its somewhat earlier beginnings in manufacturing, and due to the wider Valley (lower elevations) suitable for agriculture.

The manufacturing that was done in both counties was principally in the areas of textiles, lumber, foundries, farm tools, tanning and furniture. During the early periods of manufacturing, labor was furnished by people shifting from agriculture to this other source of livelihood but after 1850 migrants from outside the immediate area contributed significantly to the industrial labor force. Our initial impression is that, between the first and this second wave of migration, the observed growth was predominantly the result of high natural increase rather than high rates of inmigration.

In order to visually represent the distribution of population within towns, the community census sizes were plotted (Figure 4). The latter periods (1800 and 1850) seemed most appropriate for considering the results of growth, since all but one of the communities in the study area were established by 1800. The pattern that emerges is one in which the population is quite dispersed and no single community or small group of communities bears a large population. The largest community in Franklin County reported prior to 1850 numbered only 2580 individuals (Greenfield, 1850). It can be seen that, in spite of heterogeneity in community size, all communities remained as small towns for the time period under study. Towns along the Connecticut River tended to be the largest, but towns away from the area also managed to sustain moderate population sizes. This is largely due to the fact that manufacturing was quite ubiquitous in the region.

Figure 4. Population density by town in the area of the Connecticut and Deerfield Rivers, 1800 and 1850.

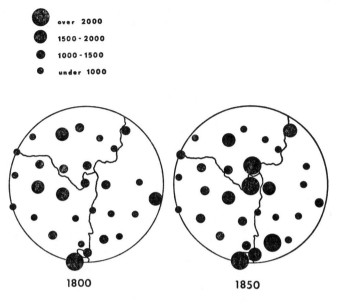

over 2000

1500 - 2000

1000 - 1500

under 1000

1800   1850

The trends described above can be better appreciated if we look at examples of specific communities in Franklin County and observe their individual patterns of growth. Klimm (1933) identified four types of communities in the Connecticut River Valley on the basis of their growth patterns. The two-county area herein described exhibits three of these patterns. These "types" should only be taken as examples of trends that occurred, and not be considered as models of settlement for all communities. We are not attempting to corroborate Klimm's original typology, but we do observe that patterns exist and that they are useful for understanding growth in the region as a whole. Basically, the types of towns discussed show patterns reflective of their geographic locations and of economic shifts occurring during the period under study. Other towns in the same environmental context as a "type" town will *tend* to reflect that pattern. In Figure 5 we plot three such towns: Deerfield, Greenfield and Shelburne.

The Deerfield pattern is representative of lowland agricultural communities that remained primarily agricultural throughout the period. Such towns can be characterized by positive growth without experiencing extreme declines or oscillating patterns. Many of these communities did experience a decline in the period 1850–1900, but were relatively successful prior to the late nineteenth century. The Greenfield pattern is characteristic of towns in the lowland region that began as agricultural communities but, because of their locations on the River or distance to other manufacturing communities, became important commercial and manufacturing centers as time progressed. Greenfield shows a pattern of moderate decline, and then rapid growth towards the end of the nineteenth century. If we were to plot Greenfield into the late nineteenth century, the curve would show a very high, exponential growth rate as a result of increasing manufacturing and mercantile activity.

The third pattern is exemplified by Shelburne. Shelburne is a town that remained principally agricultural and which is located in the uplands of the region. Soils are generally much thinner and land is very hilly. Shelburne, in its earliest period of settlement, showed a brief period of population increase and then it tended to oscillate without

Figure 5. Population growth in Deerfield, Greenfield and Shelburne, Massachusetts, 1765–1850.

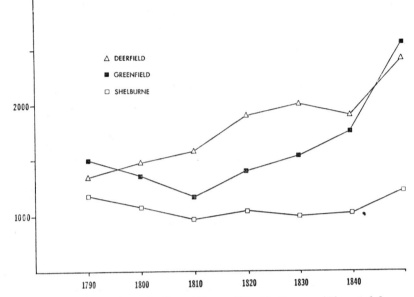

reaching a point of continued growth or decline. Towns like Shelburne, if located favorably along a stream or small river, occasionally became positive growth towns as a result of manufacturing made possible by the availability of water power. In the specific case of Shelburne, another village within the township, Shelburne Falls, took advantage of such a location and eventually grew larger than the town center of Shelburne.

The documented periods of growth, along with the economic history which suggests major causes and effects of population change, provide for a broad picture with which to view the specific demographic and genetic parameters to be estimated. Having a general understanding of the growth process in a given study area, however, does not in itself provide inference on the underlying causes of that process. In order to understand the relative contributions of fertility, mortality and population movement it is necessary to collect time-specific population data which can be translated into birth, death and migration rates respectively. Although the comprehensive analysis of these rates must await further data processing and interpretation, initial impressions have been tested in preparation for more intensive sampling.

Fertility

The analysis of fertility in historical populations has traditionally included the use of crude birth rates, refined birth rates, child-women ratios, live birth rates, mean completed family size, baptism rates and mean birth intervals as indices (see Barclay, 1958, for methods of computation for the various measures). Results from a variety of estimates for historical New England have indicated that fertility rates tend to be comparatively high over several communities and regions (e.g. Lockridge, 1966; Greven, 1970; Demos, 1970; Norton, 1971; Yasuba, 1962; Forster & Tucker, 1972), and probably higher than in many contemporaneous European populations (e.g. see Wrigley, 1969). It would appear that rates remained relatively high throughout the Colonial and Federal periods,

Table 1   **Child–women ratios, 1800–1840. Children less than 10 years of age/1000 women aged 16–44**

Year	Deerfield*	Shelburne*	Massachusetts †	Maine †	South Carolina †
1800	1450	1640	1539	1998	2089
1810	1360	1170	1470	1905	1987
1820	1440	1110	1310	1638	1888
1830	1040	1280	1148	1521	1817
1840	1020	943	1071	1489	1757

* Source: U.S. Census data.
† Source: Forster and Tucker (1972).

although a secular trend in reduced fertility also occurred (Yasuba, 1962; Forster & Tucker, 1972; Greven, 1970).

The data from the Connecticut River Valley appear to be consistent with previous observations in other areas of New England. One important point is that even though fertility was moderate to high for this time, other parts of the United States were experiencing even higher fertility in the post Revolutionary period (see Table 1). The reason for this is apparently the fact that Massachusetts, and the Connecticut Valley in particular, was already heavily settled and available farmland was limited. This limitation of resources contributed to drops in fertility from previously higher periods (Forster & Tucker, 1972)

Family reconstitution will permit more reliable estimation of fertility in the Connecticut Valley and provide for calculation of rates before 1790. The only completed family size estimates presently available are for the town of Deerfield, where 100 completed families recorded between the years 1670 and 1850 give a mean completed size of 7·06 children with a variance of 7·72. For births before 1765, a mean of 7·2 has been estimated (Suich, 1966). The parents of 1810 in this community ($N = 41$ families) had a mean complete size of 8·41 (Swedlund, 1971). See Table 2 for a comparison of various estimates.

Mortality

Mortality tends to be one of the most difficult demographic variables to study with historical records because of the problem of errors in enumeration. While it seems that births and marriage records are well represented in the civil records of Massachusetts, under-registration of deaths is a serious problem (Norton, 1971). This means that death rates based on ratios using raw counts will likely contain significant errors. Mortality is most

Table 2   **Mean completed family size in selected populations**

Population	Dates	$\bar{x}$	Source
Deerfield	1670–1850	7·06	Swedlund (1971)
Deerfield	1810	8·41	Swedlund (1971)
Plymouth, Mass.	1700	8·56	Demos (1965)
Andover, Mass.	–1704	8·7	Greven (1970)
Andover, Mass.	1705–1724	7·4	Greven (1970)
Andover, Mass.	1725–1744	7·5	Greven (1970)
Charlton, England	1800	5·2	Kuchemann, Boyce & Harrison (1967)
Charlton, England	1810	4·2	Kuchemann, Boyce & Harrison (1967)
Charlton, England	1820	4·0	Kuchemann, Boyce & Harrison (1967)

Table 3   **Representative life expectancies at birth in historic populations**

Population	Date	Male e_0	Female e_0	Source
Deerfield, Mass.	1745–1765	45·0	45·8	Suich (1966)
Sunderland, Mass.	1700–1799	48·0	45·3	Timson (n.d.)
Sunderland, Mass.	1800–1825	45·9	45·8	Timson (n.d.)
Pelham, Mass.	1772–1821	40·8	39·8	Meier (n.d.)
Pelham, Mass.	1822–1871	42·0	40·4	Meier (n.d.)
Massachusetts	1850	38·3	40·1	U.S. Bureau of the Census (1960)
United States	1850	40·4	43·0	Jacobson (1957)
England	1850	39·9	41·9	Jacobson (1957)
France	1850	39·1	40·6	Jacobson (1957)
Sweden	1850	41·3	45·6	Jacobson (1957)

frequently reported in terms of death rates, survivorship rates, burial rates, mean age at death and age-specific life expectancies (see Barclay, 1958; Wrigley, 1969).

A general consensus based on several studies in historical New England is that adjusted mortality rates were relatively quite low in comparison with those of European communities (Norton, 1971; Yasuba, 1962). Low mortality was probably the most significant reason for high rates of growth in Colonial America. An important feature of New England communities was the apparent absence or infrequency (Norton, 1971) of disease and food "crises" when compared with contemporaneous periods and populations in Europe (see Hollingsworth, 1973).

Preliminary investigations in the Connecticut Valley indicate that life expectancy was quite high in relation to Massachusetts and the United States in general. Table 3 presents some of the initial estimates made in the Connecticut Valley and indicates the favorable life expectancies present during the eighteenth century. It is interesting to note that, according to some authors (e.g. Norton, 1971; Greven, 1970), there was actually an increase in mortality in Colonial New England over time. Norton cites evidence for age-specific changes, but a possible explanation for some increase in mortality rates in the Eighteenth Century is that the age structure of certain communities was changing. A young population was becoming older and crude death rates might correspondingly go up.

Migration

The analysis of migration in historical populations has been one of the more neglected areas of research (Drake, 1972) and yet this is one of the most important variables for the population biologist. The studies cited above for England, Italy, Switzerland and Finland, as well as the Japanese studies, have dealt with migration. However, the majority of European and American studies have not devoted much attention to the subject. One of the reasons is that records that provide migration data are not nearly as common as those providing other vital statistics. A second reason is that many of the historical studies have been on the analysis of single communities and it is less interesting and informative to study migration at this level. Fortunately for a microevolutionary approach, the one type of migration data that is usually available is the one that is most significant genetically, that is, migration-at-marriage data.

Migration, in the strict demographic sense, is usually measured by rates of in-migration (immigration if across national political boundaries), out-migration (emigration if across national political boundaries) and net migration (see Barclay, 1958). Obviously of more

Table 4   **Rates of community endogamy in ten towns in the Connecticut Valley, 1670–1850**

Marriages	Percent endogamy	Years
84	0·6548	–1759
145	0·7103	1760–1769
410	0·6683	1770–1779
671	0·6393	1780–1789
991	0·5197	1790–1799
1094	0·4707	1800–1809
1163	0·4583	1810–1819
1086	0·4494	1820–1829
1175	0·3923	1830–1839
1376	0·3539	1840–1849

interest for population genetic analysis are rates of endogamy, exogamy and parent-offspring or parent-parent distances between place of origin and residence.

Migration to colonial New England was, of course, great in the early settlement period. However, our impression is that it was not immigration so much as it was intrinsic growth that accounts for increasing population in the communities studied to date (see Norton, 1971; Potter, 1965). The initial waves of migration were certainly important, but once a community was established further in-migration was not marked. In fact, we have some evidence for the Connecticut Valley and elsewhere (Haller, 1951; Zuckerman, 1972; McArdle, 1975) that towns were openly discouraging to potential migrants once the founding settlers had become established. For the years 1670–1850 we believe that most of the growth observed in the Valley was the result of internal rates.

A second dimension to migration is provided by the investigation of patterns within the region of the Connecticut Valley. One of our major concerns in this project is the observable interaction between subdivisions (towns) of the local population. In preparation for the analysis of genetic migration, we have recorded the proportions of community endogamy over time from 8195 marriages distributed in 10 neighboring townships (Table 4). We find a consistent reduction in endogamy between the founding dates of the area and 1850. This trend relates to increasing mobility as a result of *both* an increase in the number of neighboring communities over time and an increase in gross population size. The average rate over all 10 communities not only decreased over time, but the variance in rates among individual communities also decreased. Moreover, the migration distances that individuals travel for mates do not appear to be great. Information from Deerfield and Shelburne, Massachusetts, indicates that the average distance traveled for a mate over the entire period was approximately 7 to 8 miles, with a median and mode close to these values (see Norton, 1973). If endogamy is decreasing it follows that genetic microdifferentiation should also be decreasing and we will want to quantify and explain this process further in future work.

5. Population Composition

Turning now from population growth to population composition, we can offer a brief set set of observations on the nature of these towns at a single point in time. We have described some of the socioeconomic factors involved above. Of concern here are the demographic factors such as sex ratio, age structure and household and family size.

Table 5   **Sex ratio in Deerfield and Shelburne, Massachusetts, 1800–1840**

Year	Deerfield		Shelburne	
	Total pop.	Ages 16–44	Total pop.	Ages 16–44
1800	95·8	90·7	94·3	91·7
1810	98·1	97·3	93·1	97·3
1820	87·1	85·9	95·0	81·8
1830	96·3	100·0	93·8	96·9
1840	98·5	102·0	94·3	77·9

Sex ratio

One of the well documented facts about the colonization of New England is that there was an emphasis on family settlement (e.g. Moller, 1945; see Norton, 1971). This pattern was true of the Connecticut River Valley and historical accounts of the towns show the predominance of families in the early settlement structure. The effect of this familial pattern, which resulted at least partly from the influence of the Puritans, was that the

Figure 6. Age structure in Deerfield and Shelburne, Massachusetts: Census of 1830.

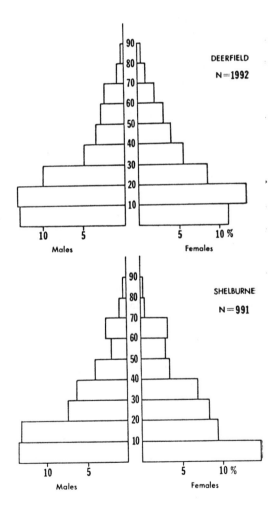

distribution of sexes was quite well balanced. An investigation of the towns of Deerfield and Shelburne, Massachusetts, between 1800 and 1850 (Table 5) confirms the even ratio for the later period. Slight imbalances may have occurred from time to time due to stochastic variation, but in general the ratios were quite even.

Age structure

The age structure in the Connecticut Valley was predominantly affected by the existence of relatively high fertility and relatively low mortality. Broad categories for age structure could be constructed for the 1790 to 1850 censuses. The towns of Deerfield and Shelburne exhibit a distribution of ages that includes about 42 percent in the ages 0 to 15, 42 percent in the ages 16 to 44 and 16 percent aged 45 and over. Age pyramids were constructed from information from the 1830 census (Figure 6) and, accounting for variation due to small population size, the pyramids exhibit the results of an even sex ratio high fertility and high survivorship.

The mean age of marriage in the Connecticut Valley ranges between 22 and 24 years for women between 1670 and 1850, and averages approximately 27 years for men over the same period. The increasing age of marriage for women is a pattern observed in other New England communities and may have contributed to the secular trend in lowered fertility. In addition, the ages are consistently younger than those reported for Europe (Wrigley, 1969) at the same time.

Family and household size

The family and household sizes reported for historical New England provide a contrast with those reported from Europe (see Laslett, 1969; 1972). In general, both household size and family size tend to be larger in New England. The Connecticut Valley data on 11 towns in the 1790 census give a mean family size of 6·25 (this should not be confused with mean *completed* size). Because of the agrarian, nuclear family structure, 95 percent of all families recorded in these towns had their own houses in 1790. Thus household size for the same communities averaged 6·54. Table 6 summarizes household size in two towns for the 1790 and 1830 censuses.

An analysis of 100 communities in England between the years 1574–1821 gave a mean household size of 4·77 (Laslett, 1969). If only rural communities are measured, it is likely that the results for England (and Europe as a whole) would be somewhat higher (see Drake, 1972). What probably contributed to the higher figures for New England are the emphasis on family, as mentioned above, the rural agrarian settlement pattern and the fact that single-member households were so rare. In contemporaneous Europe, the single-member household (particularly in more urban areas) and the presence of sojourners was apparently more common (see Hajnal, 1965).

Table 6   **Household size in Deerfield and Shelburne, Massachusetts, 1790 census and 1830 census**

Year	Deerfield			Shelburne		
	Population	Household	$\bar{x}$ Household size	Population	Household	$\bar{x}$ Household size
1790	1330	181	7·35	1183	169	7·00
1830	2003	316	6·34	995	146	6·81

Greven (1970) has described the family pattern in Andover, Massachusetts, as a "modified extended family", which seems appropriate for the Connecticut Valley communities as well. This pattern comes from the fact that the original land holders in the colonial settlements tended to practice partible inheritance in which all sons received shares of the land. As sons achieved marriageable age they would very often construct houses on the land and farm their acreage, which resulted in two or more nuclear families living on the same original farm. If the father lived a long life, he would often retain control of the land and family, thus the "extended" nature of the nuclear households.

6. Discussion

In summary, we have presented here some general aspects of population distribution, growth and composition for a region of the Connecticut Valley, Massachusetts, between 1650 and 1850. The most salient features of this survey to date include the following observations.

(1) The settlement pattern was one in which several small, principally agrarian communities are nonrandomly distributed throughout the area. The sequence of settlement is dated and well documented. We have observed that the distribution tends towards an equidistant spatial relationship between communities, and elsewhere (Swedlund, 1975) measured the regularity in pattern by nearest neighbor analysis.

(2) The region experienced considerable growth over the time considered and, with the exception of the early settlement period, our evidence suggests that the growth resulted primarily from relatively high intrinsic growth rates. Communities established late during the period of study are presumably the result of an expanding population in the earlier communities and are less dependent upon outside immigration.

(3) The structure of the communities was family-based; sex ratio was balanced and household size was comparatively large. People settling in the region were economically successful. Good levels of nutrition and low levels of exposure to infectious disease contributed to a population that was healthy for the times.

The considerable emphasis placed on social-historical factors in this paper is not offered in lieu of human biological considerations nor is it presented without clear recognition of our ultimate goal—the explanation of human biological variation. If we view the utility of historical data as primarily that of providing inference on the processes of demographic and microevolutionary change, then the cultural and social milieu is obviously important. We can briefly recount the following areas of research that are presently under investigation:

(a) One of the more interesting analyses is the assessment of fertility and mortality in a colonizing population over time. Coale & Zelnik (1963: 35, cited in Forster & Tucker, 1972) state: "The birth rate in the United States fell extensively—from 55 to 41 per thousand—between 1800 and 1860, while the population remained nearly 80 percent rural . . . To account for the decline in fertility in non-industrial environments would be a fruitful form of research."

The biological and social factors involved in population regulation are being investigated. The results of this research should be relevant to population planners as well as to human biologists. Minimally, we will be analyzing within population variation in relation to fertility and mortality as an "index of total selection" (Crow, 1958). The effects of sibship size and variance will be viewed in regard to notions of effective size. If population numbers and epidemiological information prove adequate, then other models will be employed.

(b) The analysis of migration at marriage provides a second major focus of the project. The application of spatial models of gene flow over time will provide another interesting example of the nature of population structure in subdivided populations. The opportunity to observe trends in a newly settled population is distinctive from other studies employing spatial models. The value of ethnohistorical data for time-depth studies has been demonstrated (Workman *et al.*, in press) and in this case these data are being used extensively.

(c) This project is also presently oriented toward intensive investigation of individual pedigrees, made possible by family reconstitution. The fact that similar or same surnames (isonymy) appear in several of the communities being investigated provides for the study of inbreeding by analysis of surnames.

Projected research is, of course, not limited to these areas of investigation. Many genetic models do not assume growth in their prediction of gene and genotype distributions, nor do the effects of varying demographic structures often enter into the consideration of genetic structure (see Yellen & Harpending, 1972). We see the present study as an opportunity to test the robusticity of a wide variety of models under varying demographic conditions. In addition, the potential of the socio-cultural data and the contemporary demographic structure are being investigated with respect to current problems in population planning and health care delivery, which we regard as a complement to the micro-evolutionary problems discussed here.

The basic form of this paper was first presented at the Advanced Study Institute on "Demographic Aspects of the Biology of Human Populations", Erice, Sicily (1974). We would like to thank the supporters and organizers of that conference for their support. The Connecticut Valley Project is supported in part by the National Institutes of Health (Grant HD 08979-01). We would also like to thank Peter L. Workman, University of Massachusetts, George S. Masnick, Harvard Medical School and Susan L. Norton, Health Sciences Center, University of Texas, Houston, for their constructive criticisms on a draft of this paper.

References

Bacon, E. M. (1907). *The Connecticut River and the Valley of the Connecticut.* New York: G. P. Putnam and Sons.

Barclay, G. W. (1958). *Techniques of Population Analysis.* New York: John Wiley & Sons.

Boyce, A. J., Küchemann, C. F. & Harrison, G. A. (1967). Neighborhood knowledge and the distribution of marriage distances. *Annals of Human Genetics* **30**, 335–338.

Cassedy, J. (1969). *Demography in Early America.* Cambridge: Harvard University Press.

Cavalli–Sforza, L. L. (1969). Genetic drift in an Italian population. *Scientific American* **221**, 30–37.

Cavalli–Sforza, L. L. (1973). Analytic review: Some current problems of human population genetics. *American Journal of Human Genetics* **25**, 82–104.

Cavalli–Sforza, L. L. & Bodmer, W. F. (1971). *The Genetics of Human Populations.* San Francisco: W. H. Freeman & Co.

Coale, A. J. & Zelnik, M. (1963). *New Estimates of Fertility and Population in the United States.* Princeton: Princeton University Press.

Crow, J. F. (1958). Some possibilities for measuring selection intensities in man. *Human Biology* **30**, 1–13.

Demos, J. (1965). Notes on life in Plymouth Colony. *William and Mary Quarterly* **22**, 264–286.

Demos, J. (1970). *A Little Commonwealth: Family Life in Plymouth Colony.* New York: Oxford University Press.

Dobson, T. & Roberts, D. F. (1971). Historical population movement and gene flow in Northumberland parishes. *Journal of Biosocial Science* **3**, 193–208.

Drake, M. (1972). Perspectives in historical demography. In (G. A. Harrison & A. J. Boyce, Eds.) *The Structure of Human Populations.* Oxford: Clarendon Press, pp. 57–72.

Fisher, R. A. (1930). *The Genetical Theory of Natural Selection*. Oxford: Oxford University Press.
Fitzpatrick, R. A. (1949). A survey of agriculture in the Connecticut Valley Counties in Massachusetts, 1636–1949. Master's Thesis. Amherst: University of Massachusetts.
Forster, C. & Tucker, G. S. L. (1972). *Economic Opportunity and White American Fertility Ratios, 1800–1860*. New Haven: Yale University Press.
Greven, P. J., Jr. (1970). *Four Generations. Population, Land, and Family in Colonial Andover, Massachusetts*. Ithaca: Cornell University Press.
Hajnal, J. (1965). European marriage patterns in perspective. In (D. V. Glass & D. Eversley, Eds.) *Population in History. Essays in Historical Demography*. London: Edward Arnold, pp. 101–143.
Haller, W. (1951). *The Puritan Frontier: Town Planting in New England Colonial Development, 1630–1660*. New York: Columbia University Press.
Harrison, G. A. & Boyce, A. J., Eds. (1972). *The Structure of Human Populations*. Oxford: Clarendon Press.
Hollingsworth, T. H. (1973). Population crises in the past. In (B. Benjamin, P. Cox & J. Peel, Eds.) *Resources and Population*. New York: Academic Press, pp. 99–108.
Hussels, I. (1969). Genetic structure of Saas, a Swiss isolate. *Human Biology* **41**, 469–479.
Jacobson, P. H. (1957). An estimate of the expectation of life in the United States in 1850. *The Milbank Memorial Fund Quarterly* **35**, 197–201.
King, H. R. (1965). The settlement of the upper Connecticut River Valley to 1675. Ph.D. Dissertation. Vanderbilt University. Ann Arbor: University Microfilms.
Klimm, L. E. (1933). The relation between certain population changes and the physical environment in Hampden, Hampshire, and Franklin Counties, Massachusetts, 1790–1925. Ph.D. Thesis. Philadelphia: University of Pennsylvania.
Küchemann, D. F., Boyce, A. J. & Harrison, G. A. (1967). A demographic and genetic study of a group of Oxfordshire villages. *Human Biology* **39**, 251–276.
Laslett, P. (1969). Size and structure of the household in England over three centuries. *Population Studies* **23**, 199–223.
LeBlanc, R. G. (1969). *Location of Manufacturing in New England in the 19th Century*. Hanover: Dartmouth University. Dartmouth Publications in Geography, **7**.
Lockridge, K. A. (1966). The population of Dedham, Massachusetts, 1636–1736. *Economic History Review*, 2nd series, **19**, 318–344.
McArdle, A. (1975). Population growth and regulation in Hadley, Massachusetts: 1660–1730. Master's Thesis. Amherst: Department of Anthropology, University of Massachusetts.
Meier, C. (1969). Mortality in Pelham, Massachusetts from 1772–1968: Life tables from gravestone inscriptions. Honors Thesis. Amherst: Department of Anthropology, University of Massachusetts.
Mielke, J. H., Workman, P. L., Fellman, J. & Eriksson, A. W. (n.d.). The genetic structure of the Aland Islands. *Advances in Human Genetics* **5**, in press.
Moller, H. (1945). Sex composition and correlated culture patterns of colonial America. *William and Mary Quarterly*, 3rd series, **2**, 113–153.
Morton, N. E. (1973). *Genetic Structure of Populations*. Honolulu: Population Genetics Monographs, Vol. III, University of Hawaii.
Morton, N. E. & Hussels, I. (1970). Demography of inbreeding in Switzerland. *Human Biology* **42**, 65–78.
Norton, S. L. (1971). Population growth in colonial America: A study of Ipswich, Massachusetts. *Population Studies* **25**, 433–452.
Norton, S. L. (1973). Marital migration in Essex County, Massachusetts, in the Colonial and early Federal periods. *Journal of Marriage and the Family* **35**, 406–418.
Potter, J. (1965). The growth of population in America. In (D. V. Glass & D. E. C. Eversley, Eds.) *Population in History. Essays in Historical Demography*. London: Edward Arnold, pp. 631–688.
Roberts, D. F. & Rawling, C. P. (1974). Secular trends in genetic structure: An isonymic analysis of Northumberland parish records. *Annals of Human Biology* **1**, 393–410.
Sheldon, G. (1895). *A History of Deerfield, Massachusetts*. Deerfield: Pocumtuck Valley Memorial Association, E. A. Hall & Company.
Smith, D. S. (1972). The demographic history of colonial New England. *Journal of Economic History* **32**, 165–183.
Suich, J. J. (1966). A statistical analysis of Deerfield, Massachusetts, 1705–1725 and 1745–1765. Heritage Foundation, Manuscript.
Sutter, J. (1963). The relationship between human population genetics and demography. In (E. Goldschmidt, Ed.) *Genetics of Migrant and Isolate Populations*. New York: Williams and Wilkins, pp. 160–168.
Sutter, J. & Tran-Ngoc-Toan (1957). The problem of the structure of isolates and of their evolution among human populations. *Cold Spring Harbor Symposia on Quantitative Biology* **22**, 379–383.
Swedlund, A. C. (1971). *The Genetic Structure of an Historical Population: A Study of Marriage and Fertility in Old Deerfield, Massachusetts*. Amherst: Research Reports No. 7, Department of Anthropology, University of Massachusetts.

Swedlund, A. C. (1972). Observations on the concept of neighbourhood knowledge and the distribution of marriage distances. *Annals of Human Genetics* **35**, 327–330.

Swedlund, A. C. (1975). Population growth and settlement pattern in Franklin and Hampshire Counties, Massachusetts, 1650–1850. In (A. C. Swedlund, Ed.) *Population Studies in Archaeology and Biological Anthropology: A Symposium*. S.A.A. Memoir, No. 30, 22–33.

Timson, J. (1970). Preliminary study of Riverside Cemetery, Sunderland, Massachusetts, including life tables. Manuscript. Amherst: Department of Anthropology, University of Massachusetts.

U.S. Bureau of the Census (1960). *Historical Statistics of the United States, Colonial Times to 1957*. Washington, D.C.: Government Printing Office.

Wilson, J. S. (n.d.). The geography of manufacturing in Hampshire and Franklin Counties, Massachusetts in the early nineteenth century. Manuscript. Amherst: Department of Anthropology, University of Massachusetts.

Workman, P. L., Mielke, J. H. & Nevalninna, H. R. (n.d.). The genetic structure of Finland. *American Journal of Physical Anthropology*, in press.

Wrigley, E. A. (1966). Family reconstitution. In (D. E. C. Eversley, P. Laslett & E. A. Wrigley, Eds.) *An Introduction to English Historical Demography, From the Sixteenth to the Nineteenth Century*. London: Weidenfield and Nicolson, pp. 96–159.

Wrigley, E. A. (1969). *Population and History*. New York: World University Library, McGraw-Hill Book Company.

Yanase, T. (1962). The use of the Japanese family register for genetic studies. In *The Use of Vital and Health Statistics for Genetic and Radiation Studies*. New York: United Nations, pp. 119–133.

Yasuba, Y. (1962). *Birth Rates of the White Population in the United States, 1800–1860. An Economic Study*. Baltimore: Johns Hopkins Press.

Yasuda, N. & Furusho, T. (1971). Random and nonrandom inbreeding revealed from isonymy study. I. Small cities of Japan. *American Journal of Human Genetics* **23**, 303–316.

Yasuda, N. & Kimura, M. (1973). A study of human migration in the Mishima district. *Annals of Human Genetics* **36**, 313–322.

Yellen, J. & Harpending, H. (1972). Hunter-gatherer populations and archaeological inference. *World Archaeology* **4**, 244–253.

Zuckerman, M. (1972). *Peaceable Kingdoms*. New York: Vintage Books.

M. Skolnick

*Biophysics Department
and Biology Department,
University of Utah, U.S.A*

A Preliminary Analysis of the Genealogy of Parma Valley, Italy

L. L. Cavalli–Sforza

*Genetics Department,
Stanford University, U.S.A.*

A. Moroni
E. Siri

*Laboratorio di Ecologia,
University of Parma,
Italy*

1. Introduction

In this paper, we explain the design and implementation of a methodology for the computerized reconstruction of genealogies from parish registers and present a preliminary analysis of the genealogy of Parma Valley, Italy, reconstructed using this method. The computer implementation was necessary as the study area and time period included over 125,000 entries of baptisms, marriages and deaths in parish registers. We hope that by studying an entire isolated valley defined by the 40 parishes of Parma Valley over four centuries (where possible), information would be obtained which was not present in previous studies of single parishes over short periods.

The computer problem turned out to be quite extensive and statistical methods were developed to resolve ambiguous links which arise in family reconstruction in an isolated area. These methods which were developed to be amenable to such a large data file involved approximating the likelihood that each link found was correct rather than being due to a chance matching.

The likelihood scores are based on name and demographic distributions. The rarer the matching names a link has and the more probable a link is demographically, the higher the score. The demographic distributions are also used to control the quality of the linkage.

It is beyond the scope of this paper to attempt a complete analysis of the genealogy produced, but the beginning stages and first results are described. The fertility, marriage and migration patterns are discussed, and the importance of large studies in defining these trends is emphasized. Mortality trends and the inheritance of longevity are being studied with D. Matessi and the extinction and size of genealogies is being studied with E. Lucchetti. These results and a discussion of remote consanguinity will be presented elsewhere.

2. Human Population Genetics and Genealogy

Demographic knowledge is essential to an understanding of genetic and evolutionary problems in human populations. Migration rates, population size, fertility patterns and age structure are examples of demographic observations that are basic for a description of the genetic structure of populations (Bodmer & Cavalli–Sforza, 1968; Cavalli–Sforza, 1960, 1963, 1966, 1969*a,b*; Chapman & Jacquard, 1971; Chaventre, 1972; Jacquard, 1972; Langaney, Gomila & Bouloux, 1973; Langaney & Gomila, 1974; Roberts, 1968; Skolnick *et al.*, 1971 and 1973). Age specific mortality, fertility rates and distributions of progeny sizes are similarly important for the measurement of natural selection.

We are interested, in addition, in the inheritance of some important traits such as fertility, longevity and twinning, which are themselves demographic in nature. They require studying a large area over many generations for a complete picture of their inheritance patterns to emerge.

By reconstructing a genealogy, one may look for correlations in fertility among offspring or other pairs of relatives and other factors which might tend to alter the distribution of the origin of genes among the descendants of a generation. There are known to be major differences in the mean number of children in different times and places and in different social classes. Are there also significant differences within the same class depending on parity, the marital status of sibs, and one's status as a migrant or non-migrant?

Studies of pedigrees are also essential for studies of medical problems (Cann & Cavalli–Sforza, 1968; Edwards, 1969; Haldane, 1949; Karlsson, 1968; Newcombe, 1957). With a complete genealogy linked to disease incidence data, one can begin the complex analysis of the importance of genetic composition in diseases which don't follow simple Mendelian patterns. Analysis of consanguinity data (Barrai *et al.*, 1962, 1965 & 1969; Cavalli–Sforza *et al.*, 1966, 1970; Conterio *et al.*, 1966; Hajnal, 1963; Ohkubo, 1963; Serra, 1961; Sutter, 1958; Sutter & Tabah, 1952, 1953; Woolf *et al.*, 1956; Zei *et al.*, 1971) is also an extremely important product of genealogical reconstruction. However, with the present study, we no longer have to restrict ourselves to the analysis of close consanguinity. In addition to biological inheritance, social transmission of fertility patterns can have an important effect on the genetic structure of human populations (Neel, 1970).

Finally, the socio-economic changes of the last centuries have deeply affected all demographic values and, with them, the trends and rates of biological evolution in man. For these reasons, it is useful for the geneticist to make recourse to demographic records of the past when they are available.

Because man can communicate, he can be surveyed and censused. Historical documents and man's preference for territorial possession and stability have created natural "strains" whose pedigrees can be reconstructed and whose members can be studied to increase our understanding of human nature and how it has affected and will affect our evolution. It is this approach which we have taken in this paper.

Although we cannot perform experiments, we can study man's natural mating and reproductive patterns, and select from them the matings which provide us with the most potential for further investigations. In addition, man is one of the few animals which allows us the opportunity to study a natural population structure and determine its effect on evolution.

In most animals, a long-term study of natural population patterns would be extremely difficult, and most of our information of genetic structures has come from developing highly inbred strains in the laboratory and breeding animals of known genotypes to determine the nature of many traits. With man, we can make long-term studies of natural populations.

3. Reconstructing Genealogies from Parish Registers

The method to be presented is one way of studying large human pedigrees: forming genealogies from parish registers of baptisms, deaths and marriages. These are the records which are the most useful for studying the population structure of a particular area, because individual life histories can be reconstructed by linking the baptism, marriage, and burial records in the three registries to form a complete record for each individual. Where there is enough information to link the individual's record to his spouse, parents and children, families can be reconstructed, and genealogies and pedigrees can be studied.

The habit of maintaining registers of vital events evolved in a non-uniform fashion but took shape in a more or less uniform system, due to various decrees. The uniformity of registration and the content of the registers also varies considerably, in part due to varying usage of surnames in different countries. In Scandanavia, Iceland and Polynesia, patronymics are used instead of surnames. (George, son of John, would be called George Johnson.) Children therefore have different surnames than their parents. Spanish registers, and the registers of Central and South American countries, followed the custom of attaching the mother's surname to the surname of each person mentioned in the record. There is also variation which is in part due to the degree of centralization of the religious sources of power. Where there was a central control of decisions, as in Catholic countries, the bishops and ultimately the parish priests were required to keep the registers in a very precise way. In England, where the central authority was not as strong, the registers vary considerably and the content of the data is often much scantier. Catholic registers appear to have age at death more frequently than Protestant registers. They also contain more complete nominative information. The first name of the father is almost always given (except for illegitimate births), and the surname and name of the mother are also often stated from the eighteenth century on. It appears that the richest sources of data are the French registers and the registers of countries which at one time formed part of the Spanish dominion.

The French and French Canadian records not only describe the parent of the person registered but also the witnesses, and the relationship of the witnesses to the individual or to each other. In Spanish-controlled areas, nominal identification is much more positive. Where the data are recorded completely, the grandparents are partially identified and the possibility for ambiguity is almost nonexistant.

In Catholic countries, women are recorded in death registers with their maiden name, whereas in Protestant countries, they may be recorded with their married surname, which greatly increased uncertainty in linking because one has a larger search domain for the death record, unless the link between baptism and marriage is completely unambiguous.

4. Parish Registers in the Diocese of Parma

The method presented has been designed to deal with problems in linking records from the parish registers of three communes of the diocese of Parma: Monchio, Palanzano and Corniglio. Together they form an isolated mountain valley community in the upper part of the Parma River in Northern Italy. The area is being studied genetically because

of the availability of many sources of information and because the valley itself is a genetic
isolate, a rural hilly area bounded on three sides by mountains, and thus historically, it
has had little immigration. Therefore, most marriages are between people born in the
valley. In addition, the parishes are quite small. With 40 parishes and a population of
about 10,000, the mean population per parish is around 250. As the villages of birth and
residence are included in the parish registers, it is often possible to pinpoint residence to a
cluster of houses. This detail is important, as it allows one to follow internal migration
very closely.

The division of the area into small parishes, although useful for migration studies,
causes a complication in the early period. The first Italian parish registers are found in
Siena (1379), Pisa (1459) and Piacenza (1466), some time before the systematic registry
of baptism, deaths and marriages which began with the Council of Trento (1542–1563).
However, the practice of keeping them spread slowly and irregularly, with baptism
registers often begun earlier than death and marriage registers. Since books started at
different times in different parishes, there is much missing information in the early
period, and genealogies which extend into many neighboring parishes are likely to be
incomplete. In Parma, approximately one third of birth and marriage records start
during the 17th century, but only 5 % of the death records begin this early. Table 1
gives the date of the first entry and the number of entries in each register for the forty
parishes we are studying. The parishes are in alphabetical order within each of the three
communes of Parma Valley (Corniglio, Monchio and Palanzano).

In the upper Parma Valley very few parishes have continuous data from the 17th
century. Continuity is highly desirable but is not always necessary for the reconstruction
of genealogies. It is rather the unfortunate combination of discontinuity in more than one
register which makes reconstruction very difficult. Although the reconstruction is
weakened by missing data, the presence of baptism records alone is sufficient for continuing the genealogy in cases where the information on parents uniquely identifies
appropriate parental baptism records (Skolnick *et al.*, 1971). In other cases, reconstruction becomes impossible where there are missing records. Fortunately, marriage and
baptism records, the most important for reconstruction, were usually the first to be kept.

Although the most important information used in linking two records is the surname
and names of the proband and his parents, the ages at marriage and death may be stated
on marriage and death records respectively. These provide additional information, which
is valuable for both controlling the accuracy of linkage and resolving ambiguities in cases
where one of several links must be selected. In Parma Valley, the age at death is present
in over 90 % of the records, and the age at marriage is present in about 35 % of the records.

The completeness of the nominative data in each register also varies. Often the
surname and the first name of the mother are absent, especially before 1800, and this
increases uncertainty in the reconstruction of genealogies. In these cases, the sibling
group must be linked to the father, and the mother linked to the children only through
the record of marriage to the father. Second names are present frequently enough in the
early periods for them to be of significance, but third names are too infrequent to be
useful.

Important additional data exists in some of the parish records. The parish of birth
may be given on marriage records. An indication whether the parents were alive or dead
is also usually present and illegitimate births were indicated by omitting the father's
name and surname.

Table 1   Date of first entry and frequency of baptism (B), marriage (M) and death (D) registration by parish

Parish	Baptism		Marriage		Death	
	Year of first entry	Number of entries	Year of first entry	Number of entries	Year of first entry	Number of entries
Corniglio						
Agna	1604	2530	1607	624	1604	1327
Beduzzo	1649	4545	1651	1125	1651	2873
Bosco	1569	6918	1569	1549	1630	4042
Canetolo	1628	1440	1784	252	1784	751
Corniglio	1565	7653	1529	2284	1703	3569
Graiana	1573	3034	1565	685	1630	1524
Grammatica	1632	1372	1795	154	1782	531
Marra	1680	1316	1694	379	1625	1174
Mossale	1650	1761	1652	412	1650	1065
Petrignacola	1762	1684	1808	430	1774	1042
Pugnetolo	1843	543	1844	155	1843	285
Roccaferrara	1653	1230	1920	52	1818	342
Sauna	1856	394	1856	151	1859	226
Sesta	1820	484	1820	144	1649	302
Signatico	1807	801	1808	235	1806	499
Vestana	1623	2229	1623	553	1622	1528
Villula	1566	1309	1720	217	1646	764
Monchio						
Casarola	1794	975	1870	181	1793	584
Ceda	1848	592	1889	75	1920	101
Cozzanello	1852	399	1894	73	1842	206
Lugagnano	1700	3005	1778	522	1765	1379
Monchio	1685	2900	1695	595	1748	1417
Pianadetto	1641	1734	1651	396	1630	1156
Riana	1618	1581	1619	353	1619	1140
Rigoso	1694	1346	1694	227	1695	770
Rimagna	1769	1068	1772	265	1769	609
Trefiumi	1697	1474	1698	342	1696	916
Valditacca	1800	1338	1800	327	1661	964
Palanzano						
Caneto	1766	857	1770	230	1768	572
Lalatta	1918	138	1919	73	1918	77
Nirone	1703	1054	1803	147	1782	500
Palanzano	1566	3894	1662	710	1660	2009
Pratopiano	1776	947	1776	264	1776	603
Ranzano	1710	1977	1803	483	1668	1263
Ruzzano	1633	1496	1800	259	1633	948
Trevignano	1622	783	1741	223	1832	385
Vaestano	1752	1446	1761	328	1748	934
Vairo	1710	1224	1711	290	1708	816
Valcieca	1745	761	1818	146	1877	223
Zibana	1595	1753	1566	522	1762	732
TOTAL	1565	71,985	1529	15,419	1604	40,148

5. Linking of Parish Registers to Form Genealogies

The first of two large-scale efforts to form genealogies from parish records began in the middle 1800's. M. Tanguay, a Canadian priest, reconstructed by hand the French Canadian population in its entirety from the first migrations (around 1620) to 1800 (Tanguay, 1871). The second major effort is the genealogical work of the Latter-day

Saints (Mormon) Church, which has produced the largest genealogical resource in the world and has established many files of great scientific utility.

In this century, scholars have attempted to develop systematic methods of record linking. L. Henry developed a method which gave precise rules to record linkers to avoid a product which was internally inconsistent but did not provide rules for resolving ambiguities which arise. Much has been done on the theoretical and methodological aspects of record linking (Acheson, 1964; Barrai *et al.*, 1965, 1968; Beauchamp *et al.*, 1973; Cavalli–Sforza, 1958; Cavalli–Sforza *et al.*, 1969; Charbonneau *et al.*, 1971; Felligi & Sunter, 1969; Kennedy, 1961, 1968; Kennedy *et al.*, 1964; Newcombe, 1967; Newcombe & Kennedy, 1962; Newcombe *et al.*, 1957, 1959, 1962; Skolnick, 1971, 1972, 1973, 1975; Skolnick *et al.*, 1971; Sunter, 1968; Sunter & Felligi, 1967; Winchester, 1970, 1973; Wrigley, 1966; Wrigley & Schofield, 1973). We will briefly review the methods used in Parma Valley.

Record linking by computer

The initial impetus for devising a computer algorithm was the need to link large quantities of data since results from linking isolated parishes may always be questioned in that they represent a very small population which may not be representative of a larger population. If the process could be computerized, the task of record linking could be reduced to one of data preparation, and large areas could be studied.

The method which we present follows decision-making techniques developed in artificial intelligence projects where computers are used in puzzle solving, chess playing, theorem proving, and similar examples of machine intelligence (Nilsson, 1971). The artificial intelligence approach consists of building a family of related solutions, developing a method of keeping the family of reasonable solutions small, and selecting the best solution with minimum effort and maximum accuracy.

The algorithms used attempted to follow one basic rule: find all of the possible links before making any decision. The links which appear to be unambiguously acceptable are made and distributions are generated from the records which are united by them. These distributions are then used to resolve the ambiguous cases. Manual record linking algorithms are in practice less systematic (Fleury & Henry, 1965; Wrigley, 1966). The researchers are generally instructed to solve ambiguous cases intuitively, and the result would undoubtedly reflect the biases of the researcher. No two researchers would necessarily come up with the same solution, and decisions about linking could be made to support the preconceived notions of the researcher. Because of its greater speed, the computer can be programmed to construct precise probabilities for each linkage and select the solution with the maximum probability of being correct. One can also present the other likely possibilities for examination and construct an index of confidence in each node of the genealogy.

The frequencies of the nominal identifiers (forenames and surnames) in the records to be linked form the basis of the likelihood that two records are linked by design (because they refer to the same person) or by chance. If one has the distribution of each forename and surname by time period, one can calculate the probability that a link between two records will occur by chance. Thus, if a record has much missing data, and the only data which are compatible consist of common names, the probability of a match made at random being compatible by name is quite large. If there are many identifiers, and some of them are rare names, the probability of a compatible match occurring by chance is quite low. In both cases, the probability of a chance occurrence can be estimated.

As a first approximation, each name can be considered independently. First name frequencies are considered to be the same as second name frequencies, but the surname distribution is constructed independently. The probability of a fortuitous association, P, is the product of the squares of the probabilities of all matching nominal identifiers (the person's names and his parents' names). Thus

$$P = \prod_{k=1}^{n} f_k{}^2 \qquad (1)$$

where the f_k are the relative frequencies in the population of the k matching names in the records being linked. The probability of two records chosen at random matching for the kth identifier is $f_k{}^2$, and for all k identifiers is therefore P.

The probability of a random association can be converted into a likelihood of a link being correct by using the following formula

$$L = \alpha/P \qquad (2)$$

where α is the probability of finding the link in the area of study.

The α will vary depending on whether a parish is on the border or in the middle of the area of study, on the amount of migration, and on the quantity of missing registers for neighboring parishes.

Although the number of matches between names (suggested by Wrigley & Schofield (1973) and Winchester (1973)) gives an indication of the quality of a link, the rarity of each nominal identifier is a more important factor.

Figure 1. Three examples of ambiguously linked records with log likelihoods attached to the links in the second and third cases.

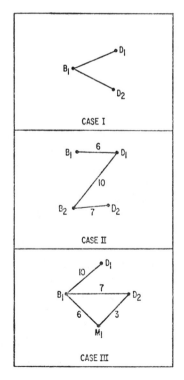

Case I of Figure 1 illustrates the importance that name frequencies may have in resolving ambiguity. In this case, one baptism (B) record can link to two death (D) records. Assume that the nominal information is the principal method of selecting a link. We might find records such as:

Baptism of   James John Smith, son of   John George and Mary Jane Jones (B_1)
Burial of   James Smith, son of   John and Mary Jane Jones (D_1)
Burial of   James John Smith, son of   John George and Mary (D_2)

In each B–D link, there are six matching names, the distinction being an additional match with the mother's surname and second name in one record and a match with the child's and the father's second name in the other. Clearly, the frequency of these four names holds the key to deciding which link to select. If one of them were rare, it would be less likely for there to be a random association, and the link with the rare name match should be selected. Random associations of this nature will occur more frequently in genetic isolates where the most common surnames often represent over one third of the residents of a parish (Skolnick, 1975; Yasuda *et al.*, 1973). Some forenames (such as Maria in Italy) are so common that they offer almost no additional identification.

Age error distributions from linked records

The likelihood of a link is made more precise by multiplying by the likelihood computed from age error distributions which are formed from records whose links are most certain. The criteria for certainty would vary from one data set to another, but in general the links which qualified as certain would be selected from unambiguous links or links which are clearly superior to their alternatives. Only those with high likelihoods, based on the name frequency distribution, should be used. The following age error distributions are calculated.

1. The difference between date of birth as estimated from the date of baptism and date of birth as calculated from the age at death and the date of death on burial records (for B–D links).

2. The difference between date of birth as estimated from the date of baptism and the date of birth as calculated from the age at marriage and the date of marriage on marriage records (for the B–M links).

3. The difference between date of birth as estimated from the age at burial and the date of burial, and the age at marriage and the date of marriage (for D–M links).

These distributions become important where the name matches are identical and age is present on the records. Where there is missing data and the date of birth cannot be estimated from death or marriage distributions, the mean value is used as the likelihood so that links with missing data will be preferred to links with poor fits. Similarly, in comparing two parent-child links, one can consider one link more likely than another if it is demographically more reasonable. For example, a mother-son link, where the mother's age at the birth of the child was 25, is much more probable than a link where her age at the birth of the child is 45. Thus, the distributions of the time between the vital events on the records of the child and the vital events on the records of the parents are calculated and converted into likelihoods.

Although considerable effort has gone into the question of scoring links to decide whether they are acceptable or not (Newcombe *et al.*, 1957, 1959; Beauchamp *et al.*, 1973; Newcombe, 1967), little attention has been given to the question of producing an overall linkage of multiple files which is maximal (Winchester, 1973). For example, consider the three links, B_1–D_1, B_2–D_1 and B_2–D_2 (Case II, Figure 1). Kennedy & Newcombe's method considers the decision to accept each of the three links as an independent problem, but several sets of solutions, i.e. B_1D_1 and B_1D_2, B_2–D_1 and B_2–D_2, B_1–D_1 and B_2–D_1 and B_2–D_2, are illogical as a person cannot be born twice nor can he die twice. The situations become more complex when marriage records and parent-child links are also considered. One of the major efforts in our reconstruction was the isolation of related sets of ambiguities for simultaneous resolution, as the most probable solution to such a problem cannot necessarily be found by sequentially selecting links and discarding inferior competitors (Skolnick, 1973, 1975).

Cases II and III of Figure 1 illustrate this problem. The numbers attached to the links represent log likelihoods. In both cases, resolution of the clump may involve rejection of the most likely individual link. In Case II, we have the choice between accepting a B_2–D_1 link and leaving B_1 and D_2 unlinked, or between accepting B_1–D_1 and B_2–D_2 links and rejecting the single highest scoring link. In Case III, the two most acceptable solutions are accepting the B_1–D_1 and M_1–D_2 links or accepting the B_1–M_1, B_1–D_2, M_1–D_2 links and leaving D_1 unlinked. In both cases accepting the highest score for the lump of links as a whole (adding the log likelihoods) means rejecting the highest scoring link. If our assumption of independence of linking decisions is correct, the log likelihoods are additive and we should accept the highest total score. While we are dissatisfied with having rejected the highest single score, we would be even more dissatisfied with rejecting two scores whose total is even greater than the highest score.

The second major problem illustrated by these cases is that the number of links in each solution varies, and the number of historical persons implied also varies (Kelley *et al.*, 1972). In Case II, one solution implies one resident, one immigrant and one emigrant; and the other solution implies two residents. Correct resolution of such cases is therefore extremely important if migration is to be accurately estimated from reconstructed genealogies.

Our idealized method of record linking first finds all potential links and ties together a number of records into a clump composed of all the records which link to one another. Where there are no ambiguities, the record linking is finished. Where there are ambiguities, they should be resolved simultaneously to produce the solution which is most likely to be correct. This ideal method was not possible to implement and in some cases not necessary. Much of the methodology required to link the records in a genealogy (Skolnick, 1973, 1975) dealt with problems of streamlining this approach without losing precision.

6. Analysis

The analysis of the genealogy is in progress, and in this paper, some of the more interesting preliminary results are reported. They fall into four broad categories: (a) the age at marriage and age difference of spouses, (b) family size distributions, (c) the length of generation, and (d) migration and the calculation of the inbreeding coefficient.

Table 2   **Means, variances and standard errors of age difference between husband and wife by husband's age and century**

		Husband's age at marriage								
		≤19	20–24	25–29	30–34	35–39	40–44	45–49	≥50	TOTAL
	Before 1799									
	Mean	−8·58	−2·81	1·41	4·56	7·44	10·03	19·19	27·09	4·34
	Variance	79·15	62·93	57·56	81·71	80·11	130·55	75·71	215·53	137·07
	Standard error	1·37	0·68	0·50	0·66	0·84	1·49	1·47	2·29	0·40
	Frequency	42	135	232	190	114	59	35	41	848
Age difference between husband and wife	**1800–1899**									
	Mean	−7·56	−1·30	2·14	5·27	8·45	10·22	12·35	21·63	4·75
	Variance	65·90	45·72	31·47	36·20	48·35	53·68	91·89	140·04	75·81
	Standard error	1·41	0·38	0·22	0·28	0·18	0·63	1·38	1·20	0·20
	Frequency	33	316	632	451	267	134	48	98	1979
	1900+									
	Mean	−2·80	0·88	3·45	5·31	8·32	10·18	12·54	16·13	4·29
	Variance	42·10	16·77	17·50	26·86	31·46	62·04	55·94	143·54	36·37
	Standard error	0·93	0·18	0·13	0·22	0·37	0·80	1·11	1·63	0·12
	Frequency	49	544	1042	566	229	96	45	54	2625
	TOTAL									
	Mean	−6·03	−0·31	2·77	5·18	8·21	10·17	14·29	21·25	4·47
	Variance	66·97	34·07	27·58	38·97	47·90	71·55	82·78	170·00	66·36
	Standard error	0·73	0·19	0·12	0·18	0·28	0·50	0·80	0·94	0·11
	Frequency	124	995	1906	1207	610	289	128	193	5452

Table 3   **Marriages by age of husband by century for marriages with both husband and wife linked to baptism records**

	≤1799	1800–1899	≥1900	Total
Husband's age				
≤19	0·05	0·02	0·02	0·02
20–24	0·16	0·16	0·21	0·18
25–29	0·27	0·32	0·40	0·35
30–34	0·22	0·23	0·22	0·22
35–39	0·13	0·13	0·09	0·11
40–44	0·07	0·07	0·04	0·05
45–49	0·04	0·02	0·02	0·02
≥50	0·05	0·05	0·02	0·04
Age at marriage				
Mean	32·04	31·97	29·73	30·90
Variance	89·36	72·40	46·78	63·95
Standard error	0·32	0·13	0·11	0·08
Total Marriages	848	1979	2625	5452

Age and age differences at marriage

The mean age at marriage, age differences at marriage, and secular changes in these patterns are of fundamental socio-economic interest. They are also important for the population geneticist in that they are an important factor in determining and controlling family size and variance in the distribution of family size, which in turn is an important component of genetic drift.

Table 2 gives the age difference between husband and wife by century of marriage. The age difference has been nearly constant over time but the variance in the age difference has dropped considerably, for both the total and the age specific age differences. Table 3 shows that the mean age at marriage is quite high but has fallen in recent years, and that the variance in the distribution has also fallen considerably. The distribution is skewed to the right but this skewedness has also decreased.

Figure 2 presents an interesting phenomena. When the age difference is negative, the

Figure 2. Mean age at marriage for husbands and wives by difference in age at marriage.

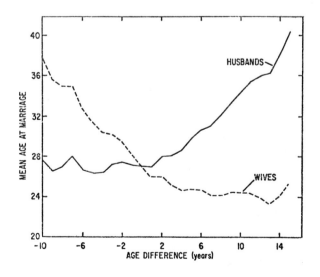

mean age of the male is constant and rather high, and the age of the female increases. Similarly, if the husband is more than three years older than the wife, her age remains approximately constant and his age increases. Therefore, models which incorporate age difference at age of marriage must also account for the fact that the mean age difference is age specific and that the pattern of age difference also has a characteristic form.

Family size distributions

Four measures of family size have been tabulated. They are all measures of children ever born and allocation by century was based on the date of marriage. The first three are attempts to measure family size for all producing couples, varying the criteria for being considered a producing couple and the child of the couple as follows.

Criterion I—accept all couples and their children even if only the death record is found.

Criterion II—exclude couples where only the death record is found for the parents and don't count children if only a death record is attached to the parents. If the marriage record is missing, calculate the date of marriage as the baptism date of the father plus 30 years.

Criterion III—the parents must have a marriage record, and the children with only death records are excluded.

Criterion IV measures completed family size for producing couples and couples are selected in the following manner: If the baptism, marriage, and death records are present for the wife, then she must either die after age 45 or be married for 25 years. If the baptism record is missing, she must live for 25 years after her marriage. The effective number of reproductive years of the marriage is then calculated as the minimum of 25 and the date of her death minus the date of her marriage, and the husband must live that number of years after the date of marriage.

Table 4	Number of children ever born by three criteria and for completed families by century					
	<1699	1700–1799	1800–1899	1900+	Missing date	TOTAL
Criterion I						
Mean	3·19	3·51	4·53	2·82	2·77	3·37
Standard deviation	2·76	3·13	3·62	2·32	2·50	2·99
Standard error	0·06	0·06	0·05	0·04	0·03	0·02
Frequency	1918	2860	5293	4278	6424	20773
Criterion II						
Mean	3·24	3·52	4·24	2·76		3·46
Standard deviation	2·58	2·82	3·19	2·23		2·82
Standard error	0·05	0·05	0·04	0·03		0·02
Frequency	2200	2900	5725	5804	3	16632
Criterion III						
Mean	4·07	4·56	4·95	2·93		3·99
Standard deviation	2·80	3·11	3·24	2·26		2·96
Standard error	0·08	0·08	0·05	0·03		0·03
Frequency	1155	1553	4011	4592	2	11313
Completed family size						
Mean	—	6·79	7·53	6·50		7·34
Standard deviation	—	3·27	3·28	3·08		3·26
Standard error	—	0·25	0·10	0·26		0·09
Frequency	20	170	1059	135	0	1384

Figure 3. Family size distributions by three criteria (see text).

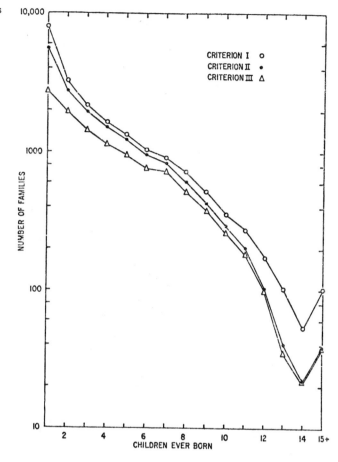

Table 4 summarizes the results by criterion and century, Figure 3 compares the distributions for the three criteria, and Figure 4 shows the secular trend for the third criterion. Family size distributions under all four criteria show a peak in the 19th century with family size dropping considerably in the 20th century. The figures for the 20th century are too low for the first three distributions since some families will not have completed their fertility. Only the measure of completed fertility is accurate in the 20th century and it is only slightly lower than during the 18th century. Given the high standard errors in these periods, even this comparison is uncertain. Figure 5 gives the distribution of completed fertility which is characterized by a mean smaller than the mode and by skewedness to the right.

One interpretation of the rise in family size during the 19th century is that as death rates fell, families were not being broken up as often, the mean reproductive period increased in length, and therefore, without extensive birth control, family sizes increased.

The distributions based on the first two criteria are nearly the same. The families missing the date of marriage by the first criterion are distributed by the second criterion. However, the family size for the third criterion is considerably higher and this may be caused by several factors.

Figure 4. Family size distributions by century.

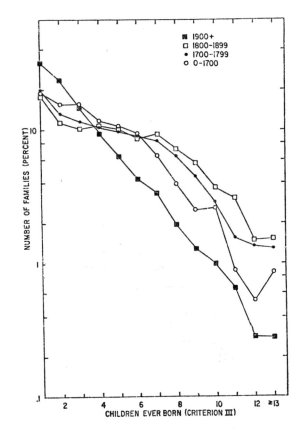

Figure 5. Family size distributions for couples with maximum reproductive periods.

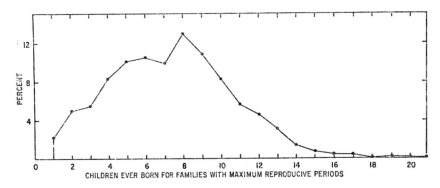

Some of the families counted under I and II but not under III are migrants. Figure 6 gives family size for migrants and non-migrants and Table 5 summarizes the means and variances of migrant and non-migrant fertility by century. It is interesting to note that if the mother is a migrant, family size decreased slightly, but if the father is a migrant, then the family size is greatly reduced. This is as one would expect since it is fairly normal in this area for a woman to change parishes when she marries but less normal for a man to do so.

Figure 6. Family size distributions by migrant status.

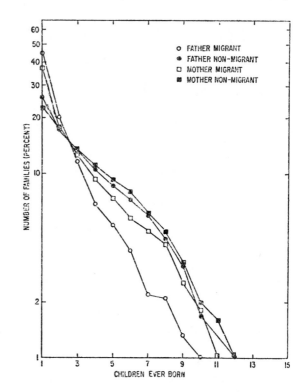

Table 5   **Fertility of migrants and non-migrants**

	Father		Mother	
	Non-migrant	Migrant	Non-migrant	Migrant
<1799				
Mean	3·59	2·36	3·92	3·42
Variance	2·66	2·07	2·73	2·87
Standard error	0·05	0·10	0·09	0·14
1800–1849				
Mean	4·62	3·33	4·57	3·93
Variance	2·97	2·69	2·89	2·95
Standard error	0·09	0·19	0·11	0·14
1850–1899				
Mean	4·91	3·13	4·77	3·92
Variance	2·97	2·59	2·97	2·88
Standard error	0·07	0·15	0·08	0·10
>1900				
Mean	2·74	2·08	3·39	2·80
Variance	2·03	1·59	2·52	2·33
Standard error	0·04	0·07	0·05	0·07
TOTAL				
Mean	3·74	2·57	3·97	3·40
Variance	2·73	2·21	2·79	2·70
Standard error	0·03	0·06	0·04	0·05

Two factors may act to reduce fertility of migrant males. The first is that the lands which migrants can settle in the area may be less productive. Fertility differentials may also be related to the cause for migration. Since the Parma Valley is not capable of supporting sustained expansion, it is not incorrect to assume that many of those who migrate did so because they did not inherit the homestead or were forced to migrate for other economic reasons. As the farms were generally not divided if there were several potential heirs, the reduced fertility might be due to a differential age at marriage for migrants. A first son would generally be a non-migrant and could marry immediately, being economically secure with his inheritance. He would continue to work the fields already under cultivation and he would have to make no investment to house his family. A migrant, on the other hand, would have to seek funds to build a house and clear the fields. His circumstances could cause him to be older at his marriage. Their relatively disadvantaged economic status may cause greater infant mortality among their offspring or increased morbidity or mortality for themselves. They may have decreased fecundity, either voluntary or because of a lowered nutritional level, or they may delay family building after marriage until they have achieved more economic stability.

Once the burdens of migration were overcome, one might expect that these families would function normally in society. One might also find that migrants who move short distances are also supported to a certain extent by being members of a greater family at close proximity. As the distance of migration increased, or in the rare instances that the family was known to migrate during the formation of the family (measured by the distance between the birthplaces of a sibship), the above effects might be exaggerated. Further analysis of the effects of migration on family building are in progress so that the overall fitness of migrants can be evaluated. These differences cannot be explained in terms of data biases. One might say that some children of migrants are born out of the study area, but this explanation ignores the large differences found between male and female migrants. Another possibility is that in the absence of a marriage record, the children assigned to baptism and deaths are broken into several families but this would require a greater difference between the distributions found by criteria I and II. This analysis of migrants demonstrates the danger of analyses based on single parishes. The differences shown between families of migrants and non-migrants are of major demographic importance and further analyses may show still other differences between families which can be reconstructed from a single parish and families whose vital events cross parish boundaries.

Length of generation

Two important parameters in determining the genetic structure of populations are the mean and variance of the length of generation. Figure 7 gives three measures of this distribution: (a) the time between the baptism of a child and the baptism of his father, (b) the time between baptism of a child and the baptism of his mother, and (c) the time of marriage of the parents and marriage of the child. It is interesting to note that the mean length of generation measured with baptism records is longer and has a larger variance if measured using the father's date than with the mother's date. In particular, the right hand tail of the distribution is missing because of menopause. Table 6 gives the means and variances of these distributions computed from totally unambiguous links. There is considerable difference in the mean of the three measures and although the distribution of marriage length has an intermediate mean, its variance is greater than

Figure 7. Three measures of the length of generation.

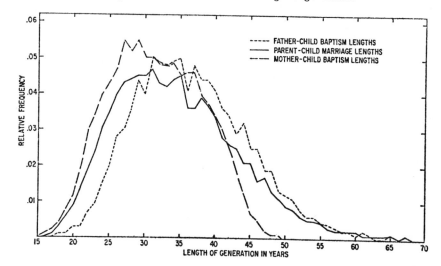

Table 6	**Means and variances of three measures of the lengths of generation**			
	Number of links	Mean	Variance	Standard error
Father-child birth intervals	9528	36·75	66·88	0·08
Parent-child marriage intervals	8950	34·89	83·55	0·10
Mother-child birth intervals	9620	31·68	42·14	0·07

either the father–child or the mother–child baptism lengths. To resolve this dilemma, one might compute an effective length of generation to make an analogy with effective population size. This would require weighting the generation length of individuals by their reproductive success, since fitness may be parity specific and generation time is, by its nature, parity specific.

Migration and calculation of the inbreeding coefficient

A migration matrix has been prepared to compare the calculation of the inbreeding coefficient using the method of Bodmer & Cavalli-Sforza (1968) with a calculation based on gene frequencies. The migration matrix which has been summarized in Table 7 is the cumulation of father–child and mother–child birthplaces. As migration from the outside world cannot be directly measured, the most remote parishes are kept within the migration matrix and migration from the other known parishes is used as an indicator of migration from the outside world. The sixteen parishes most isolated from the outside world were included in the migration matrix and their effective population sizes were estimated from the average number of marriages per generation. The parent–child matrix gives an equilibrium inbreeding coefficient of 0·0265 after 30 generations. This rather high value does compare favorably with the observed variation of gene frequencies which gives a value of 0·0356. The factors which contribute to this difference are being examined. No correlation was found between effective population size and rate of migration.

Table 7   **Parishes included in the migration matrix
and their estimated effective population sizes**

Parish	Effective population size	% Non- migrants	% Internal migration	% Migration from outside
Bosco	100	95·9	3·4	0·7
Grammatica	40	93·0	4·5	2·5
Mossale	50	83·8	15·3	0·9
Sesta	30	51·5	41·1	7·4
Casarola	65	88·4	7·1	4·5
Ceda	33	88·2	9·2	2·6
Lugagnano	80	55·0	33·2	11·7
Monchio	85	83·4	7·2	9·5
Pianadetto	45	88·2	13·1	4·7
Riana	33	80·8	10·8	8·4
Rigoso	50	94·0	5·3	0·7
Rimagna	50	73·7	20·6	5·8
Trefiumi	50	80·0	18·0	2·1
Valditacca	60	86·5	10·0	3·5
Nirone	40	82·5	9·3	8·2
Valcieca	45	80·3	13·2	6·5

7. Conclusion

A genealogy was constructed of Parma Valley, Italy, using records of baptisms, marriages, and deaths in parish registers which go back to the 16th century. This was accomplished by computerized record linking. Methods were devised for efficiently generating a maximum likelihood linkage of multiple files. Ambiguities were resolved by generating likelihood scores for a clump of ambiguous links and accepting the overall solution with the highest total likelihood score.

Various demographic parameters were examined using this data. The mean age at marriage is quite high but has fallen in the 20th century, along with the variance in the distribution. The age difference between partners at marriage has been nearly constant over time but the variance in the age difference has dropped considerably for both the total and the age specific differences. The mean age difference is age specific and the pattern of age difference has a characteristic form. When family size was compared by centuries, it was found to peak in the 19th century and drop off in the 20th century. A distribution was shown for children ever born for families with maximum reproductive periods. When family size was compared for migrants vs. non-migrants, it was found that migrants tended to have smaller families, but this trend was much more pronounced when the father was the migrant. Factors affecting fertility of migrant males were discussed. Generation length was estimated by comparing the date of baptism of a child with its parents and between the marriage of a child and the marriage of its parents, and the inbreeding coefficient was calculated using a migration matrix.

We wish to thank L. Soliani, C. Matessi, B. Baty, J. Gillette and K. deNevers for comments and assistance in preparing this manuscript.

This research has been supported by an Italian C.N.R. grant for historical demography (number 72.0020.10/115.3976), a U.S. Atomic Energy Commission grant (number AT (04-31-326)), and a PHS Grant No. RR07092 to the University of Utah.

References

Acheson, E. D. (1964). The Oxford Record Linkage Study. A review of the method with some preliminary results. *Proceedings of the Royal Society of Medicine* **57**, 11.

Acheson, E. D. (1968). *Record Linkage in Medicine.* London: E. & S. Livingstone, Ltd.

Azevedo, E., Morton, N. E., Miki, C. & Yee, S. (1969). Distance and kinship in Northeastern Brazil. *American Journal of Human Genetics* **21** (1), 1–22.

Bachi, R., Baron, R. & Nathan, G. (1967). Methods of record-linkage and applications in Israel. *Bulletin of the I.S.I.* **42**, 766.

Barrai, I., Cavalli–Sforza, L. L. & Moroni, A. (1962). Frequencies of consanguineous marriages and mating structure of the population. *Annals of Human Genetics, London* **25**, 347–376.

Barrai, I., Cavalli–Sforza, L. L. & Moroni, A. (1965). Record linkage from parish books. In *Mathematics and Computer Science in Biology and Medicine.* London: John Blackburn Ltd. pp 51–60.

Barrai, I. & Moroni, A. (1965). Variazione secolare della consanguineita nella Diocesi di Reggio Emilia. *Atti A.G.I.* **10**, 320–326.

Barrai, I., Cavalli–Sforza, L. L. & Moroni, A. (1969). The prediction of consanguineous marriages. *Japanese Journal of Genetics* **44** (Suppl. 1), 230–233.

Barrai, I., Moroni, A. & Cavalli–Sforza, L. L. (1968). Further studies on record linkage from parish books. In (E. D. Acheson, ed.), *Record Linkage in Medicine.* London: E. & S. Livingstone Ltd.

Beauchamp, P., Charbonneau, H. & Lavoie, Y. (1973). Reconstitution automatique des familles par le programme 'Hochelaga'. *Population* **26**, 39–58.

Bodmer, W. F. (1968). Demographic approaches to the measurement of differential selection in human populations. *Proceedings of the National Academy of Sciences* **59** (3), 690–699.

Bodmer, W. F. & Cavalli–Sforza, L. L. (1968). A migration matrix model for the study of random genetic drift. *Genetics* **59**, 565–592.

Bodmer, W. F. & Jacquard, A. (1968). La variance de la dimension des familles. *Population* **23**, 870–878.

Buchanan, B. G., Sutherland, G. L. & Feigenbaum, E. A. (1969). Heuristic dendral: a program for generating explanatory hypotheses in organic chemistry. In (B. Meltzer and D. Mikie, eds.), *Machine Intelligence IV.* Edinburgh: Edinburgh U. Press. pp 209–254.

Cann, H. M. & Cavalli–Sforza, L. L. (1968). Effects of grandparental and parental age, birth order, and geographic variation on the sex ratio of liveborn and stillborn infants. *American Journal of Human Genetics* **20**(4), 381–391.

Cavalli–Sforza, L. L. (1958). Some data on the genetic structure of human populations. *Proceedings of the Tenth International Genetics* **1**, 389–407. Toronto: U. of Toronto Press.

Cavalli–Sforza, L. L. (1960). Demographic attacks on genetic problems. In *The Use of Vital and Health Statistics for Genetic and Radiation Studies* (Proceedings of the seminar sponsored by the United Nations and the World Health Organization). New York: United Nations.

Cavalli–Sforza, L. L. (1962). Demographic attacks on genetic problems. Some possibilities and results. In *The Use of Vital and Health Statistics for Genetic and Radiation Studies* (Proceedings of the seminar sponsored by the United Nations and the World Health Organization). New York: United Nations.

Cavalli–Sforza, L. L. (1963). The distribution of migration distances: models and applications to genetics. In *Human Displacements* (Entriens de Monaco en sciences humaines, Premiere session 1962), pp. 139–158.

Cavalli–Sforza, L. L. (1966). Population structure and human evolution. *Proceedings of the Royal Society B* **164**, 362–379.

Cavalli–Sforza, L. L. (1969a). Human diversity. *Proceedings of the Twelfth International Congress on Genetics* **3**, 405–416.

Cavalli–Sforza, L. L. (1969b). Genetic drift in an Italian population. *Scientific American* **221**(2), 20–37.

Cavalli–Sforza, L. L., Barrai, I. & Moroni, A. (1969). Family reconstitution by computer. *World Conference on Records and Genealogical Seminar* Salt Lake City, Utah, U.S.A., pp 1–7.

Cavalli–Sforza, L. L., Conterio, F. & Moroni, A. (1970). Valutazione del carico genetico in relazione ai matrimoni fra consanguinei. *54th Cong. Naz. Soc. Ital. di Ost. e Ginecol.* Milano, pp 10–22.

Cavalli–Sforza, L. L., Kimura, M. & Barrai, I. (1966). The probability of consanguineous marriages. *Genetics* **54**, 37–60.

Chapman, A. M. & Jacquard, A. (1971). Un isolat d'Amérique Centrale, Les Indiens Jicaques du Honduras. Paris: I.N.E.D, Cahier No. 60.

Charbonneau, H., Lavoie, Y. & Legare, J. (1971). Etude des caracteristiques nominatives dans l'etat civil et les recensements Canadiens du XVII e Siecle: prelude a l'utilisation des ordinateurs pour le jumelage des donnees. *Colloque Int. de Demographie Historique.* XVII–XVIII Siecles.

Chaventre, A. (1972). I.—Les Kel Kummer, isolat social. *Population, Paris* **27**, 771–783.

Conterio, R. and Barrai, I. (1966). Effetti della consanguineita suila mortalita e sulla morbilita nella popolazione della diocesi di Parma. *Atti Ass. Genet. Ital.* **11**, 378–391.

Edwards, A. W. F. (1972). *Likelihood.* Cambridge: Cambridge University Press.

Feigenbaum, E. A., Buchanan, B. G. & Lederberg, J. (1970). On generality and problem solving: a case study using the dendral program. Stanford Artificial Intelligence Project Memo AIM-131.

Felligi, I. P. & Sunter, A. B. (1969). A theory for record linkage. *Journal of the American Statistical Association* **64,** 1183–1210.

Fisher, R. A. (1958). *The Genetical Theory of Natural Selection, 2nd Edition.* New York: Dover. (First edition of this book published in 1930.)

Fleury, M. & Henry, L. (1965). *Nouveau Manuel de Depouillement et D'Exploitation de l'Etat Civil Ancien.* Paris: Ed. de l'Institut National d'Etudes Demographiques.

Gautier, E. & Henry, L. (1958). *La population de Crulai, parcisse normande; etude historique.* Paris: I.N.E.D., Cahier No. 33.

Glass, B., Sacks, M. S., Jahn, E. F. & Hess, C. (1952). Genetic drift in a religious isolate: an analysis of the causes of variation in blood group and other gene frequencies in a small population. *American Naturalist* **86,** 145–159.

Godbout (1951–65). [Partial revisions of the Dictionnaire genealogique des familles Canadiennes by Tanguay appeared frequently in *Rapport de l'Archiviste de la Province de Quebec,* Quebec City, Canada.]

Hajnal, J. (1963). Random mating and the frequency of cosanguineous marriages. *Proceedings of the Royal Society B* **159,** 125–177.

Jacquard, A. (1967). La reproduction humaine en regime malthusien. *Population* **22,** 897–920.

Jacquard, A. (1972). II.—Evolution du patrimoine genetique des Kel Kummer. *Population, Paris* **27,** 784–800.

Kelley, R., Skolnick, M. & Yasuda, N. (1972). A combinatorial problem in linking historical records. *Historical Methods Newsletter* **6**(1), 10–16.

Kennedy, J. M. (1961). *Linkage of Birth and Marriage Records Using a Digital Computer.* Document No. AECL-1258, Atomic Energy of Canada Ltd, Chalk River, Ontario.

Kennedy, J. M. (1968). File structures for the automatic manipulation of linked records. In (Acheson, E.D., ed.), *Record Linkage in Medicine.* London: E. & S. Livingstone Ltd. pp 109–119.

Kennedy, J. M. *et al.* (1964). List processing methods for organizing files of linked records. Doc. No. AECL-2078, Atomic Energy of Canada Ltd, Chalk River, Ontraio.

Langaney, A. & Gomila, J. (1973). Bedik and Niokholonko: intra- and inter-ethnic migration, *Human Biology* **45**(2), 137–150.

Langaney, A., Gomila, J. & Bouloux, C. (1972). Bedik: bioassay of kinship. *Human Biology, Wayne State U. Press* **44**(3), 475–488.

Lederberg, J., Sutherland, G. L., Buchanan, B. G. & Feigenbaum, E. A. (1969). A heuristic program for solving a scientific inference problem. Summary of motivation and implementation. Stanford A. I. Memo AIM-104.

Major Genealogical Record Sources for Italy. The Genealogical Society of the Church of Jesus Christ of Latter-day Saints, Inc. Research Paper, Series G, No 2. Salt Lake City: Publishers Press.

Moroni, A. (1960). Sources, reliability and usefulness of consanguinity data with special reference to Catholic records. In *The Use of Vital and Health Statistics for Genetic and Radiation Studies,* UN-WHO Seminar Sept, 1960, U.N., New York. *World Health Organization Chronicle* **15,** 465–472.

Moroni, A. (1963). Consanguinity studies in Italy. *Proceedings of the 11th International Congress on Genetics.* In *Journal of Genetics* **64.**

Moroni, A. (1969). *Historical Demography, Human Ecology and Consanguinity.* London: International Union for the Scientific Study of Population, General Conference. p. 2427.

Morton, N. E. (1961). Morbidity of children from consanguineous marriages. In (A. G. Steinberg, ed.) *Progress in Medical Genetics, Vol.* 1. New York: Grune and Stratton.

Neel, J. V. (1970). Lessons from a "primitive" people. *Science* **170**(3960), 815–822.

Newcombe, H. B. (1965). Record linkage: concepts and potentialities. In *Mathematics and Computer Science in Biology and Medicine.* London: Medical Research Council. pp. 43–49.

Newcombe, H. B. (1967). Record linking: the design of efficient systems for linking records into individual and family histories. *American Journal of Human Genetics* **19**(3), 335–359.

Newcombe, H. B. & Kennedy, J. M. (1962). Record linkage: making maximum use of the discriminating power of identifying information. *Communications of the Association of Computing Machinery* **5,** 563–566.

Newcombe, H. B. & Rhynas, P. O. W. (1962). Family linkage of population records. U.N./W.H.O. Seminar on *Use of Vital and Health Statistics for Genetic and Radiation Studies.* U.N. Pub. Sales No. 61, XVII, i (1962), 135–154.

Newcombe, H. B., James, A. P. & Axford, S. J. (1957). Family linkage of vital and health records. *CRB-717.* Atomic Energy of Canada Ltd, Chalk River, Ontario.

Newcombe, H. B., Kennedy, J. M., Axford, S. J. & James, A. P. (1959). Automatic linkage of vital records. *Science* **130,** 954–959.

Nilsson, N. S. (1971). *Problem Solving in A.I.* New York: McGraw-Hill.

Ohkubo, T. (1963). Consanguineous marriages in West-Southern Sado. *Japanese Journal of Human Genetics* **8**(2), 128–135.

Roberts, D. F. (1968). Genetic effects of population size reduction. *Nature* **220,** 1084–1088.

Serra, A. (1961). La consanguineita e i suoi effetti nelle popolazioni umane. In (L. Gedda, ed.) *De Genetica Medica*. Rome: Apud Mendelianum Institutum.

Skolnick, M. (1971). A computer program for linking historical records. *Historical Methods Newsletter* **4**, 4.

Skolnick, M. (1972). Heuristic searches in data reconstruction. *Proceedings of 2nd Int. Congress of Cybernetics and Systems*. Oxford, August.

Skolnick, M. (1973). Resolution of ambiguities in record linking. In (E. A. Wrigley, ed.), *Identifying People in the Past*. London: Edward Arnold Ltd. pp. 102–127.

Skolnick, M., Moroni, A., Cannings, C. & Cavalli–Sforza, L. L. (1971). The reconstruction of genealogies from parish registers. In (Hodson, F. R., Kendall, D. G., and Tautu, P., eds.), *Mathematics in the Archeological and Historical Sciences*. Edinburgh: Edinburgh University Press. pp. 319–334.

Skolnick, M., Cavalli–Sforza, L. L., Moroni, A., Siri, E. & Soliani, L. (1973). A reconstruction of historical persons from the parish registers of Parma Valley, Italy. *Genus, Rome* **29**, 103–155.

Skolnick, M. (1975). The construction and analysis of genealogies with a case study of Parma Valley, Italy. Ph.D. Thesis, Stanford University.

Sunter, A. B. (1968). A statistical approach to record linkage. In (E. D. Acheson, ed.) *Record Linkage in Medicine*. London: E. & S. Livingstone Ltd. pp. 89–109.

Sunter, A. B. & Felligi, I. P. (1967). An optimal theory of record linkage." *Bulletin of the I.S.I.* **42**, 809–839.

Sutter, J. & Tabah, L. (1952). Effets de la consanguinite et de l'endogamie. *Population* **7**, 249–266.

Tanguay, Abbe Cyprien (1871). *Dictionnaire Généalogique des Familles Canadiennes*. Montreal: Eusebe Sénécal.

Winchester, I. (1970). The linkage of historical records by man and computer: techniques and problems. *Journal of Interdisciplinary History* **1**, 107–124.

Winchester, I. (1973). On referring to ordinary historical persons. In E. A. Wrigley, ed.) *Identifying People in the Past*. London: Edward Arnold Ltd. pp. 17–40.

Wrigley, E. A. (1966). *An Introduction to English Historical Demography*. London: Weidenfeld and Nicolson.

Wrigley, E. A. & Schofield, R. S. (1973). Nominal record linkage by computer and the logic of family reconstitution. In (E. A. Wrigley, ed.) *Identifying People in the Past*. London: Edward Arnold Ltd. pp. 64–101.

D. F. Roberts
M. Mohan

Department of Human Genetics,
University of Newcastle upon Tyne,
19 Claremont Place,
Newcastle upon Tyne,
NE2 4AA, England

History, Demography and Genetics: The Fiji Experience and its Evolutionary Implications

1. Introduction

Had it been technically and physically possible in 1870 to examine the ABO blood groups of all the inhabitants of the Fiji islands, the survey would have shown the blood group B gene to be present at a frequency of about 9 %. Such a survey today would give double that frequency, about 18 %. A change of gene frequency as great as this in any other species would suggest the operation of natural selection and, by analogy, one might suppose that individuals with the B gene were endowed with improved survival in the conditions on Fiji, greater successful fertility, or a combination of both. This is not the explanation. It is a direct result of a succession of quirks of history, and illustrates a type of evolutionary process different from the usual interpretation of natural selection as favouring fitter individuals.

The historical events which had such repercussions took place on the other side of the world from Fiji. First, there was the demand in fashionable Europe for spices and scents. This led to the search for and exploitation of sandalwood; many of the traders so engaged were unprincipled adventurers seeking fortunes at the cost of ruthless shedding of native blood, and Fiji suffered greatly. Before their coming, the Fijian social system incorporated intermittent warring between groups, in the usual Melanesian pattern, which undoubtedly had demographic effects, but did not pose a threat to the survival of the population as a whole. The intrinsic balance of the strife, however, was upset by the European contacts, for when the competition for sandalwood was keen, captains offered the help of their crews in war as an independent inducement to cut cargoes, with massive destructive effect on the population. Moreover, from its previous relative isolation, the Fiji population provided virgin soil for foreign diseases. Disastrous epidemics consistently followed the first contact with Europeans, and for a century death-dealing epidemics swept through the islands.

Secondly, in the sophisticated world there were the technical advances of the 1840's; coconut oil came to be used in the manufacture of soap and candles, trade in coconut oil from Fiji developed, and indeed this became the principal export. In 1855, phosphate was found in Fiji, companies for its exploitation were established, and by about 1870 peak production was attained. Thirdly, there was the occurrence of the American Civil War in 1861; the cotton supply to the north was cut off, so the Union (and other countries similarly affected) started looking towards the Pacific Islands to compensate the loss. In Fiji cotton replaced coconut oil as the principal export as early as 1866, and by 1870 the cotton industry in Fiji was worth over £90,000. There was a flow of incomers from many European nations to settle and exploit the agricultural or commercial potential of the islands, disputing amongst themselves but the majority believing that their interests should predominate when there was any conflict with those of the natives.

But the key development for the purposes of the present analysis was that of sugar-planting, again in response to the continually increasing demand for sugar in Western Europe, again a quirk of fashion. The establishment of the sugar industry in Fiji in 1873 created a strong demand for labour. The Fijians had proved unsuitable for plantation labour, so this demand could not be met by them nor by workers from the other Pacific Islands, and negotiations were commenced in 1877 with the Government of India, to obtain Indian labourers. Their advent was eagerly anticipated in Fiji "to avoid a period of stagnation and paralysis, most damaging and disastrous to all interested in the prosecution of agricultural enterprise" (Colonial Office, 83/20, 27 October 1879). An ingenious indenture system was devised, by which after 5 years of service and then a further 5 years of residence in the colony the Indians were entitled to the return passage free to India.

The first group of 481 Indian recruits arrived in Fiji from Calcutta in May 1879. Thus, all the movement of this population falls within the period over which census data are available for analysis (registration of births and deaths of Fijians began in 1875, and the first census was made in 1879). Over the years the immigrants came to be in great demand and the numbers rose (Table 1). For instance, in 1882, 908 immigrants were able to satisfy the plantations' needs, but in 1884 applications for new labourers totalled 1790. The cost of their introduction fell from £21 4s 1¼d in 1884 to £16 15s 7d in 1890. In 1889 return passages began, but while a number of Indians left the colony every year, others chose to remain as settlers. It was not always possible for immigrants to come as members of families, since most men only made the decision through sheer

Table 1   **Immigrant voyages 1879–89**

Name of vessel	Year	Length of voyage (days)	No. embarked	No. of births	No. of deaths	Rate of mortality (%)	No. disembarked
Leonidas	1879	72	498	1	19	3·80	480
Berar	1882	93	431	4	6	1·37	429
Poonah	1882	81	491	2	14	2·83	479
Poonah	1883	74	518	1	23	4·43	498
Bayard	1883	86	499	3	6	1·19	496
Syria	1884	58	497	1	4	0·80	494
Howrah	1884	78	513	6	18	3·46	501
Pericles	1884	54	487	—	25	5·13	462
Newnham	1884	58	592	3	20	3·36	575
Main	1885	72	723	2	2	0·27	723
Ganges	1885	76	540	1	18	3·32	523
Boyne	1886	73	549	6	19	3·42	536
Bruce	1886	70	463	2	7	1·50	458
Hereford	1888	69	537	4	3	0·55	538
Moy	1889	67	675	3	1	0·14	677

Table 2   **Indian migration 1890–1900**

Year	Number introduced	Births	Total in colony	Returned to India	Deaths	Percentage of deaths	No. remaining in colony at end of year
1890	1161	125	7712	149	181	2·34	7382
1891	1040	222	8644	427	229	2·65	7988
1892	1534	209	9731	496	245	2·51	8990
1893	777	253	10 020	573	280	2·79	9167
1894	1085	277	10 529	1067	295	2·79	9167
1895	1418	274	10 859	608	397	3.56	9854
1896	1191	273	11 418	684	258	2·26	10 476
1897	1331	441	12 248	35*	253	2.01	11 960
1898	573	506	13 039	413	229	1·75	12 397
1899	931	501	13 829	571	258	1·86	13 280
1900	2275	559	16 114	403	343	2·13	15 368

* Emigration from Fiji was restricted on account of the famine in India 1896–7.

necessity, but the Indian Emigration Acts had laid down that there should be a proportion of at least 40 women to every 100 men. A number of children were born en route or in Fiji, and indeed amongst the first return passages in 1889 were 67 such children (Table 2). As a result of the Indian presence, the colony, which during the previous 26 years had been trying to balance on precarious funds, at the turn of the century found itself on the road to prosperity. Recruitment of labour in India was stopped under the Defence of India Act, 1917, indenture was categorically abolished in 1920, and in 1922 the Government of India specifically prohibited the emigration of Indian unskilled workers. Thus, the steady flow of Indian immigrants into Fiji that had continued over 38 years came to an end. Migration thereafter was sporadic.

The arrival of the first shipload initiated the development of a population new to Fiji. For this the Indians paid a price. The voyage occupying 72 days itself was perilous, and every ship records mortality during the journey, on one occasion reaching 5%. On the islands, the "chronic loss of life and health among the indentured immigrants and their children" (F.R.G. No. 60, 31 December 1895) was of serious concern. Many men did not serve their full term of indenture, the cumulative percentage loss due to death rising to over 25% by the end of the 5th year of indenture. The mean death rate for indentured Indian labourers varied from year to year, usually about 4%.

Besides this mortality was loss by repatriation through incapacity. There was also infant mortality among the babies of indentured parents, 19·7% in 1896 dying within a year of birth, 21·2% in 1897, 17·0% in 1898, 19·5% in 1899 and 20·7% in 1900. Among children up to the age of 15, the average death rate was 11·1% between the years of 1887 and 1900 (F.R.G. No. 60, 31 December 1888; No. 37, 29 October 1890; No. 60, 31 December 1895; No. 41, 22 August 1900; No. 45, 18 October 1901). This mortality among the infants and children was attributed to the mother's absence at work and, to some extent, to the debility and want of proper nourishment of mothers (F.R.F. No. 60. 60, 31 December 1895). Other reasons suggested were social maladjustment due to the sex disproportion and the length of the indenture period.

Nevertheless the Indians settled to the conditions of the colony, the polulation grew and continued to do so, not only because of the priming of immigration, but by natural increase among those already there; whereas in 1911 only 27%, and in 1921 44%, of

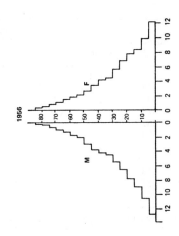
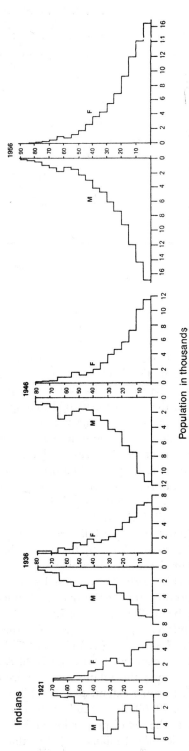
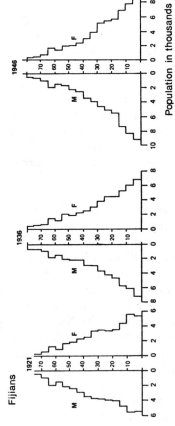

Figure 1. Population pyramids of Fijians and Indians in Fiji.

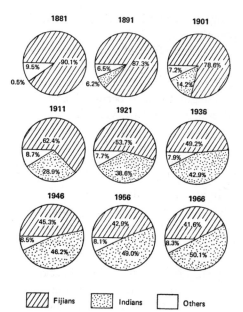

Figure 2. Population replacement by Indians in Fiji.

the Indian population had been born in Fiji, in 1936 this figure rose to 72% and in 1946, 85%.

The population pyramids of the Indians of Fiji's population at the censuses of 1921, 1936, 1946, and 1956, show how a population that was initially entirely migrant, largely dependent on immigration for its growth, became less transitory, and relatively independent of migration (Figure 1). The 1921 pyramid shows a bulge between the age of 25 and 45 years, a very low proportion of females, and a rapid decline in the older age groups, indicating the largely immigrant origin. This bulge had largely disappeared by the 1956 pyramid, which shows, by its broad base, the growth potential. The disproportion between the sexes is generally confined to cohorts born before 1901.

Here, then, is a situation of fully documented population movement. A century ago, there were virtually no Indians on Fiji; the 1956 census showed that the 169,403 Indians outnumbered the Fijians by more than 14%, and today the figure is nearer 20%. For this change in proportion, migration alone is not responsible. The total number of Indian immigrants arriving in the islands over the total indenture period was 61,121. A number departed to India at the end of their indenture period, in the years 1890–1911 totalling some 10,700. By the early thirties, more Indians were leaving the colony than entering it. There was the further loss through endemic and epidemic mortality among adults, children and infants. But despite this loss, population growth continued, and certainly from 1911 onwards it was due primarily to natural causes. The total picture, of steady replacement of the Fijian population by the Indian in Fiji, is summarized in Figure 2.

2. Demographic Explanation

The Fijians

The coming of the European brought disaster to Fiji. With the introduction of firearms, the nature of native warfare changed and, to a society geared to a relatively harmless system of strife, the new barbarism brought losses impossible to assess. There is no conception of the number of men, women and children of all ages who died, but certainly many of the victims during this period were of the age groups of the greatest reproductive potential.

A second effect of European contact was the scourge of epidemic disease. This was particularly heavy on the Fijians who, by reason of their geographical isolation, possessed little immunity to the more usual infections of the outer world. The first Fijian epidemic is thought to have occurred about 1791–2 followed by an outbreak of dysentery in 1802–3, both with devastating mortality. In 1874–5 measles was introduced, the epidemic swept through the almost totally susceptible native population, reputedly causing the deaths of roughly 40,000 or one-quarter of Fijians. Describing this epidemic, the Commission, set up in 1893 "to enquire into the decrease of the native population" in Fiji, deplored the Fijian's attitude to illness generally, and particularly as it applied to infants and children, many of whom, it was considered, died unnecessarily through neglect. The high mortality rate among the infants, more than thrice that in London, was, in the Commission's opinion, one of the most important causes of the Fijian population decline, for the birth rate was higher than that in England. In 1884, a major epidemic of whooping cough carried off another 3000 lives, followed by dysentery and influenza in 1885–6 resulting in about 1500 Fijian deaths. The secondary effects of these epidemics on the population number cannot be evaluated, since there are no details of incidence in terms of age. There were further outbreaks of influenza and whooping cough in 1891, causing about 1500 deaths and diminishing the total number of Fijians still further. Influenza continued to attack the Fijians annually in the cool months. In 1903 a measles epidemic took many lives, for which no figures are available, but Boyd (1911) comments that the decrease among the Fijians from measles was 2481. It is also estimated that the total deaths from epidemics within a period of less than 30 years numbered approximately 47,000.

In these epidemics infection was widespread. It can be assumed that after the first measles epidemic only those persons born after 1875 were susceptible to measles infection in 1903; that is, in the 1903 outbreak persons at risk were under the age of 28 years, the potential reproducers. Their mortality would naturally lead both to immediate and delayed effects on the numbers of births in subsequent years, while any reduction of the numbers of deaths each year for the next few years would be very small. The epidemic in fact depleted the reproductive capacity of the population. It seems that the total number of deaths continued to exceed the number of births each year until 1905. From then until 1912 the numbers fluctuated, but after 1912 a numerical superiority of births was established, though interrupted in 1918 when influenza swept Fiji. There was relatively little immunity to this epidemic in Europe and Asia, certainly not amongst the Fijians. Montague (1919) reported that the heaviest mortality occurred at ages below 45 years, so again from the age incidence it is the reproductive capacity of the population that suffered. This is confirmed in the figures for Fijian births in each year from 1921–1936 (Lambert, 1938) which show that the epidemic reduced the increase of the population for the subsequent 25–30 years.

Comparison of the two populations

At the time of the Indian arrival, the Fijian population was still in a state of cultural shock. Its demographic and social structure was reeling from the impact of European contact, particularly through internal warfare, the arrival of new diseases, and commercial development. The Fijian took time to accustom himself to the changing conditions, and meanwhile the Indian slowly but surely gained economic and numerical ascendancy over him. For the indentured Indians, by contrast, had to adapt in order to survive. On arrival in the colony, they had no choice but to labour in order to earn money to keep themselves; "to grow food often on insufficient areas of land, to make housing materials; a stranger in a strange land, knowing nothing of the customs and traditions obtaining therein". Bringing his own customs and social ideas based on the freedom of individuals or family units, he worked hard for his survival. But adjustment took time. Still by 1893, the year of the Commission, the 9167 Indians in the colony were little, if at all, better off than the Fijians, for they lived in poor conditions, with women outnumbered by men, and with deaths exceeding births.

Besides their continuing heavy endemic mortality, the Indians too succumbed to the epidemics. Those born in India presumably had some immunity to the common disorders, but certainly they were affected by the 1918 influenza epidemic; deaths amongst Fijians were 5154, amongst the Indians 2553, representing respective rates percent of population of 5·7 and 4·2. However, for both Fijian and Indian populations the trends soon changed. For the Fijians, the tide of decrease turned midway between the two major epidemics of 1903 and 1918; certainly, despite outbreaks of dysentery in 1921, whooping cough in 1925 and epidemic dysentery in 1929–30, the population increased steadily year by year. The period of recovery of the Fijian population coincided with the peak period of Indian immigration. It is not possible to measure the relative growth of the two populations from 1911 on account of Indian movement into and from Fiji, but figures from 1921 onwards are acceptable.

Table 3 shows the average annual rate of increase for the Indians and the Fijians in the three intercensal periods. In each period, particularly in the first, the Indian growth outpaced the Fijian.

A conspicuous difference between the two populations is seen in their birthrates (Table 4). For the years 1929–1938, the birthrate in Indians is the higher in every year but three.

These differences in birth rates are attributable to several factors. Age at marriage is particularly relevant, for earlier marriage age gives a potential difference in the age of commencement of, and in the total, reproduction of great importance to the population growth rate. Table 5 shows, for Fijian and Indian females by selected age groups, the percentage married in both census years 1936 and 1946. There is a striking contrast between the percentages in the age groups 15 to 24, showing the strong tendency for the Indian female to marry earlier than her Fijian counterpart.

A second factor is population composition. There has always been an excess of Fijian females over males, a situation resolved in Fiji society by polygyny; also to increase their wealth and prestige, Fijians liked to accumulate as many women as possible.

Table 3   **Growth of the two populations**

Population	Average annual rate of increase in intercensal period			Percentage increase in 15 years 10 years 10 years		
	1921–36	1936–46	1946–56	1921–36	1936–46	1946–56
Fijians	0·98	1·92	2·29	16	21	26
Indians	2·27	3·55	3·46	40	42	41

Table 4   **Birthrate comparison. Birthrates (per thousand) in the two populations, 1929–38**

Year	Fijian	Indian
1929	31·9	34·9
1930	36·4	36·0
1931	35·3	33·4
1932	34·3	38·4
1933	35·1	38·7
1934	37·5	37·2
1935	36·5	37·4
1936	37·8	40·2
1937	34·5	37·6
1938	37·6	39·5

The usual effect of polygyny is to reduce fertility per female, and in Fiji this effect is enhanced still further by the tendency for the Fijian female to be in many respects self-sufficient, cultivating her own plot of communal land. The number of Fijian and Indian women in paid occupations, per thousand female population, in 1956, was 65 for Fijians and only 28 for Indian females. The Fijian woman has left the sphere of her own village community, appreciates the need for money and independence, and has therefore become less available for marriage. There are many unmarried Fijian females in such occupations as nursing, schoolteaching and paid domestic services. The Indian woman is customarily unprepared to enter into public activities of her own on anything like the same scale as her Fijian counterpart. The sex composition in Indians is the reverse. Indian women customarily married at an earlier age than the Fijian women, on account of the Indian cultural pattern of marriage of an established man to a teenage wife, tending to increase fertility. This effect was enhanced in Fiji by the disproportion of the sexes, for the paucity of Indian women meant they were more in demand, and this perhaps may have tended to further lower female age at marriage.

Thus, the factors age at marriage, population composition, and activities, together exert an obvious effect on the fertility of each race; from these one would expect that the Indian mother would have a larger family than the Fijian in the early stages of married life, and a greater proportion of the total population would do so. That this is so is shown by comparison of fertility by maternal age (Table 6). The modal number of liveborn children for Indian mothers aged 20–24 is 3, for Fijian 1; the modes for those aged 25–29 respectively 5 and 3. The higher fertility of Indian women is due to the fact that they are younger mothers than the Fijian and that the proportion of wives is higher in every age group. Indian fertility seems to be some 36% higher than Fijian, though

Table 5   **Number and proportion of females married by age group**

Age group	1936				1946			
	Number of married females		Percentage of female total		Number of married females		Percentage of female total	
	Fijian	Indian	Fijian	Indian	Fijian	Indian	Fijian	Indian
15–19	559	3522	11·9	83·2	779	4285	13·8	71·6
20–24	2789	2043	59·3	93·0	3667	4392	66·6	94·9
25–29	3112	1577	80·6	94·0	4078	3855	81·2	94·7
30–34	2659	1297	87·4	93·2	3423	2772	86·9	94·4
35–39	2247	1386	89·9	89·6	2764	1802	91·9	88·3

Table 6 Number of married women by age group and fertility

Number of children born alive — Married women

Age group	0 Fijian	0 Indian	1 Fijian	1 Indian	2 Fijian	2 Indian	3 Fijian	3 Indian	4 Fijian	4 Indian	5 Fijian	5 Indian	6 Fijian	6 Indian	7 Fijian	7 Indian	8 Fijian	8 Indian
Under 15	— (—)	367 (—)	— (—)	33 (—)	— (—)	2 (—)	— (—)	— (—)	— (—)	— (—)	— (—)	— (—)	— (—)	— (—)	— (—)	— (—)	— (—)	— (—)
15–19	418 (6878)	1782 (6657)	288 (503)	1326 (1397)	50 (73)	803 (597)	17 (8)	267 (140)	5 (2)	88 (23)	— (—)	15 (1)	1 (1)	4 (—)	— (—)	— (1)	— (—)	— (—)
20–24	913 (2516)	559 (1235)	1129 (1885)	575 (1168)	828 (1207)	940 (1475)	494 (573)	1004 (1381)	182 (187)	686 (908)	59 (48)	386 (389)	32 (8)	160 (155)	15 (1)	49 (26)	15 (1)	33 (11)
25–29	678 (835)	383 (389)	644 (866)	242 (256)	753 (944)	354 (506)	688 (1004)	414 (686)	623 (885)	581 (906)	264 (542)	702 (909)	244 (203)	557 (804)	113 (57)	316 (449)	71 (30)	306 (416)
30–34	460 (518)	250 (199)	388 (442)	138 (205)	327 (455)	169 (270)	325 (473)	210 (302)	396 (617)	258 (409)	529 (680)	332 (529)	401 (618)	400 (653)	298 (317)	362 (627)	299 (241)	653 (1184)

Those figures shown without brackets refer to the year 1946; those figures shown within brackets refer to the year 1956.

Table 7   **Secular trend in gross birth and death rates (per thousand)**

Year	Fijians Death rate	Fijians Birth rate	Indians Death rate	Indians Birth rate
1891	52	37		
1896	45	35		
1901	45	37		
1906	38	38		
1911	37	36·8		
1916	25	34		
1921	27·2	32·2		
1926	23·1	35·0		
1931	22·22	35·34	10·19	33·44
1936	28·03	37·80	12·32	40·15
1938	20·94	37·63	11·20	39·52
1940	15·77	36·00	8·15	40·96
1941	15·94	36·78	7·94	45·09

this may perhaps be partly due to nonregistration of some Fijian children under the age of 5.

Turning to general mortality, amongst the Fijians (Table 7) the death rate outstripped the birth rate, often considerably, until 1905, but the reverse was not firmly established until after 1911 (again to be interrupted in 1918 and 1919). All years for which there are figures show Fijian general mortality rates to be higher than Indian. For instance, death rates for 1938, 1940 and 1941 were respectively Fijians 20·9, 15·8, 19·9; Indians 11·2, 8·2, 7·9. The overall crude death rate in Fijians is about twice as high. But it is early mortality that is important for population growth. Infant mortality in Fijians was high. On this account the Fijian infant welfare campaign was inaugurated in 1927, and as a result the infant mortality rate for Fijians improved and in 1937 compared very favorably with that for other tropical countries. In the meanwhile the Indian infant mortality rate had improved and, for those years in which internal comparison in Fiji is possible, remains appreciably better than the Fijian. So too does early childhood mortality. Table 8 shows the percentages of children who did not survive the first year of life, and the first 5 years of life.

It is not easy to identify the causes of this differential mortality. They may be attributed to a low standard of hygiene in Fijian women associated with general insanitation

Table 8   **Child mortality**

Year	Percentage of children dying in the first year of life Fijians	Indians	in the first 5 years of life Fijians	Indians
1929	16·7	6·5		
1930	18·6	9·1		
1931	11·3	7·7		
1932	10·0	5·2		
1933	9·8	7·1		
1934	12·6	8·3	20·5	10·6
1935	12·7	6·3	22·5	8·1
1936	14·1	8·1	27·9	11·9
1937	9·6	5·6	20·5	8·7
1938	10·7	7·7	21·1	10·4
1940	7·0	5·2		
1941	8·0	4·0		

for which there is little quantitative evidence and early European observers in their ignorance of exotic childrearing practices were quick to condemn. However, the age specific mortality rates for 1946 and 1956 (McArthur, 1959) give some support to this interpretation. But whatever the cause, the relatively high infant mortality of the Fijians, and the excessive number of deaths of children under 5 years old with some contribution from other mortality, obviously account for very much of the difference in growth of the two populations.

Thus, as a result of all these differences, the numerical preponderance of Indians in Fiji is today well established. The difference between them this elementary demographic analysis shows to be attributable first to the level of mortality, which in Indians is about two-thirds that of the Fijians, and secondly to the level of fertility which is about 40% greater in the Indians. Of all Indian infants born, a much higher proportion reach reproductive age. The average age of Indian women at the birth of their first child is lower than in their Fijian counterpart, though there is roughly the same average interval between births as in the Fijian. A larger number of children are born to Indian women at younger ages.

3. Conclusion

Here, then, is a situation of population replacement. Had this occurred in any other species it would be interpreted as interpopulation selection reflecting biological advantage in some character. In this case however there is sufficient material to allow examination of the mechanisms responsible for it, and to explore its dynamics. In a very short space of time, the human gene pool of a particular territory has become very much modified.

There has been partial replacement of the indigenous, presumably adapted, gene pool by that from an alien population. This has been brought about by differences in the demographic structure and behaviour of the two populations. The demographic differences are a direct reflection of the cultural differences between them, and their recent cultural history. There is no doubt that the changes in gene frequency in the Fiji islands after the initial Indian immigration have been primarily due to interpopulation differential mortality and fertility. Yet there is no evidence at all that they are selective, making for increased fitness and increased adaption of the population to the Fijian environment. Instead they represent the effects of intergroup cultural differences, which are of little if any relevance to the adaptive value of the individual's biological characters.

This reasoning appears acceptable in respect of the fertility differential. It may however be argued that cultural factors are not entirely responsible for the mortality differences, but that these have occurred in response to real but unidentified biological differences in ability to survive in the Fiji environment. But many other situations of population replacement that have occurred demonstrate the cultural element in differential mortality. What would have happened say if the Tasmanians instead of the Europeans had had the guns? In many situations of culture competition that have occurred, often to a grosser extent than in Fiji, which indeed contribute greatly to the world distribution of modern man and his genes, the solution has come through differential mortality, related to cultural rather than biological advantage. It is the whole population which is favoured, and thereby the characters of all its component members irrespective of whether they are biologically advantageous and disadvantageous.

For how much of man's biological history, past and present, is such "unnatural selection" or "hitch-hiking evolution" responsible?

References

Boyd, J. (1911). *Fiji Census Report, 1911.*
Colonial Office Series. Original correspondence and despatches from Fiji, 1860–1902. **83,** No. 20, 27 October 1879.
Fiji Royal Gazette No. 60, 31 December 1888; No. 37, 29 October 1890; No. 60, 31 December 1895; No. 41, 22 August 1900; No. 45, 18 October 1901.
Lambert, S. M. (1938). Indians and Fijians: their changing numerical relations. *Bishop Museum Special Publication* No. 32.
McArthur, N. (1959). Fijians and Indians in Fiji. *Population Studies* **12,** 202–213.
Montague (1919). *The Montague Report, Fiji Legislative Council Report* No. 31.

L. B. Jorde
H. C. Harpending

Department of Anthropology,
University of New Mexico,
Albuquerque, New Mexico 87131,
U.S.A.

Cross-spectral Analysis of Rainfall and Human Birth Rate: An Empirical Test of a Linear Model

1. Introduction

Much of ecological anthropology is concerned with structural regularities in human societies in relation to climatic and environmental variables, as well as to intrinsic variables such as population density. The treatment of these interrelations is generally in terms of statics or in terms of variables changing very slowly (see, e.g. Spooner, 1971). In view of the substantial amount of archeological and historical information available about human populations, we feel that there is much understanding to be gained from examining the dynamic relations among environmental and cultural variables. There is an analogy to an electrical engineer presented with an unknown device; he might dissemble it to contemplate its structure, but he is more likely to pass signals through it and to observe the effect of the device on the signals. Similarly, we propose to regard climatic events as one of several inputs to a cultural "system", to regard crude birth rate as one of several outputs, and to apply techniques of time series analysis to study the characteristics of the system. We have tentatively confirmed a very simple working hypothesis: that technologically simple societies should show more response to short term or "high frequency" variation in input, while more complex system should filter high frequency input more effectively.

It is a consequence of simple models, and it is an intriguing hypothesis that complex systems in stronger interaction with environmental variables are in general more sensitive to long term trends, or "low frequency" input and are ultimately more unstable, although this instability should be manifest over long time periods, on the order of centuries.

Thus, for example, an interior Eskimo group is very vulnerable to sporadic environmental disturbance, such as a severe decline in the caribou herds, but the system persists over long time periods relatively unchanged. On the other hand, a complex agricultural system will survive the occasional bad year with little change, perhaps through food storage, but it is likely to set up long term changes in the ecosystem, such as soil erosion or desert formation, which will render it ultimately extinct.

There is considerable evidence that there exists a causal relationship between fluctuation in climate and food supply and fluctuation in crude birth rate. For example, it has been shown that dietary deficiencies lead to increased frequencies of stillbirths, spontaneous abortions (Sauvy, 1969; Bender, 1971), and, in severe cases, spontaneous amenorrhea (Nag, 1962). A common response to a decreased food supply is a prolongation of the

10

lactation period in nursing women (Skolnick & Cannings, 1972), which, in turn, prolongs postpartum amenorrhea (Jain et al., 1970). Diet has been shown to affect the age of menarche (Kralj–Cercek, 1956; Keys, 1950), which exerts an effect on overall reproductive potential. Finally, Eversley (1965) notes that a decrease in food supply will cause postponement of marriage, which lowers birth rate. All of these factors lead to results such as those of Thomas (1941): high positive correlations between food supply (determined largely by rainfall) and birth rate.

Since our data on climate, harvests, birth rates, and comparable phenomena consist of sequences of events, familiar methods of regression and correlation analysis are not adequate, since the data are autocorrelated and thus are not independent replicates of each other. The methods of time-series analysis are appropriate for the examination of temporal (or spatial) sequences of data.

Using the example of rainfall and birth rates, we may wish to detect two sorts of complexity which do not occur with non-sequenced data. First, relations may be out of phase. Thus, at the simplest level an increase in birth rates in response to favorable rainfall should occur at least a year later. Second, relations may be of a different nature in different frequency bands. Populations might show increased birth rates in response to runs of favorable years, yet show no response to year to year fluctuations in climate. If the response to the longer runs of climatic variation were mediated by slow changes in the ecosystem, a substantial lag between the climatic events and the change in birth rate might occur. Time-series analysis reveals these kinds of relations.

In regression and correlation analysis the explicit models upon which statistical analyses are based are usually of little independent interest. For example, if x and y are height and weight, one studies the regression of one upon the other by a least squares fit to a model of the form

$$y_i = ax_i + b + \text{error.}$$

This linear relation is usually considered to be a local approximation to a more complex relationship, but as long as x and y are static variables this is the most general kind of linear form relating them.

If x and y represent series of events, or functions of time, the corresponding model becomes

$$y = L(x) + \text{noise}$$

where L is a linear operator, a combination of algebraic relations, integrals, derivatives, and time delays. There is considerable latitude for generating interesting models purely from theory and then comparing them with empirical relations in a body of data. For example, let I represent a (continuous) harvest, and F be the food available. A simple model corresponding to buffering of the irregular harvest by storage is given by

$$I \rightarrow \boxed{\text{buffer}} \rightarrow F$$

$$F(t) + \beta \frac{\mathrm{d}f}{\mathrm{d}t} = I(t).$$

This corresponds to a linear operator on the function I, yielding F as its output; an alternate terminology is that the operator filters I to yield F. We discuss below some consequences of this filter. Again, linear filters are often regarded as approximations to more complex dynamic relations among variables.

The analyses and the presentation of results on time-series analysis are often done in the frequency domain rather than the time domain; thus, a series can be described in terms of its power spectral density. The power spectrum of a process is a representation of the variance in the process as it is accounted for by various frequency bands; peaks in the spectrum correspond to cycles or "tendencies" to cycle at a given frequency or in a given frequency range. The polar extremes of power spectral densities are, on the one hand, a wave of fixed frequency corresponding to a spike in the power spectrum at that frequency and, on the other hand, white noise, which is a mathematical abstraction with a uniform spectral density at all frequencies. In computing spectra one need not distinguish deterministic from random periodicities in data since both will simply appear as a sharp peak in the power spectrum (Koopmans, 1974). It is usually desirable to remove such a concentration of power from the data by filtering.

Linear dynamical models are conveniently conceptualized as operating on the power spectral density of an input process and yielding a power spectral density of the output process by multiplying the input power at each frequency by the squared gain of the filter at that frequency. Consider, as an example, an agricultural group in the American southwest which stores food. An equivalent way of writing the filter discussed above is:

$$f(t) = \int_0^t I(t-a)^{-\beta a}\,\mathrm{d}a$$

Thus, the food availability at any time is an exponentially weighted sum of the past harvests. The power spectrum of f is given by

$$\Gamma_f(\omega) = \frac{\Gamma_I(\omega)}{\omega^2 + \beta^2}$$

where $\Gamma_I(\omega)$ is the harvest power spectrum and ω is the frequency in radians per year. (See Jenkins & Watts (1968) or Koopmans (1974) for a derivation of these relations.) Take $\beta = 1$ so that after one year approximately $e^{-1} \simeq \frac{1}{3}$ of a harvest input remains. The spectral peak of rainfall corresponding to one cycle every three years, or $2\pi/3 \sim 2$ radians per year, is reduced in the spectrum of f by

$$\Gamma_f(2) = \frac{\Gamma_I(2)}{1 + 4}$$

or by approximately one-fifth. For a forty-year cycle, corresponding to $2/40 \sim 0\cdot 15$ radians per year, the damping is

$$\Gamma_f(0\cdot75) = \frac{\Gamma_I(0\cdot15)}{1 + 0\cdot023}$$

so, as one would intuit, two- to three-year food storage does not buffer long term variations in harvest quality, but it reduces the variance of a three-year cycle by a factor of one-fifth.

We have been experimenting with a model of a human population in interaction with a resource in an attempt to understand how various reproductive patterns, patterns of resource use, and environmental characteristics condition the stability of human subsistence systems. We sketch here our model to show how a simple formulation can generate interesting relations between climatic variables and human populations. This is a slight elaboration of a scheme given in Harpending & Bertram (1975).

Let $K(t)$ be a resource, $P(t)$ the size of the consuming human population, $B(t)$ the births at time t, and let $I(t)$ represent some exogenous stochastic input such as rainfall. The resource is governed by the equation

$$\frac{dK}{dt} = -\delta P - \varepsilon K + I$$

where δ is the rate at which humans degrade the resource base and ε is the turnover rate of the resource. The births at time t are given by

$$B(t) = \int_0^t B(t - a)\phi(a)\, da + g(K - P) \tag{1}$$

where $\phi(a)$ is the net maternity function and g is a positive constant which measures the strength with which the population regulates its births according to the difference between population P and resource level K. There is latitude here for experimenting with different forms of regulation, for example, delayed regulation or regulation according to the derivative or the integral of $(K - P)$. Finally, population is given by

$$P(t) = \int_0^t B(t - a)e^{-la}\, da$$

where we are assuming exponential survivorship for convenience. These equations are conveniently studied by their Laplace transforms, indicated here simply by functions dependent upon s instead of time t. Keyfitz (1972) shows how to approximate equation (1) with the first several roots of the characteristic equation associated with the integral. Write (1) as its Laplace transform:

$$B(s) = B(s)\phi(s) + g(K(s) - P(s))$$

or

$$B(s) = \frac{g(K(s) - P(s))}{1 - \phi(s)};$$

the denominator term $1 - \phi(s)$ is approximated by

$$1 - \phi(s) \approx \prod_{i=1}^{m}(s - r_i)$$

where the r_i are the first m eigenvalues of the Lotka integral (1). The first three roots are given in Coale & Demeny (1966) for many populations of the world, and Coale (1972) gives a large number of roots from a few censuses. This is a slightly different method of approximating the Lotka integral from those given by Coale (1972) and Lee (1974). In Laplace transform notation our equations are

$$SK(s) = -\delta P(s) - \varepsilon K(s) + I(s)$$

$$B(s) = -[gK(s) - gP(s)]/\prod_{i=1}^{m}(S - r_i)$$

$$P(s) = B(s)/S + l$$

or, in input-output block diagram form:

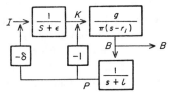

The filter characteristic (gain function) of this feedback system is easily derived from this Laplace transform representation, but it is algebraically complex. Graphically there is a peak in the gain at a cycle length of two to three generations, as found by Lee (1974) with a different model, and several lesser peaks for intervals corresponding to fractions of the generation length. Demographers sometimes consider the effect of the fourth and higher roots of the Lotka equation to be small (Keyfitz, 1972). We find in our model that including the fourth and fifth roots leads regularly to increased gain in the region of one cycle every twenty to forty years. The dominant root ordinarily has little or no effect on the frequency response, although it changes the equilibrium population under constant input.

By manipulating the parameters of our model, one can find conditions leading to long term instabilities on the population's relation to the subsistence base. These instabilities are, in general, difficult to avoid if the potential for human degradation of resources (δ) is moderately high. This reveals the wisdom of the strategy which Douglas (1966) considers widespread among human groups-regulation according to something very divorced from the resource base such as the supply of palm fronds for roofing huts. When a population regulates itself by a quantity which it in turn effects, the strength of the feedback is destabilizing. Thus, by regulating itself according to some environmental variable whose dynamics are independent or nearly independent of the level of the human population, a human group is more nearly homeostatic. In addition to the examples given by Douglas, the regulation by land available per person as occurs among many hunter–gatherers would function in this way.

Our interest in this model and the reports and speculations in the demographic literature about relations between climate, harvests and birth rates, have led us to examine spectral densities of birth rates, climatic variables and the relations between them for several human groups. In general, records are of inadequate length to study the low frequency (i.e. several generations long) dynamics of the interaction between populations and climate, but we can examine the effects of technology and cultural complexity on filter characteristics in the higher frequency bands. For example, we chose the Ramah Navajo with the idea that pastoralists without substantial food storage would reflect more the higher frequency variation in rainfall than would Pueblo peoples with greater food storage. Agricultural productivity in the arid southwest should be directly related to rainfall. In England and Scotland the relation may be weaker and more complex. For example, insolation would be inversely related to rainfall, and if insolation were the most relevant input, it would simply change the phase relations in our material but would not otherwise affect our results.

2. Methods

Rainfall and birth rate data for four populations are used. We took the Ramah Navajo and San Juan Pueblo because they represent societies of simpler technology, while Scotland and England were the most convenient complex societies.

Crude birth rates for England for the years 1841 through 1950 were taken from Mitchell (1962) and Mitchell & Jones (1971). These sources were also used to obtain Scottish birth rates from 1855 through 1950. Birth rates for the Navajo population of Ramah, New Mexico, and for San Juan Pueblo, New Mexico (1853–1934 for both) were provided by J. N. Spuhler (personal communication). Rainfall data for Greenwich, England; Edinburgh, Scotland; and Santa Fe, New Mexico were taken from Exner *et al.* (1927), Simpson *et al.* (1934), Clayton & Clayton (1947), and U.S. Department of Commerce (1959).

A brief discussion of cross-spectral analysis follows; much more detailed accounts can be found in standard texts on spectral analysis (e.g. Jenkins & Watts, 1968; Otnes & Enochson, 1972; Koopmans, 1974).

Cross-spectral analysis is a method by which two time series (input and output) may be studied in terms of their interrelationships in various independent frequency bands. In one method of computing cross-spectra, a cross-correlation function between the two series is computed, and the Fourier transformation of the even (positive lag) and odd (negative lag) components of this function is performed, resulting in a cross-spectral density function.

The frequency response diagram (or Bode plot), the logarithm of the gain of the system plotted against frequency, allows direct examination of the response of the system to "input" at a given frequency (see Di Stefano *et al.* (1967) for a good discussion of the Bode plot). Gain is computed as the cross-spectral density divided by the spectral density of the input series (spectral density is the Fourier transform of the autocorrelation of a single series). Thus, gain is directly analogous to a regression coefficient in statistics.

Confidence intervals for the gain estimates are not shown here for two reasons. (1) The asymmetric intervals for the logarithm of the gain estimate are difficult to manage and interpret. (2) Anderson & Koopmans (1963) point out that confidence interval theory in spectral analysis was developed for stationary Gaussian processes with reasonably smooth spectral densities. When confidence interval estimation is used for processes of unknown stochastic structure, peaks of real power are often dismissed as "insignificant". Since the system under study here does contain series, the stochastic nature of which is questionable, traditional confidence interval estimation is inappropriate.

We give in Table 1 coherence and phase for the maximum gain for each population. Coherence is computed as the cross-spectral density divided by the product of the square roots of the spectral densities of the input and output series. Thus, it expresses the amount of variation in amplitude at a given frequency and is interpreted in the same manner as the statistical correlation coefficient. The phase spectrum is computed as a function of the Fourier transform of the odd component of the cross-correlation function, and it estimates the extent to which the input series either lags or leads the output series at a given frequency.

A few "missing values" were encountered in the rainfall data. These were estimated using simple linear interpolation, a method which, as Jones (1971) has shown, produces very little distortion when the percentage of missing values is small.

For the Scottish and English populations, the erratic birth rates during and immediately following World Wars I and II were replaced with interpolated values. This was done to remove the artificial high frequency effect of these two events.

Prior to computing the cross-spectral functions, linear and polynomial trend was removed from all of the time series, since trend will cause high gain values near zero frequency (infinite period). This can cause distortion of the estimated spectrum at neighboring frequencies. A least squares technique was used to subtract the linear trend in the San Juan Pueblo and Ramah Navajo birth rate series, and third degree polynomial equations were used to extract the polynomial trend in the Scottish and English birth rate series. This technique is preferable to the more commonly used difference filter.

The Tukey spectral window was used in computing the smoothed spectral estimates for gain and phase. Maximum number of lags in all four cases is approximately equal to $N/5$, where N is the number of data points in the time series (see Jenkins & Watts (1968) for discussion). This maximum lag number is considered by most authorities to be reasonable *vis-à-vis* the bias variance compromise (Granger & Hatanaka, 1964; Blackman & Tukey, 1958).

3. Findings

Figure 1 shows the frequency response diagrams for each of the populations. Table 1 shows the coherence values, phase angles and time lags associated with the peak gain for each population.

Figure 1. Frequency response of the birth rates for four populations to variability in rainfall. The response is denoted by the gain of the system (frequency distribution of births) for frequencies of the input system (variability in rainfall). The Y axis is $\log_{10}$ of gain and the X axis is the frequency in cycles per year. The four populations are Ramah Navajo, San Juan Pueblo, Scotland, England in order from top to bottom.

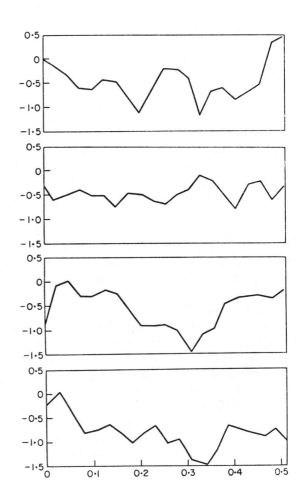

Table 1

Population	Peak gain	Coherence	Phase angle	Time lag
Ramah	2 years	0·95	−180°	1 year
San Juan	3 years	0·38	−65°	7 months
Scotland	20 years	0·52	−325°	18 years
England	40 years	0·34	−75°	9 years

4. Discussion

For the Ramah Navajo population, maximum gain is at a frequency of 0·5 cycles per year which indicated birth rate response to a two-year periodicity in rainfall. This would be expected, since this group has had a semi-nomadic pastoral subsistence strategy with a very limited potential for filtering rainfall fluctuations. It is interesting to contrast this with the frequency response for San Juan Pueblo, since this shows the response of a group dependent primarily on agriculture (much of which was irrigation agriculture) to the same rainfall input (that of Santa Fe). The primary response here is centered at a period of three years but what is more significant is that the very high coherence at high frequency is not present. This means that this group possesses sufficient filtering technology to be able to ignore the two-year periodicity to which the Navajo respond; however, a three-year periodicity in rainfall results in some stress on the system, and a high response in the birth rate is seen at this frequency. This response is of particular interest in that ethnohistorical accounts cite a one-year food surplus as the "ideal" maintained by most southwest Puebloans (Titiev, 1944; Judd, 1954) as well as by San Juan Pueblo itself (Ford, 1968).

For the Scottish population, one would expect less response to high frequency periodicity than in the preceding cases. Indeed, one large peak in the frequency response diagram is seen at a period of about eight years. The small two-year peak seen here may be due to the pastoral adaptation of a portion of this population during the period under study.

The English population, being the most heavily industrialized and technologically advanced of the four groups, should respond principally to low frequency rainfall variation. The frequency response for England, with its highest peak at forty years, shows that this is indeed the case. The second peak for the English population, at eight years, is interesting in that business cycles of this periodicity have been noted in British economic history (Harberler, 1946).

The phase angles and time lags shown in Table 1 must be interpreted with caution. While a polynomial regression filter was applied to the English and Scottish birth rates, it would have been methodologically unsound to have applied it to the rainfall input for these two groups. Koopmans (1974) has noted that application of different filters to the input and output series, as we have done here, can result in artificial shifts in the phase relationship between the series. Nevertheless, Table 1 does reveal an interesting pattern. As one proceeds from less to more technological sophistication, the lag between birth rate and rainfall tends to increase. This is what one would expect: the more a human system is "buffered" from environmental influences by technology, the slower its response to environmental changes should be.

5. Summary

The notion of adaptation in cultural evolution is poorly developed, but it is taken by many anthropologists to involve, at least in part, homeostasis. We suggest that it may be fruitful to conceive of disturbances as partitioned into different frequency bands and to consider homeostasis with respect to phenomena in various bands. We suggest that simple societies are less homeostatic at high frequencies, that is year to year kinds of variation in the environment. Complex cultural systems, as they evolve mechanisms to buffer these short term disturbances, may render themselves less stable in the face of long term phenomena. Some evidence for such a view is presented by examining the frequency domain relations between rainfall and birth rate for four societies.

We are grateful for the advice and assistance of J. B. Bertram, W. J. Chasko, H. T. Davis and J. N. Spuhler. L. H. Koopmans was especially helpful in providing criticism and guidance. Any errors are our own.

References

Anderson, R. Y., & Koopmans, L. H. (1963). Harmonic analysis of varve time series. *Journal of Geophysical Research* **68**, 877–893.

Bender, D. R. (1971). Population and productivity in tropical forest bush fallow agriculture. In *Culture and Population* (S. Polgar, ed.). Cambridge, Mass.: Schenkman Publishing Company.

Blackman, R. B., & Tukey, J. W. (1958). *The Measurement of Power Spectra from the Point of View of Communications Engineering*. New York: Dover Publications.

Clayton, H. H., & Clayton F. C. (1947). World Weather Records, 1931–1940. *Smithsonian Miscellaneous Collections*, **105.**

Coale, A. J. (1972). *The Growth and Structure of Human Populations*. Princeton, N.J.: Princeton University Press.

Coale, A. J., & Demeny, P. (1966). *Regional Model Life Tables and Stable Populations*. Princeton, N.J.: Princeton University Press.

De Stefano, J. J., Stubberud A. R. & Williams, I. J. (1967). *Feedback and Control Systems*. New York: McGraw-Hill.

Douglas, M. (1966). Population control in primitive groups. *British Journal of Sociology* **17**, 263–273.

Eversley, D. E. C. (1965). Population, economy, and society. In *Population in History* (D. V. Glass and D. E. C. Eversley, eds.). Chicago: Aldine Publishing Company.

Exner, F., Walker, G. Simpson, G. C. Clayton, H. H. & Mossman, R. G. (1927). World Weather Records. *Smithsonian Miscellaneous Collections* **79.**

Ford, R. I. (1968). *An Ecological Analysis Involving the Population of San Juan Pueblo, New Mexico*. Ann Arbor, Michigan: University Microfilms.

Granger, C. W. & Hatanaka, M. (1964). *Spectral Analysis of Economic Time Series*. Princeton, N.J.: Princeton University Press.

Harberler, G. (1941). *Prosperity and Depression: A Theoretical Analysis of Cyclical Movements*. Geneva, Switzerland: League of Nations.

Harpending, H. C. & Bertram, J. B. (1975). Human population dynamics in archaeological time: Some simple models. In *Population Studies in Archaeology and Biological Anthropology: A Symposium*, (A. C. Swedlund, ed.). Society for American Archaeology Memoir, No. 30.

Jain, A. K., Hsu, T. C., Freedman, R. & Change, M. C. (1970). Demographic aspects of lactation and postpartum amenorrhea. *Demography* **7** 255–271.

Jenkins, G. M. & Watts, D. G. (1968). *Spectral Analysis and its Applications*. San Francisco: Holden-Day.

Jones, R. H. (1971). Spectrum estimation with missing observations. *Annals of the Instute of Statistical Mathematics* **23** 387–398.

Judd, N. M. (1954). The material culture of Pueblo Bonito. *Smithsonian Miscellaneous Collections* **124.**

Keys, A. (1950). *The Biology of Starvation*. Minneapolis: University of Minnesota Press.

Keyfitz, N. (1972). Population waves. In *Population Dynamics*, (T. N. E. Greville, ed.). New York: Academic Press.

Koopmans, L. H. (1974). *The Spectral Analysis of Time Series*. New York: Academic Press.

Kralj–Cercek, L. (1956). The influence of food, body build and social origin on the age of menarche. *Human Biology* **28,** 393–406.

Lee, R. (1974). The formal dynamics of controlled populations and the echo, the boom and the bust. *Demography* **11**, 563–585.

Mitchell, B. R. (1962). *Abstract of British Historical Statistics*. London: Cambridge University Press.

Mitchell, B. R. & Jones, H. G. (1971). *Second Abstract of British Historical Statistics*. London: Cambridge University Press.

Nag, M. (1962). *Factors Affecting Human Fertility in Nonindustrial Societies: A Cross-Cultural Study*. Yale Publications in Anthropology, No. 66.

Otnes, R. K. & Enochson, L. (1972). *Digital Time Series Analysis*. New York: Wiley.

Sauvy, A. (1969). *General Theory of Population*. New York: Basic Books.

Simpson, G. C., Walker, G., Mossman, R. C., Clayton, H. H. & Clayton, F. L. (1934). World Weather Records, 1921–1930. *Smithsonian Miscellaneous Collections* **90**.

Skolnick, M. H. & Cannings, C. (1972). The natural regulation of population size for primitive man. *Nature* **239**, 287–288.

Spooner, B. (ed.) (1972). *Population Growth: Anthropological Implications*. Cambridge, Mass.: MIT Press.

Thomas, D. S. (1941). *Social and Economic Aspects of Swedish Population Movements, 1850–1933*. New York: Macmillan.

Titiev, M. (1944). Old Oraibi: A Study of the Hopi Indians of Third Mesa. *Papers of the Peabody Museum of American Archæology and Ethnology* **22**, no. 1.

U.S. Department of Commerce (1959). *World Weather Records, 1941–1950*. Washington: U.S. Government Printing Office.

Albert Jacquard

*Institut National d'Etudes Demographiques,
27 Rue du Commandeur,
75675 Paris, France*

R. H. Ward

*CDMRC and Department of
Anthropology,
University of Washington, Seattle,
Washington* 98195, *U.S.A.*

The Genetic Consequences of Changing Reproductive Behaviour

> *"And nothing 'gainst Time's scythe can make defence*
> *Save breed......"*
> Shakespeare
> Sonnet 12

1. Introduction

In the unremitting battle against the relentless erosion of time, our only hope of even a provisionary victory lies in procreation. Of the genes that we transmit to our children there will be some that in their turn will be transmitted unaltered to our grandchildren. The individual can only enjoy a hopeless battle—without hope. A gene may defy the march of centuries.

A human population is perceived in terms of the ensemble of individuals that constitute it; yet each individual disappears to be replaced by another. If the group has any real permanent existence it is because it is something fundamentally distinct from a collection of evanescent individuals. It is a population of genes. To be sure, every society has a degree of temporal permanence as it can be characterised in terms of a system of rites, myths, beliefs and rules—all persisting to some extent through time. Even so, amidst the intertwining strands of genetic and cultural elements that define a human group in time and space, each individual's contribution flashes for a spark of time and then is lost. However, our prime concern is with the biological domain. Hence, to adequately define a human group, it is both necessary and sufficient to describe the ensemble of alleles it carries and which constitute its biological heritage.

Indeed, while we are not indifferent to the history of individuals, because it is our own heritage, in the long run it is the history of our genes that counts most. Ultimately it is the set of events that shaped the genetic past that will mould the individual's future. Genes are the very essense of any human group. The component individuals are merely their temporary products, resulting from the chance union of gametes. Our real heritage is cut from a genetic cloth and it is this rich tapestry of interweaving threads of genetic descent that we must evaluate.

The study of the shifting patterns of our genetic heritage is the provenance of population genetics; a relatively new discipline richer in mathematical models than in collections of well understood data. Despite its youth (a little more than half a century), the discipline can provide unquestionable insights by illuminating the probable consequences of a variety of factors. Taking the elementary principles of Mendelian inheritance and elaborating upon them, one can effectively evaluate the changes in the genetic composition of a population resulting from the following factors: The effect of selection, where specific alleles confer a greater fitness to certain individuals, either in terms of increased viability (because of greater resistence to disease, etc.) or of increased fertility. The effect of consciously choosing a mate as opposed to random mating—a choice which favours consanguineous unions in some societies whereas the marriage of related individuals (carrying alleles indentical by descent with a high probability) is proscribed in other societies. The effect of migration which can introduce new alleles or modify the frequency of alleles already present. The effect of mutation which is the ultimate origin of all new alleles, albeit at a very low initial frequency. Finally there is the all pervasive effect of chance.

The role of chance is often forgotten, or under estimated, because it cannot be represented by a specific cause. It is, rather, the absence of a specific cause which will have certain inevitable consequences. For chance lies at the heart of the process whereby the genes are transmitted: the procreation of a child. For every genetic character each child receives one of two alleles from the father and one of two alleles from the mother. Chance alone dictates which particular allele is transmitted by each parent. The essential characteristic of sexual reproduction is to provide a mechanism for the operation of chance. The reality of a particular individual's existence results from this chance draw from an infinity of possibilities.

Less evident, but no less real, is the mediation of stochastic events in the transmission of the genetic heritage of a population, once the effective size of the group becomes small. These days, one of the major trends in population genetics is the emphasis on the stochastic aspect of the evolutionary process. On one side are arrayed those researchers who choose to evoke "Non-Darwinian evolution" where chance plays a paramount role. Their opponents emphasise the importance of the effects of natural selection, in the name of classical "Neo-Darwinism".

These debates, frequently hotly contested, are essentially concerned with natural populations of plants and animals. For Man an additional attribute must be taken into account: his behaviour. Far from passively submitting to the selective pressures about him, Man struggles to modify his environment. If the temperature should become too low, long before there is any increase in alleles conferring resistance to cold, shelter and modes of heating will have been invented. So for our species the additional dimension of culture provides an alternative mode of adaptation to the exigencies of the environment—a mode which may be vastly more efficient than natural selection in as much as the individual and his immediate offspring are concerned. However, this does not preclude the concomitant action of natural selection even though overt interactions may be harder to discern than in other natural populations. Rather, we should view culture as an extension and elaboration of the phenotypic plasticity which our species has always possessed. Hence in Man, as in certain colonising species, the ability to react to immediate environmental stimuli in a homeostatically responsive way will be at a selective premium (c.f. Bradshaw, 1965). In our own species we may presume this plasticity to be expressed by "cultural" adaptations arising as a consequence of selection for mental adroitness and other factors embodying a high "cultural fitness", rather than by selection for physiological and developmental flexibility. In both instances selection need be no less important than when it is invoked to explain obvious morphological adaptations to environmental pressure.

Aside from the modification of the immediate environment, the hallmark of culture rests in the expression of free will by the members of each human society. Instead of drifting at random, each individual will have a specific behaviour that results from choosing an objective freely decided upon. However, this set of voluntary actions (as opposed to the involuntary behaviour of the members of theoretical populations) does not have more than a relatively mild effect on the constitution of the gene pool. Even the choice of mates, which is often regulated by a complex set of rules in the majority of societies, has no more than a very modest effect on the rate of genetic evolution.

On the contrary, those attitudes of our species which are directly concerned with the transmission of life, (i.e. matters of reproduction and the care of the newborn) have rather important consequences that are manifest relatively rapidly. As it happens, for our species in the short space of a century two radical changes have been experienced in these attitudes. As a consequence, the possibility of major changes in the transmission of our genetic heritage has arisen in a few scant generations. It is these modifications of human behaviour that, for the first time in the history of our species, raise the possibility of a drastic alteration in the manner by which we transmit our genetic endowment. These dramatic changes in the reproductive attitudes of our species are twofold (and here we recognise that what has changed may be less the desire for certain reproductive ends than the means to achieve them). Both changes lie close to the core of the reproductive process and hence have considerable influence on the tramsmission of genes from one generation to the next. The two aspects are: first, the ability to virtually ensure the survival of an infant, once it has been born; and second, the ability to modulate the rate and extent of reproduction. By reason of their profound effect on the demographic structure, these changes are commonly referred to as the first and second demographic revolutions repectively.

Respect for the life of infants and children even if not quite a universal rule, appears to have been generally subscribed to in most societies. Nevertheless, unable to combat the ravages of nature, this sentiment could never be fully realised, no matter how forcibly expressed. Now, after the decisive progress accomplished by modern medicine, matters have changed. The death of an infant is often wholly preventable. Consequently such deaths are considered a scandal against which medical resources in all their potency are mobilized. Given the technological advance, our concern has been universally expressed by a dramatic drop in infant mortality—the first demographic revolution.

Once accomplished, this first revolution ushered in a second—a revolution that we are now in the process of experiencing at first hand. This is the struggle, not against life, but rather against the excessive production of newborns as well as against the indeterminate nature of conception. Hereafter it is hoped that each birth will correspond more and more to a deliberate decision, rather than our passive submission to a fortuitous event.

These two revolutions have been rendered possible by technical progress resulting from chance discoveries by laboratories that have only rarely had such specific aims in mind. For the most part, they were the by-products of research directed in quite a different direction. The comment by Alexis Carrel, "Nous avons modifié les conditions de notre existence au hasard des inventions, des nos appetits, et de nos illusions, sans aucun égard pour notre esprit et pour notre corps", is nowhere more appropriate than in this domain. Not only are our individual faculties and feelings affected but so is the well-being of our whole species: the transmission of life.

We shall now attempt to understand the genetic consequences of these two changes, both recent and radical, in human behaviour. In evaluating the effect of these demographic changes on the manner by which we bequeath our genetic heritage to our distant offspring, we shall consider each effect in turn. Finally, having considered the genetic consequences for these two changes in the reproductive behaviour of our species, we shall examine the possibility of a third revolution which would advocate directed changes in the transmission of our genetic heritage.

2. The Struggle Against Infant Mortality and Genetic "Deterioration"

The success of the first demographic revolution has been so overwhelming, that our species may ultimately become consumed by it. The social, economic and ecological ills of a rapidly increasing population due to lifting the restraints of early mortality are well known and need not be documented here. On the genetic front, this revolution has likewise been perceived in a negative fashion. It is commonly held that the techniques mediating the drop in infant mortality will also encourage the inexorable spread of deleterious genes throughout the population.

The reasoning is simple and is often stated in the following terms. A child that, on the whole, is more feeble than others, more susceptible to infectious diseases, less capable of struggling against the onslaughts of its environment, has a genetic constitution that is less favourable than the average. In curing such infants, medicine is viewed as slowly but surely degrading the gene pool. It is held that to aid such a child in surmounting its "genetic handicap"; to allow it to reproduce and transmit the "bad" genes it possesses, will cause their increase. The slow accumulation of these deleterious genes is viewed as dysgenic for the population as a whole.

The argument can be made for three distinguishable phenomena that are influenced by the drop in infant and childhood mortality. They are the effect of medical progress on: (a) genes causing diseases transmitted as simple Mendelian characters; (b) genes implicated in multifactorial diseases (such as hypertension); (c) changing the differential survival of offspring and hence the rate of increase in fitness of a population. We shall examine the arguments for each case in turn, before evaluating whether or not there is any justification for viewing such effects as dysgenic.

The accumulation of deleterious genes by curing diseases with Mendelian inheritance

This situation is the clearest to comprehend, since the algebraic arguments follow directly from Mendelian principles and specific examples abound. Phenylketonuria is a recessive disease whose spontaneous onset results in a profound mental retardation. This onset can be averted and a normal physical development assured by means of a diet lacking phenylalanine—if it is applied almost immediately after birth. The homozygous baby, bearing two of the deleterious alleles (designated by ϕ), develops more or less normally. On attaining the age of reproduction, such a child will no longer be incapable of reproducing and will thus transmit the allele ϕ to any children it may have. To be sure, there is only a small probability that it will produce, in its turn, a child afflicted with phenylketonuria. The spouse of such an individual will almost certainly furnish a normal allele and the resulting offspring will be heterozygotes and, by virtue of the recessive nature of ϕ, unharmed. But from the standpoint of the population, an equilibrium has been broken. Under the hypothesis that the deleterious effects of the allele has been totally eliminated, there is now nothing to oppose the slow increase of ϕ. Whereas previously, the frequency was maintained at very low levels by the elimination of homozygotes before the age of reproduction, now the frequency will rise.

The same argument holds for deleterious sex-linked alleles, such as hemophilia. The advance in the solicitous care for males carrying this allele and formerly afflicted by this malady, now allows them to live a relatively normal life. This will inevitably augment the frequency of the allele in the population.

To be sure, there are now a multiplicity of ways of averting the production of afflicted offspring—all arising as a consequence of genetic counseling. Couples who have been identified as both bearing a deleterious allele may consciously choose to abstain from reproduction. This behavioural modification by the potential parents will reduce the number of afflicted offspring. It will also be eugenic since the deleterious alleles that they possess will henceforth cease to be transmitted to future generations. However, even supposing such a modification of reproductive behaviour to become more widespread than at present, the efficacy of such restraint will be dependent on whether counseling is retrospective or prospective, as well as on the desired family size (Mayo, 1970). At present, most genetic counseling is retrospective (i.e. couples at risk are ascertained by the birth of an affected child). Also, the desire for smaller families has caused a drop in both the mean and variance of the number of offspring. As a consequence, the proportion of afflicted individuals averted by such procedures will be small (Fraser, 1973). Similarly, the reduction in the rate of transmission of the deleterious alleles will be virtually negligible.

Besides such voluntary acts of limiting reproduction, a variety of modern technical accomplishments allow us to envisage the possibility of detecting affected embryos before they manifest as afflicted offspring. However, even these resources will not avert a "deterioration" of our gene pool. Suppose, for example, that it was possible to detect all embryos carrying the two alleles ϕ. (Here we imagine prospective antenatal screening so we could detect every pregnancy which would terminate in a newborn afflicted with phenylketonuria.) Suppose also, that all such embryos should be eliminated. At first sight, such an attitude (and here we choose to skirt the ethical problems raised by such a decision) would seem to exhibit the advantage of eliminating deleterious alleles and thereby enhancing the gene pool of the population, besides averting the production of affected offspring. In fact, this conclusion will not hold if reproduction is planned about a modal value for family size. In countries where family size can be controlled (and these will be countries where the detection of the homozygote ($\phi\phi$) embryo is feasible) the eliminated embryo will be "replaced" by a healthy child which will have a two-thirds probability of being a heterozygote carrier of the allele ϕ. Thus the frequency of the allele ϕ in the population will still continue to slowly accumulate (Fraser, 1972).

The result will be the same for sex-linked deleterious alleles. Women who are carriers (i.e. those with hemophiliac fathers as well as those ascertained by other means) can avoid having hemophiliac sons (which would occur 50% of the time) by only producing daughters. This could be achieved either by eliminating male fetuses, or in the future, by the technique of separating the spermatozoa bearing X and Y chromosomes. However, every daughter produced will have the same probability (50%) of being a heterozygote. They will thus propagate the allele throughout the population to the same extent as if afflicted males were produced and allowed to reproduce normally (with the help of medical care).

These two examples display an essential aspect of the eugenic problem: the often contrary interests of the individual and the population. A measure that is salutary for the well-being of an individual may well be unfavourable for the community at large. The inescapable conclusion is that the price for the well-being of each individual today, as a consequence of medical programs, is paid much later by the collective majority as generation by generation our genetic endowment is progressively degraded.

This conclusion must be put in perspective however. Later we shall examine whether this kind of analysis is justifiable. Here we make two important caveats in assessing the relative importance of the processes we have described.

First, not only are such complete cures scarcely realised today, but the individuals afflicted by diseases of a simple Mendelian character form a rather small proportion of the total population. The proportional number of such deleterious alleles, in terms of the species gene pool, is likewise small—though they cannot be entirely disregarded if we are to think in terms of "lethal equivalents". The genetic consequences are somewhat less significant for our species than proponents of the above arguments generally allow. Similarly, it needs to be pointed out that much of the demographic revolution that we have witnessed has occurred by conquering infant mortality through relatively non-specific public health programs. Only in the past few decades, has medical technology had any significant impact on the amelioration of genetic diseases attributable to single loci—and then only for a few favoured countries with a high level of technological achievement. Indeed, the proportion of "genetic deaths" has probably only become appreciable for a relatively small segment of our species over the time span during the past generation. As the bulk of this first demographic revolution has occurred by averting "non-genetic" infant mortality, the burden imposed on the whole species, by the application of sophisticated medical techniques to a few favoured populations, must be regarded as being rather small.

Secondly, we need to be aware of the time scale against which these dysgenic effects are to be measured. One of the essential characteristics of evolution is its relative slowness—the dysgenic aspects of medical progress are no exception. In terms of genetic transmission, the unit of time is a generation (for man this is a quarter to a third of a century), and for the members of each generation the amount of change will hardly be noticeable. The actual rate of change will depend on: whether the allele is dominant or recessive; whether the "natural" equilibrium existed as a result of mutation pressure, of heterozygote advantage, or of varying frequency dependent selective values. The specific models allowing us to predict rates of change in allelic frequencies will differ, but in all cases a mathematical analysis shows that the changes involved will be extremely slow (Cavalli–Sforza & Bodmer, 1971).

An example is afforded by the case of cystic fibrosis of the pancreas, a genetic disease scattered over much of Europe and the United States. Due to a recessive allele which we designate by m, this disease manifests with a frequency of 1/1000 to 1/3000 according to the country. The mean may be approximated by 1/2000. The frequency of the allele m is thus of the order of

$$p = \sqrt{1/2000} = 2\%.$$

The children that are homozygous mm are, at present, not very viable. They do not attain reproductive age so their fitness is effectively zero. The maintenance of this allele in the gene pool, despite the elimination of the homozygotes, is not due to mutation pressure, because the allele frequency has attained an appreciable level. Most likely, the heterozygote bearing only a single allele m enjoys a specific selective advantage (perhaps, for example, they are better able to withstand certain illnesses). With this hypothesis and assuming that the present situation represents an equilibrium, the fitness of the respective genotypes can be given by

$$mm:0 \qquad mM:1\cdot02 \qquad MM:1.$$

If we imagine (and this is far from the case) that medical progress will one day result in a total cure for this disease, the fitness of the mm genotype will become equal to one. One can show that under such conditions, the frequency of the allele will increase, little by little, to attain an equilibrium frequency of $p = 50\%$.

The rate of this transformation will be such that the change in frequency from one generation to the next will be given by

$$\Delta p = 0\cdot04p(1 - p)(p - 0\cdot5).$$

This indicates that in order for the present frequency to double (from 2% to 4%) more than thirty generations will be required—virtually a millennium. Thus any fears that have been kindled regarding the dysgenic effect of modern medical practices should not be urgent. The consequences, if they exist at all, will not be manifest until the far distant future.

Accumulation of deleterious genes by treatment of multifactorial diseases

Another consequence of the application of modern medicine in reducing infant mortality is the rise in prevalence of multifactorial diseases such as diabetes, hypertension, etc. To the extent that such diseases have a genetic component, the influence of medical care in allowing afflicted individuals to live normal lives will be dysgenic. As the fitness of the alleles at the various loci involved increases, their rate of transmission to succeeding generations will also increase. However, this rate will be far slower for a given locus than in the case of the allele associated with Mendelian disease. Even if the heritability of the disease in question is close to one (this is usually far from the case), the rise in incidence of the disease will still be very slow as the effect of independent assortment will prevent the deleterious genotypes from accumulating.

Of the few cases that can be cited in support of these affirmations, an example can be given by the diabetic. After treatment with insulin he is not hindered from leading a normal life, nor from normal reproduction. The frequency of diabetics is steadily increasing and for certain advanced countries, has attained 3–4% of older age groups. But does this perspective of matters really conform to a dysgenic effect?

In the case of diabetes, and undoubtedly for other diseases, the rise in prevalence occurs less from an increase in frequency of the responsible alleles than from a modification of life style. It is essentially a disease that is becoming all the more prevalent as dietary habits become richer. In periods of scarcity two factors may operate. First, the majority of the alleles concerned will remain unexpressed. Second, the "diabetic genotype" may well enjoy a selective advantage under conditions of partial famine (Neel, 1962). Hence, the observed increase in the prevalence of diabetics need not reflect any detrimental change in the genetic structure. Similar arguments hold for other multifactorial diseases where environment plays a key role in the expression of the character. In all cases, whatever the effect on the genetic structure, it will only be altered at a very slow rate.

Accumulation of deleterious genes due to a relaxation of prereproductive selection

Now, after two centuries, the extremely rapid progress of medicine is most dramatically evidenced by changing life expectancies (see Table 1). While this rise in life expectancy

Table 1   **Changing mortality schedules in France and Western Europe as reflected by values for life expectancy and survivorship**

	Western Europe		France			
	17th century	18th century	19th century	1900	1940	1970
Men						
Life expectancy at birth	28·1	36·1	39·1	43·4	56·5	68·6
Life expectancy at age 15	30·2	39·5	—	44·7	48·2	55·3
Survivorship to age 15 per 1000 born	628	664	684	731	853	969
Women						
Life expectancy at birth	33·7	38·2	40·6	47·0	62·5	76·1
Life expectancy at age 15	36·2	39·9	—	47·1	53·5	62·5
Survivorship to age 15 per 1000 born	628	664	702	758	880	979

has been manifest for all ages of life, it is particularly noteworthy for the years of infancy. In Western Europe during the 17th century, 37% of all infants died before fifteen years of age. This proportion had diminished to 26% by 1900 and now it is actually less than 3%.

Such a drastic reduction in mortality necessarily reduces the scope for the beneficial action of natural selection by the elimination of unfavourable genes. One measure of the potential magnitude of natural selection is furnished by the Index of Opportunity for Selection (Crow, 1958, 1966). Utilizing the celebrated "Fundamental Theorem" of natural selection (Fisher, 1929) Crow demonstrated that the rate of increase in genetic fitness of a population can be measured by an index composed of (1) a component due to the differential mortality; (2) a component resulting from differential fertility. This index will actually reflect the magnitude of natural selection only to the extent that differential mortality and differential fertility are correlated across generations. Since much of the observed variability in fertility and mortality will not be genotype specific, the index will provide a rather generous estimate of the possible action of natural selection.

The component due to mortality is usually expressed in terms of prereproductive mortality. This first part of the index can be given by

$$I_m = \frac{1 - S_a}{S_a}$$

where S_a is the rate of survivorship to the reproductive age, let us say 15 years. Utilising the figures given in Table 1, we obtained for this index the following values:

I_m	17th century 0·59	18th century 0·51	19th century 0·42	1900 0·32	1940 0·14	1970 0·02

Without giving these figures too absolute an interpretation, we can at least conclude that the opportunity for the action of natural selection, due to differential mortality, has been practically reduced to zero in the space of a few centuries. Even if a high proportion of infant mortality was originally due to "non-genetic" deaths so that two centuries ago a regime of "soft selection" (Wallace, 1968) prevailed, the change in the index is sufficiently marked that some decrease in selection pressure seems likely.

We have now discussed the possible dysgenic effects of modern medical progress from three distinct perspectives. We have seen that for each of the three dysgenic effects under consideration, the issues are complex. Also it is virtually impossible to disentangle eugenic consequences from dysgenic consequences. However on the balance the above reasoning indicates that the overall effect of medical progress is dysgenic—to an unknown extent. We now have to pay more attention to the following question.

Are these fears truly justified?

All the above arguments are based on the assumption of "good" *versus* "bad" alleles. However, this concept is not as simple as it first appears. For each elementary genetic character we are endowed with not one, but two alleles. The attribute "good or bad" is attributable not to a single allele, but to an association of two alleles (i.e. the genotype). The transition from evaluating the worth of a genotype to evaluating a specific allele is not always simple. Sometimes such a procedure can be devoid of sense. Let us reconsider the case of cystic fibrosis. One can define as "best", that genotype with the highest fitness. Under existing conditions this will be the heterozygote, mM. Likewise, the worst genotype will be the homozygote, mm. However, the classification of genotypes by the decreasing series—Mm, MM, mm, by no means allows us to make valid distinctions between the alleles m and M. If the Mm genotypes are very numerous and the mm genotypes are very rare, then possession of the allele m will on the average be advantageous. However, if the proportions are reversed then this same allele, m, will be unfavourable.

A similar argument obtains for the allele for hemoglobin S. This allele may lead to death from anemia (for the SS homozygote) or confer a much greater resistence against malaria (for the AS heterozygote). In a highly malarious environment, the allele is "good" because it increases the chance of survival of the group. In an environment not infected with malaria the allele is evidently deleterious, since its sole effect is to give rise to illness and increased mortality for children who possess it in a double dose.

A dualistic Manichean doctrine, which constitutes the logical underpinning of most of our judgments, has no place in genetics. The question "Is this allele good or bad?" lacks meaning unless one specifies in addition: for whom—"for the individual?" or "for the population?"; for which objective—"for the longest survival in the population?" or "for the production of the greatest number of offspring?"; for which environment . . . .

Even if, for a given epoch, we had good reason to consider a certain allele as deleterious, this judgment is based on the specific environment at that time. Medical techniques have now created a "new" environment for humanity and we have to evaluate alleles in this context.

11A

Let us return to cystic fibrosis and the hypothesis of a perfect cure for this disease. This reasoning implies that in ten centuries the frequency of the allele m will double. Using France as a reference point, under this hypothesis, the number of affected individuals now of the order of 20,000, will become multiplied by four to yield 80,000. But how will this constitute a dysgenic effect? By our hypothesis the disease will be curable and will no longer constitute a genetic blemish. The only consequence for society will be the cost of the necessary care that these 80,000 people would require. It will no longer be a question of a genetic load, but rather of an economic load.

Even better, this load would have a compensation by a doubling of the number of heterozygotes. If they have a superior selective value, as at present, this would be a benefit. In the above example this number would rise from two million to four million.

Ever since our species developed an efficient mind it has intervened in its evolution by its own behaviour. Much of our development during the past millenia occurred through cultural evolution. This means our species did not submit passively to selection imposed by the external environment. Medical progress is nothing other than the continuation of this response. The discovery of an antibiotic is neither more nor less dysgenic than the invention of fire or the utilization of animal hides.

To attribute a lack of conscience to those who heal, by invoking the interest of future generations, corresponds to a far too simplistic viewpoint. The distinction between "good" and "bad" alleles, often impossible, is always limited to a specific environment. It is precisely this environment that Man is capable of modifying. If our technology does not fail us, we have the potential for choosing our own fitness values for alleles and for genotypes.

3. Family Planning and Genetic Evolution

The struggle against an excessive number of births is the ineluctable consequence of the victories won in the battle against infant mortality. A new equilibrium is necessary. This can only be attained by limiting reproduction. The most striking effect of this novel attitude is the reduction in total births. More important, in the long run, are the consequences for our gene pool. Some of these consequences result almost mechanically from planning reproduction, without being deliberately sought. Other consequences, on the contrary, may themselves constitute an implicitly chosen objective.

In all instances, the application of family planning modifies the conditions of genetic transmission. The size of the family (i.e. the number of genes that the parents transmit), was at one time a function of the biological capacity of the couple. Now it will increasingly depend on the results of their intention. The very heart of the evolutionary mechanism is at stake. We shall now specify various aspects of these consequences.

Age of parents

The limitation of births generally brings about a reduction in the mean age of parents at the time of birth. The attached table gives the distribution of births according to the age of the father and mother in France, Japan and Chile.

In France, in a century and a half, the mean age of mothers has diminished by more than three years while the age of fathers has been reduced by 2·5 years since the beginning of the century. Simultaneously, for the mothers, the dispersion of ages at the time of birth has been notably reduced. The variance in age of mothers at birth is now only three quarters of what it was in the 19th century. For both sexes the principle change has been a reduction in reproduction at the more elevated ages. Births to females of more than forty years represented 7·3 % of the total at the middle of the 19th century, 5·7 % in 1900 and only 2·9 % today.

In Japan the transformation is similar but has been more dramatic and more rapid From the figures given by Matsunaga (1972) women of more than forty years do not contribute more than 0·5 % of all births, compared to 6·4 % before the introduction of family planning.

Similarly in Chile the massive introduction of family planning since 1965 has had extremely rapid effect. The mean age of mothers has diminished by two years in a six year period. This can essentially be attributed to the effect of family planning.

The concentration of births into a relatively small fraction of the span of female fertility, (from 20 years of age to a little beyond 30 years) has important genetic consequences. Birth anomalies of children are a little more frequent for very young women and much more common for older women. Characteristically the curve representing the incidence of such anomalies as a function of maternal age has a J shape.

One knows, for example, that the number of Down's syndrome children born rises rapidly as the age of the mother increases beyond 35 years. Matsunaga has calculated that the modification of the reproductive period in Japan has been sufficient to diminish the proportion of such births by 40 %.

However, one cannot affirm that the evolution of the gene pool has been modified as a result of such a reduction in prevalence of a "genetic" disorder. In a "natural" reproductive regime, Down's syndrome children may well be more numerous than in a "planned" regime. This difference is a change in the incidence of individual afflictions without any collective biological consequence because Down's syndrome individuals rarely reproduce. The same affirmation holds for those other various chromosomal abnormalities that arise as a function of maternal age which also tend to be incapable of reproducing. Even for those few who might reproduce, the risk of producing an affected offspring is not appreciably greater than for the general population.

The case of mutations in another matter. To be sure, our knowledge in this area is very insufficient. However, one can note that for certain diseases an apparent increase in the proportion of mutations as a function of age, especially to men older thn 35 to 40 years.

Finally, we note that for certain diseases the reduction in age of parents may attenuate selection pressure, and thus by dysgenic. This reasoning applies to diseases such as schizophrenia or Huntington's chorea which have a late age of onset. When an appreciable proportion of births occur to older parents these illnesses may have their onset during the period of reproducton. This will prohibit or discourage further reproduction of affected individuals. With the fall in parental age this aspect of selection will now only operate on a very small proportion of births. Bodmer (1968) has calculated the change in fitness for schizophrenics where the disease is not manifest until after thirty years of age. He finds that the changing reproductive patterns between 1940–1960 in the United States has caused the selective disadvantage for this disease to fall from 86 % to 51 % for men and from 40 % to 22 % for women. One of the essential obstacles to the spread of the responsible alleles has thus to a large extent been eliminated. However, the advent of genetic counseling will result in a similar form of selective pressure against these alleles, though it will now be intergenerational in nature (i.e. individuals may limit their own reproduction as a consequence of observing the manifestation of the disease in their parents).

Variability in number of children per couple

We have seen that rate of genetic change are due to a mortality component before the age of reproduction and another component due to differences in fertility. The importance of this second factor can be measured by the index I_f (Crow, 1958):

$$I_f = \frac{V}{N^2}$$

where V is the variance and N the mean number of children to couples. The greater the index I_f the more rapid the change in fitness. The variance, V, of the number of offspring is thus an essential parameter.

To demonstrate this by way of an intuitive example, it will suffice to consider the extreme case of two populations in which the mean number of children per family is equal to two (both populations are thus replacing themselves). In the first population the variance in offspring is zero (all families have exactly two infants), whereas in the second it is equal to four (half of the families have no infants and the other half have four).

For a single locus we consider one of the two alleles carried by an individual. Each time he reproduces, the probability that this allele will not be transmitted is equal to one half. If he has n children, the probability of never transmitting this allele is thus $(\frac{1}{2})^n$. In the first population, the probability of not transmitting an allele taken at random is thus

$$(\tfrac{1}{2})^2 = 0.25.$$

In the second population, this allele will be present half the time in an individual without children and half the time in an individual who will have four children. The probability of non-transmission is therefore equal to

$$\tfrac{1}{2} \times (\tfrac{1}{2})^0 + \tfrac{1}{2} \times (\tfrac{1}{2})^4 = 0.53.$$

The role of chance in altering the gene pool from one generation to the next is therefore twice as important in the second population as in the first.

In addition, the magnitude of this variance is an important factor in dictating the frequency of consanguineous marriages. These in turn will effect the manifestation of diseases due to recessive alleles. In the first of the two extreme populations that we have considered every child has two parents who are derived from sibships of size two. Every child will therefore have one uncle and one aunt (assuming constancy of sex ratio) and consequently four first cousins. In the second population each child will have two parents derived from sibships of four children (no parent can be derived from a sibship of zero children!). Every individual will thus have six uncles/aunts (3 of each) and on the average twelve first cousins. In the absence of any rules regulating the choice of marriage partner, the probability of marrying a cousin is therefore three times higher in the second population than in the first. This result holds in similar vein for all forms of consanguineous marriages.

Now, while family planning has as its primary objective a reduction in the mean number of births, it also has the important consequence of reducing the variance. The genetic consequences of this effect may be most striking. Unfortunately, records in this field are poor because the object of the measure is the number of genetically "successful" children, where "success' is defined as attaining the age of reproduction. This

Table 2 **Temporal changes in the distribution of births by age of parent for three selected countries**

Country		Date	Percentage of births to parents of age							Age of parent	
			<19	20–24	25–29	30–34	35–39	40–44	>45	Mean	Variance
France	Mothers	1830*	4·3	22·1	28·1	22·6	15·6	6·3	1·0	29·8	44·6
		1900	5·1	26·2	29·1	20·6	13·3	5·0	0·7	28·1	42·3
		1970	6·5	39·3	26·8	16·0	8·5	2·7	0·2	26·5	34·1
	Fathers	1900	0·2	6·0	28·0	27·3	20·0	11·3	7·2	33·7	44·8
		1964	0·7	14·4	32·7	27·0	15·1	7·1	3·0	31·2	45·5
Japan†	Mothers	1925	6·0	27·2	26·6	19·7	14·1	5·7	0·7	28·9	45·5
		1968	1·2	25·2	49·2	19·6	4·3	0·5	0·0	27·6	17·8
	Fathers	1952	0·3	9·8	31·2	26·6	18·1	9·5	4·6	32·5	45·4
		1968	0·1	7·0	38·6	39·2	12·3	2·2	0·6	30·8	21·2
Chile‡	Mothers	1963	12·9	27·6	22·6	21·6	11·6	3·4	0·3	27·6	45·7
		1969	20·8	34·2	21·0	11·7	9·0	2·8	0·4	25·6	56·2

* Approximate date.
† After Matsunaga (1972).
‡ After Cruz–Coke (1971).

is not equivalent to the total number of births because a child dying in infancy is equivalent to a stillborn infant as far as the evolution of the gene pool is concerned. However, two examples can be as follows.

1. In the United States, the average total number of children was 3·9 for white females born around 1870 while the variance in offspring number was 10. For women born about 1930 the mean family size was 3·1 and the variance 4. This would give an apparent reduction in I_f of 50 % (from 0·81 to 0·42). It is quite plausible that there was a similar fall in the variance of the number of "successful" children during this period.

2. In his analysis of the demographic history of the 19 families, that constitute the "Bourgeoisie de Genève", Henry has analyzed births and mortalities for each of the 903 couples that were members of this group since the 17th century. From these records one can calculate with some precision the number of "successful" children to each of these lineages (Table 3).

Table 3 **The changing relationship between number of liveborn children and the proportion that attain reproductive maturity in the Bourgeoisie of Geneva over three centuries (from Henry, 1956)**

Date of husband's birth	Total number of offspring to each family		Number of offspring that survive to maturity	
	Mean	Variance	Mean	Variance
1600–1650	5·5	20·1	3·1	7·0
1650–1700	3·6	10·3	2·4	5·0
1700–1750	2·9	5·9	2·0	2·7
1750–1800	2·8	4·3	2·3	2·6
1800–1850	2·7	4·9	2·4	3·4
1850–1900	2·0	3·2	1·9	2·9

The demographic history of these families is characterized by a rapid decline in the number of births since the beginning of the 18th century. Birth control had been adopted and become widespread in this small human isolate in less than a century. The total number of infants born to women married before the age of 24 was:

9·6 for those where the husband was born between 1600 and 1650, and

3·4 for those where the husband was born between 1700 and 1750.

Simultaneously, the variance was also considerably reduced (see Table 3). The comparison between the two sets of figures indicates that the apparent change in I_f calculated from total number of births is not always closely related to changes in I_f calculated from this distribution of "successful" offspring.

In a general way, by reducing the variance of fertility, birth control restricts the opportunity for the action of natural selection. This implies that the opportunity for selection, already drastically reduced, may have been practically eliminated by the adoption of family planning.

In addition to the above, there is another important matter. The very essence of selection is changing. Not only has the field of action for selection been considerably contracted, as measured by the variance in family size, but the factors by which it operates are no longer the same. The mechanism of evolution may have lost some of its force. It also may have changed in nature.

In a regime of "natural" reproduction, the number of children per couple is largely a function of their biological potential. Alleles favouring high levels of fertility will be selected for, little by little. In a regime of "controlled reproduction", the number of children is dictated by the desires and intentions of each couple. Hence psychological factors of selection have been substituted for physiological factors. Henceforth, any alleles selected for will be those which are associated with psychological factors.

To take an extreme example, let us imagine that to a certain extent the need to reproduce is linked to certain psychological conditions which in turn are dependent upon specific alleles. These alleles, formerly neutral, will now be acted upon by selection. Any such alleles increasing the desire for numerous children will be rapidly propagated. If such a state of affairs actually existed, family planning would eventually become aborted. If economic or ecological factors did not intervene a new demographic explosion would result.

Of greater interest is the effect of family limitation on the mean level of intelligence. In his work entitled *Hereditary Genius*, Francis Galton drew attention in 1869 to the dangers of the low level of reproductive performance for families of high status. Numerous other workers, especially R. A. Fisher, have reiterated this theme in terms of the deleterious effect for society. However, such an attitude stems from incomplete knowledge. While a depressed fertility of the very gifted may have occurred in Great Britain in the 19th century it is not a systematic feature of all populations. The following data indicates some of the complexities.

The data presented by Bajema (1963) for a United States population (Kalamazoo). They show that the reproductive rates follow a U-shaped function with respect to I.Q. rather than a uniformly decreasing function. Since the relationship between net fertility and generation length varies for each I.Q. class, the actual genetic consequences will be complex.

The figures extracted by Kirk from *Who's Who in America* which records individuals of recognized social success. This analysis shows that for the older generations, men who figure in the list had a fertility slightly inferior to that of their contemporaries. However, this situation was reversed for the younger men. Although married later, on the average they have larger families than other Americans of their generation. In the space of a quarter of a century, the trends in fertility with respect to "social class" have become reversed.

These changes shed light on a modern characteristic of genetic transmission: its increasing susceptibility to modifications of the environment, especially the cultural environment. Undoubtedly the surroundings will interact with the mode of transmission in a regime of natural selection. However, modifications will be slow and the process of genetic transmission will proceed in a relatively stable manner.

In contradistinction the cultural milieu has been modified rapidly—at the whim of fashion; of propaganda; or of political pressures. It is possible to guess at the subtle influences that could be exercised to favour a higher fertility for one group and ensure that the "voluntary" limitation of births was most strict in another. The alarming feature of such an eventuality is the rapidity of the response to such shifts in attitudes.

In natural regimes the essential characteristic is stability. Some hundreds of generations are necessary for a selective differential to effect a demonstrable change. As we have seen, despite their efficiency, medical techniques by themselves will only have consequence for the very distant future. To the contrary, the effect of altering the number of desired births will be rapidly achieved. We can imagine two groups of equal size, endowed with distinct gene pools. Each group experiences psychological and economic pressures such that the mean number of children judged to be ideal for a couple is 2·5 in one population and 1·9 in the other. With this rather small difference a single generation will suffice for the first group to become 32 % larger than the second. At the end of two generations this superiority will increase to 70 %.

Without doubt it is this last feature which is the most important. With the intervention of free will in the reproductive process, our genetic heritage has been placed within the domain of objects which we can manipulate. So far, the transformation of our gene pool has not occurred as the direct consequence of deliberate actions. Rather, it has changed in an unforseen way, as an involuntary consequence of strategies directed towards different objectives. But the increasingly precise knowledge of the mechanisms of genetic change will in turn allow a greater possibility of deliberate action The question is: how to define the goal of such a course?

4. A Third Demographic Revolution: Directed Evolution?

It is tempting to deduce the consequences of our new knowledge and to imagine we might peer ahead to some future time when we will have become, to use the expression of J. de Grouchy, the "New Pygmalions", shaping humanity of the future at will. Having gained victory in the combat against infant mortality having struggled against the excesses of increasing populations' humanity may accomplish a third demographic revolution by taking in hand the development of our genetic heritage.

However, in this sphere, just as in so many others, we risk creating the means before we define the ends.

We have illustrated some of the complexities above. How difficult it is to classify alleles as "good" or "bad". How often the biological interest of the individual and the population will be at odds. How the genetic consequences of specific changes in technological progress may be favourable in some respects and unfavourable in others. How impossible it is to be able to distinguish any clear genetic tendency.

In fact, in this area, our knowledge is essentially piecemeal. It is uncertain and certainly insufficient to initiate any valid action. For the present, the most urgent need is to be well aware of this insufficiency. The worst danger is to make decisions by taking for scientific certainty what is no more than a hypothesis; to take as a definitive explanation what is no more than a provisionary model. For the sake of our future it would be well to admit that knowledge is not usually reversible. If the concept of eugenics is well founded then we must appreciate that various social and technological innovations with genetic consequences (directly or indirectly) are inevitable. We must face the issue and acknowledge that some coordination is desirable, that the definition of a genetic "manifesto" cannot be indefinitely avoided.

The key issue is to increase the biological richness of humanity (as measured by our genetic diversity). More modestly it entails avoiding the degradation of our heritage. Now, as a species our strength is due less to favourable alleles, less to gifted individuals and less to the specific accomplishments of societies than to the diversity of people; in terms of themselves as individuals and in terms of the alleles they bear.

The preservation of this diversity should undoubtedly be the prime objective of such a "manifesto". In order to succeed, it would be necessary to convince each person and each group, that "the other person" is enriched by the extent of the differences between them. This is a weighty task! In order to realize such a lofty objective, it will be necessary to create the "composite Aristotle" as advocated by A. Carrel "Pour amalgamer les données de la biologie et de la sociologie, il est besoin d'un centre de pensée collective, d'un institution consacrée à l'intégration des connaissances, d'un organisme capable d'élaborer une véritable science ce l'Hommee".

References

Bajema, C. (1963). Estimation of the direction and intensity of natural selection in relation to human intelligence by means of the intrinsic rate of natural increase. *Eugenics Quarterly* **10**, 175–187.
Bradshaw, A. D. (1965). The evolutionary significance of phenotypic plasticity. *Advances in Genetics* **13**, 115–155.
Bodmer, W. F. (1968). Demographic approaches to the measurement of differential selection in human populations. *Proceedings of the National Academy of Science (U.S.)* **51**, 690–699.
Carrel, A. (1937). La construction des Hommes civilisés. Lectures given at Dartmouth College.
Cavalli–Sforza, L. L. & Bodmer, W. F. (1971). *The Genetics of Human Populations*. San Francisco: Freeman.
Crow, J. F. (1958). Some possibilities for measuring selection intensities in man. *Human Biology* **30**, 1–13.
Crow, J. F. (1966). The quality of people: Human evolutionary changes. *Bioscience* **16**, 863–867.
Cruz–Coke, R. (1971). Problèmes biologiques liés à la contraception. In *Génétique et Populations*. Paris: I.N.E.P. Presses Universitaires de France.
Fraser, G. R. (1972). The implications of prevention and treatment of inherited disease for the genetic future of mankind. *J. Genet. Hum.* **20**, 185–205.
Fraser, G. R. (1973). The short term reduction in birth incidence of recessive diseases as a result of genetic counseling after the birth of an affected child. *Human Heredity* **22**, 1–6.
Henry, L. (1954). *Fécondité des mariages*. Paris: Presses Universitaires de France.
Kirk, D. (1957). The fertility of a gifted group. In *The Nature and Transmission of the Genetic and Cultural Characteristics of Human Populations*. New York: Milbank Memorial Fund.
Matsunaga (1972). Effect of changing parental age pattern on chromosomal aberrations and mutations. In *Recent Progress in Biology and Medicine*. C.I.O.M.S.
Mayo, O. (1970). On the effects of genetic counseling on gene frequencies. *Human Heredity* **20**, 361–370.
Wallace, B. (1968). *Topics in Population Genetics*. New York: Norton.

Index